SOUTH ASIA

SOUTH ASIA

Selective studies of the essential Geography of
India, Pakistan, and Ceylon

B. L. C. JOHNSON

Professor of Geography
Monash University
Victoria

HEINEMANN EDUCATIONAL
BOOKS LTD · LONDON

Heinemann Educational Books Ltd

LONDON EDINBURGH MELBOURNE TORONTO
AUCKLAND SINGAPORE JOHANNESBURG IBADAN
HONG KONG NAIROBI NEW DELHI

ISBN 0 435 34480 3

Published by Heinemann Educational Books Ltd
48 Charles Street, London W1X 8AH
Printed in Great Britain by
Fletcher & Son Ltd, Norwich

CONTENTS

To my Wife

PREFACE

This book aims to provide an introduction to essential themes in the geography of South Asia: India, Pakistan, and Ceylon. To some extent what is essential is necessarily a matter of opinion, and some would deplore the neglect of particular topics. However, the reader is not offered a 'complete' geography: for that he is referred to Spate and Learmonth's *India and Pakistan* which stands alone as the authoritative work on the region. The present study is sketched in a more impressionistic manner with the writer's particular areas of interest making themselves very evident. It is intended to be read as a whole, since much of what is written about the development problems in Indian agriculture, for example, is true of Pakistan and Ceylon. The plates have been selected to show something of the range of landscapes and activities to be found in South Asia. They should be seen as representative of the quality of cultural and economic adaptation in South Asia's various environments rather than as illustrating purely local phenomena.

BIBLIOGRAPHICAL NOTE

The following are among the major general sources drawn upon in preparing this work and to which readers are referred for further and more detailed treatment.

Spate, O. H. K. and Learmonth, A. T. A., *India and Pakistan* (Methuen, London, 1967).
Ginsburg, Norton (Ed.), *The Pattern of Asia* (Constable, London, 1958).
Spencer, J. E., *Asia, East by South* (John Wiley, New York, 1954).
Ahmad, Kazi S., *A Geography of Pakistan* (Oxford University Press, Karachi, 1964).
Ahmad, Nafis, *An Economic Geography of East Pakistan* (Oxford University Press, 1968).
Tayyeb, A., *Pakistan, A Political Geography* (Oxford University Press, London, 1966).
Cook, E. K., (revised Kularatnam, K.), *Ceylon* (Macmillan & Co., London, 1953).
Farmer, B. H., *Pioneer Peasant Colonization in Ceylon* (Oxford – R.I.I.A., London, 1957).
Farmer, B. H., *Ceylon, A Divided Nation* (Oxford University Press, London, 1963).

ACKNOWLEDGEMENTS

In writing about India, Pakistan, and Ceylon, I am very conscious of the debt I owe to many people for inspiration, help, and friendship over close on thirty years. Before World War II the late Sir Dudley Stamp stimulated my interest in the region where I was to soldier through the war years in the Indian Army. To those many friends, military and civilian, Hindu, Moslem, Sikh, Buddhist, and Christian, who in wartime sowed in me the seeds of a lasting affection for the region's peoples, I am deeply grateful. With the war's end Professor O. H. K. Spate helped discipline academically the demobilised soldier seeking to rehabilitate himself as an undergraduate, and I was among the fortunate number who heard as lectures chapters of his then embryonic masterpiece.

More recently I have had cause to be thankful to many others, particularly academics and officials in India, Pakistan, and Ceylon who have gone out of their way to offer me hospitality and to smooth my path on the journeys I have made into many corners of the region. To try to name them all would inevitably leave unmentioned some whose help is none the less valued though their names escape my memory. My thanks go to academic geographers in Dacca, Karachi, Multan, Lahore, Delhi, Calcutta, Madras, Colombo, and Peredeniya; to many administrators, to casual acquaintances of railway-carriage, bus, and plane, and to the very many courteous cultivators who shared with me their *chapatti* and *dhal* or cut me down green coconut for refreshing *dab* in the heat of the day.

For permission to draw upon their studies of specific agricultural areas I am grateful to Professor A. T. A. Learmonth, Professor P. P. Karan, and Professor Mohd. Shafi. My thanks are due to Mr. B. H. Farmer for helpful comments. Finally the willing help over several years, of clerical and technical staff at Birmingham and Monash Universities and the critical advice of many academic colleagues are acknowledged with gratitude.

B. L. C. J.

Monash University,
Clayton, Victoria.
December 1968.

FIGURES

Numbering of figures is by chapter and section

x

TABLES

Numbering of tables is by chapter and section

PHOTOGRAPHS

ACKNOWLEDGMENTS FOR PHOTOGRAPHS

The author is grateful to the following for the photographs listed:

Burmah Oil Company: 42.

High Commissioner for Ceylon, Canberra: 45, 46, 49.

High Commissioner for India, Canberra: 6.

High Commissioner for India, London: 7, 9, 13, 14, 15, 17, 18, 22, 23, 24, 25.

High Commissioner for Pakistan, London: 29, 33, 43, 44,

Professor A. T. A. Learmonth: 20.

Associate Professor W. M. Rivers: 10.

Other illustrations are from photographs taken by the author.

CHAPTER ONE

INTRODUCTION: SOUTH ASIA

One-fifth of mankind occupies this region which forms the westernmost part, and so that closest to Europe, of the populous and humid marginal lands of Asia. South Asia has closer links to the Western world in its culture and its history than the other major divisions of the marginal lands – China and Southeast Asia. Its early civilisation, revealed in the cities of the Indus plains, Mohenjodaro and Harappa dating from 2500 B.C., had contacts with the earlier Sumerian civilisation of Mesopotamia. The languages spoken by the majority of the region's inhabitants share a common ancestry with those of Europe. The people themselves could also claim that their genetic make-up owes a great deal to forbears common to peoples in the Mediterranean area.

In religion South Asia developed its own distinctive and widely influential theocracies, and the size of the debt of Graeco–Judaeic–Christianity to Buddhist ideas has yet to be fully appreciated. From Hinduism, still the faith and way of life of about 400 million of the region's 625 or so million people there sprang Buddhism as a reformed religion which, although claiming only about ten million adherents today and now the majority faith only in Ceylon, spread vigorously through Southeast and Eastern Asia. The two other religions claiming sizeable numbers of followers are of foreign origin. Christianity, the faith of about twelve million, came to South India in the early centuries of its existence, and there persisted to be reinforced as the faith of the European mercantile nations from the fifteenth century. Islam arriving later from the Middle East, both through Arab trade and through overland invasion, flourished more strongly to become the faith of upwards of 130 million, and the *raison d'être* for Pakistan as a separate nation.

The history of South Asia over nearly four centuries has brought the region close to the West, and although the bonds of empire have been shed in recent decades, the political and economic heritage remains. India and Pakistan, before their partition and independence the Empire of India, and Ceylon experienced in common, but as separate entities, several centuries of British rule, which culminated in their independence being achieved by governments in which the ideal of democracy was a basic assumption. Whether or not democracy as it is understood in the West can survive its transplantation to South Asia is an open question, but one of vital interest to the 'free nations' of the world. Some of South Asia's most sympathetic friends in the West may sometimes wonder whether its problems are of a kind and scale that require for their solution a measure of authoritarian leadership that universal suffrage seems unlikely to produce. India is attempting what some have called the greatest experiment in democracy, giving all adults the vote, and making it possible for illiterate peasants to take a meaningful part in elections. Ceylon also has followed the democratic pattern of Britain, her one-time tutor. So did Pakistan, until irresponsibility in the democratic process so seriously threatened the country's unity and progress that a more authoritarian rule was imposed and a fresh approach was made towards creating responsible democratic government from the village level upwards.

In part because of their interest and concern to see democratic ideals, as they understand them, upheld in South Asia, the wealthier non-Communist countries of the West, in particular the U.S.A., have been generous in the assistance they have given to India, Pakistan, and Ceylon. But help has come also from the countries of the Communist bloc; the Soviet Union has given technical and material aid to India to help expand heavy industry; Ceylon has engaged in barter trade with China, exchanging rubber for rice; Pakistan has received military equipment from China.

These three countries of South Asia have much in common both in their past and in their present. Their pasts are closely interwoven. Even though they are now separate sovereign states within the Commonwealth, and despite the bitterness that taints their interrelationships – the Kashmir issue between India and Pakistan, which has twice flared into warfare, and the less violent but intractable issue of the large Tamil minority in Ceylon – they are still closely tied by human bonds. The huge Moslem minority still living in India stands hostage to Pakistan's behaviour towards India.

All three are badly in need of economic development to enable them to raise living standards. Their peoples are mostly subsistence farmers; the proportion of people employed in industry or living in cities is still small, though increasing. Capital in the form of finance, materials, equipment, and technological skill is desperately needed so that jobs can be created for the rapidly expanding population.

High rates of population increase, and low rates of capital accumulation are common problems. Standards of living are dismally low for the majority, and the spectre of famine still stalks the land – particularly in India where all problems assume a formidable scale.

To maintain unity within diversity is a common problem for all three. Pakistan has the obvious problem of forging the widely separate and different wings of West and East into a national unity, of trying to create more bonds than the single one of religion. India's problems stem rather from size and linguistic diversity which tends to give everyone a dual loyalty: to his immediate cultural group, speaking his own language, and self-governing to a degree within the linguistic state, and to the Union of States that is India. In Ceylon the problem is smaller in scale but no less acute: the problem of satisfying the national aspirations of the Sinhalese-speaking Buddhist majority while preserving the rights of the Tamil-speaking Hindu minority, many of whom could claim their ancestors have resided a millennium in Ceylon.

CHAPTER TWO

THE PHYSICAL BACKGROUND

1. FOUNDATIONS AND FORM OF THE LAND*

In its rocks and their physiographic expression in the landscape, South Asia reveals great contrasts. South India contains some of the oldest rock formations known, and some of its landscapes have been exposed to subaerial erosion through scores – perhaps hundreds – of millions of years. On the other hand, parts of the Himalaya form one of the youngest mountain chains in the world and a zone of instability is associated with the whole Himalayan system and its contact with the stable 'shield' of central and Peninsular India. The alluvial sediments which have filled the depression flanking the rising Himalaya to form the Indo-Gangetic Plains have themselves been involved in structural movements persisting into historic time.

Structural and Physiographic Evolution

The principal events in the geological history of South Asia are reviewed here only in so far as they seem important to an understanding of the present geography of the region. Attention is focused on those aspects of geological structure and landscape morphology that affect man's ability to make a living: on gentle slopes and productive soils to cultivate, on economically useful minerals to work, on water resources to harness for irrigation or power.

Fig. 2.1.1 shows the main features of the geology of South Asia.

The structural relationships of the major formations in the subcontinent are shown diagrammatically in the sections in Fig. 2.1.2.

* It is assumed that the reader has access to a good atlas (e.g. *Oxford Atlas* or *Philips' Library Atlas*) in which most places mentioned in the text can be located. The official form in which Indian geographical names are now transliterated sometimes varies from their customary spelling in English language texts and atlases. A list of the more important variations in spelling will be found as an appendix.

The stable 'shield' of Peninsular India and Ceylon is regarded by some geologists as having formed part of an ancient continental landmass referred to as Gondwanaland, which is thought to have broken up, through the process of 'continental drift' to form parts of what are now South Africa, Brazil, and Western Australia. In common with these areas the Peninsular Shield is made up largely of very ancient formations. Granites and gneisses are widespread and are probably the oldest rocks. The *Dharwar–Aravalli* series include a great variety of metamorphosed sedimentary and igneous material, possibly as old as the granites and gneisses, and conveniently bracketed with them as of Archaean age, i.e. early Pre-Cambrian. These Archaean formations cover much of the Peninsula and occur also in the Shillong Plateau, which has been detached from the main mass by the foundering and alluviation of the Ganges–Brahmaputra Delta region. The Archaean rocks in places contain valuable minerals: India's major iron ores of Bihar and Mysore, the manganese of Madhya Pradesh, gold, copper, asbestos, and mica.

The younger Pre-Cambrian (*Cuddapah*) series represent the sediments deposited in basins within the Archaean basement rocks and are found principally in Madhya Pradesh, and Andhra Pradesh where they form impressive scarplands. In the latter area they are overlain by Vindhyan sedimentary rocks (? Lower Palaeozoic, Cambrian–Ordovician) which are more extensively found in the north of the Peninsula. The Vindhyan Range along the line of the Narmada–Son rivers is the most impressive outcrop.

Of greater economic importance are the Gondwana Group, in geological age extending from Upper Carboniferous through Permian and Triassic

3

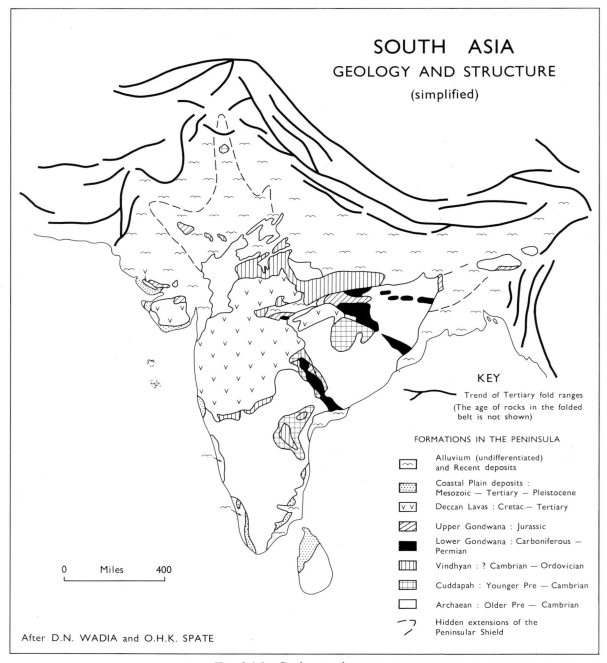

FIG. 2.1.1   Geology and structure

time into the Lower Jurassic. The deposits of this group are preserved in rift-like troughs still followed in the main by major drainage lines, e.g. the Damodar and Godavari valleys. Coal seams, often of great thickness and little disturbed by folding, are found along the troughs and probably extend westwards beneath the Deccan lavas. The coal is known to lie beneath the older alluvial deposits of the Ganges Plain in East Pakistan.

The Gondwana deposits are continental in origin,

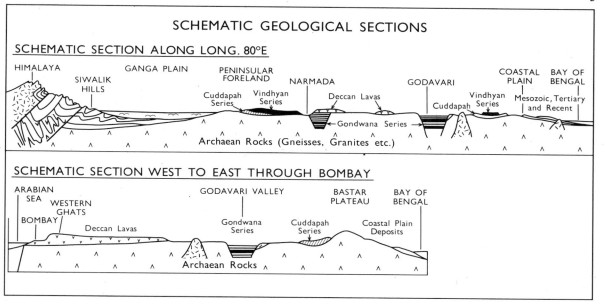

FIG. 2.1.2 Schematic sections

and one has to turn to the coastal plains of the Peninsula to find appreciable areas of marine formations of Mesozoic–Tertiary age. Apart from a small marine deposit in the watershed of the Narmada–Son rivers, evidence of marine transgression is lacking in the interior. It would seem that the Peninsula remained a relatively stable landmass over long periods of geological time, while the seas worked gently on the Coromandel coast to produce a narrow zone of plain built up of low cuestas of marine sediments.

Early in the Tertiary and beginning in late Cretaceous time, there occurred fissure eruptions of lava on an immense scale, which buried the northwestern part of the Peninsula beneath thousands of feet of basalt. Near Bombay the lava is 10,000 ft. thick, and it is surmised that it must have extended some way westwards and now lies deep beneath the Arabian Sea. Faulting along the line of the Western Ghats, and tilting of the lava plateau generally eastwards produced the main features of the present landscape.

It may well be that eruptions of the Deccan lavas were connected with the crustal instability associated with the Himalayan orogeny. To the north of the Peninsular 'shield' of mainly ancient rocks covered in places with younger continental, coastal, and extrusive igneous rocks, there lay a more or less broad depression, or geosyncline, into which the

bordering continental landmasses of the Peninsula and Central Asia had long been discharging through their rivers the products of erosion. During Tertiary time the deposits in the geosyncline dating from Pre-Cambrian to Tertiary were folded and thrust upwards to form the Himalaya. The process was long-continued and as the mountain chains grew, erosion fast worked upon them, and great rivers carried vast quanties of material into the marine gulfs that separated the young ranges from the Peninsular 'shield', then probably a large island. Continued uplift and fracturing raised more ranges, incorporating some of the recent deposits, which in turn were exposed to erosion. As the marine gulfs retreated, conditions were locally favourable at various times to the formation of coal and petroleum and the accumulation of salt. Coal of Cretaceous and Tertiary age is found in workable quantity in Assam, Jammu, the Salt Ranges, and Baluchistan; oil-bearing structures are located in the Salt Ranges, the Assam Valley, Gujarat, and the Tamilnadu coastal plain, natural gas-wells at Sui (West Pakistan) and Sylhet (East Pakistan); the Salt Ranges have long been a source of rock salt. Vertical movement of the Himalaya may not yet have ceased, and certainly during the Pleistocene period displacements measured in thousands of feet took place. The mountain belt still suffers earthquakes;

severe shocks have taken place at places as widely separated as Quetta, Kashmir, Himachal Pradesh, Bihar, and Assam. On the geological map (Fig. 2.1.1) the various formations of the Himalaya have not been distinguished. The Outer Himalayan belt, with the hills of the Assam–Burma border, and the mountain belt of Baluchistan and the northwest are largely of Mesozoic and Tertiary age. Rocks of almost all ages are found incorporated into the main Himalaya.

The youngest element in South Asia's structure is

changes in course by some of the major distributaries and tributaries, such as the 'Old' Brahmaputra and the Tista, have had important repercussions on navigation and settlement over the past two hundred years, a very short time geomorphologically speaking.

A distinct type of deposit associated with the Pleistocene in northwest Pakistan is loess which mantles parts of the Potwar Plateau between the Salt Ranges and the outer ramparts of the Himalaya. Disturbance of the vegetation cover through

1. *Baluchistan–Indus Plains:* The semi-arid Kachhi Plain and bare rocky Sulaiman Range beyond a mud-walled village with its mosque in the centre

the alluvium of the Indo–Gangetic Plains and the numerous smaller lowland areas. It is important to realise the variety of materials that are generally grouped under the heading 'alluvium' and the way in which differences in site in relation to present rivers affect their agricultural value. The term alluvium includes fluvial deposits laid down at various times through the Pleistocene up to the present. The most recent floodplain deposits include some very fertile material, while the older alluvia, long exposed to the leaching effect of rainfall and standing often above the levels where present-day floods might introduce fresh plant nutrients in the form of soluble salts and silt, tend to give rise to poorer soils.

There is evidence, particularly in the Ganges Delta, that the alluvium has not been entirely stable even in recent historic time. The 'older', Pleistocene, alluvial surfaces of the Ganges–Brahmaputra have been dislocated by faulting, with subsequent influence upon the local drainage pattern. Striking

over-grazing has led to severe gullying in the loess.

Major Physiographic Regions

The scheme of physiographic regions outlined below and shown in Fig. 2.1.3 leans heavily on Spate's work. Its purpose is to provide a regional framework within which to fit the varied facts of human, physical, and biogeographic significance. The relationships between man and his physical environment are further elaborated in later sections.

1. Baluchistan.
2. Northwestern Hills and Submontane Region.
3. Karakoram and Western Himalaya.
4. Eastern Himalaya.
5. Hills of the Burma border.
6. The Plains.
7. Peninsular Foreland.
8. Plateaus, troughs, and basins of the Peninsular Interior.

FIG. 2.1.3 Physiographic regions

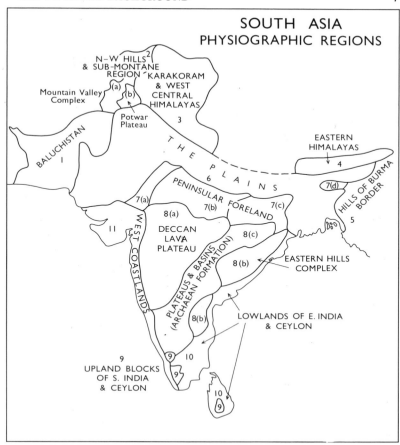

SOUTH ASIA
PHYSIOGRAPHIC REGIONS

9. Upland blocks of Southern India and Ceylon.
10. Lowlands of Eastern India and Ceylon.
11. West Coast lowlands.

1. In **Baluchistan** the influence exerted on the structure of the Tertiary fold mountains by the hidden northwesterly projection of the Peninsular Shield can be seen in the north–south trend of the Sulaiman and Kirthar ranges (north of Karachi), which break the generally east–west trend of the folds forming the Himalaya and the ranges of the Iranian complex. Fringed to the east by alluvial fans, the Sulaiman and Kirthar ranges present to the traveller from the Indus Plains a forbiddingly bare and rugged front, rising in the volcanic Takht-i-Sulaiman, to over 11,000 ft. Westwards the east–west trend of the system is restored in the ranges of Central Baluchistan and the Makran coast. Between the Chagai Hills and the Siahan Range are several basins of internal drainage, containing *playa* lakes,

such as Hamun-i-Mashkel. In the Makran and the eastern half of Baluchistan the intermontane basins drain eventually to the sea.

2. **The Northwestern Hills and Submontane Region.** The Gomul River just north of Takht-i-Sulaiman effectively separates the Baluchistan region with its predominance of broad high upland features from the region to the north where valleys and mountainous spurs make up much of the terrain. Structurally this is a most complicated corner, where the massive southeast–northwest-trending ranges of the Great Himalaya and Karakoram point across the Indus and Hunza valleys to the east–west and northeast–southwest-trending systems of the Pamir and Hindu Kush. The mountain and valley complex is best described in terms of its rivers and their basins, several of which constituted the territories of feudal states. The Kurram waters the Bannu Plain. To its north is the smaller Kohat Plain. The broad Vale of Peshawar is floored with

alluvium brought down from the west by the Kabul River and from the north by the Swat and its parallel tributary the Panjkora, these latter two valleys forming the territory of the former 'tribal' states of Swat and Dir respectively. The valley of the Upper Kunar which flows south to join the Kabul in Afghanistan, is the state of Chitral. Almost as isolated is the basin of the Gilgit River in the western extension of the furrow occupied by the upper course of the Indus before it cuts south and west in its spectacular gorge around the flanks of Nanga Parbat (26,629 ft.) which marks the western extremity of the Great Himalaya. South from this bastion the Kagan and Kishen valleys drain to the Jhelum.

Enclosed between the Salt Range, the Himalayan foothills, and the Indus, the Potwar Plateau is a distinctive region characterised by close-textured low rocky ridges following the strike of the Siwalik formations and masked in places by a cover of water-sorted loess.

3. **The Karakoram and Western Himalaya.** In Kashmir and the mountain zone extending eastwards into Nepal the parallelism of structural elements provides a key to the landscape. Approaching the Himalaya from the Punjab Plains, the first evidence that one is entering the orogenic belt is the abrupt change in scenery in the Siwalik Hills. Carved by erosion out of the fractured and distorted deposits of mainly coarse detritus derived from the Himalayan ranges as they grew to full stature in late Tertiary and early Pleistocene times, the Siwaliks strike parallel to the mountain front for hundreds of miles, presenting a formidable barrier to transverse movement on account of the ruggedness of the terrain rather than its relief which is rarely as much as 3000 ft. above sea-level (cf. the 1000 ft. or so of the adjacent plains). Between the Siwaliks and the Outer or Lesser Himalaya there are occasional breaks in the close succession of rocky scarp and jungly vale, and the landscape opens out in a submontane alluvial basin a few miles in width, e.g. the 'dun' of Dehra Dun and the Kangra Valley east of Pathankot.

The Outer Himalaya are 'lesser' only in comparison to the world's greatest range to which they form a broad pedestal. Away from this context, the Pir Panjal which separates the Vale of Kashmir from the Punjab Plains, and the Dhaola Dhar in Himachal Pradesh, rising to over 15,000 ft., would be sub-

stantial mountain ranges in their own right. Further east in the Kumaon Division of Uttar Pradesh the Outer Himalaya are less impressive in altitude but form a broad belt of deeply and maturely dissected plateau 70 miles wide, with crest levels rising from 6000 ft. to 12,000 ft. towards the flanks of the Great Himalaya.

Only in the Vale of Kashmir 20–25 miles wide and more than 80 miles along its axis parallel to the Pir Panjal, is the progression of steps upward to the grand peaks interrupted. The synclinal basin of the Vale is floored with a variety of alluvial deposits, lacustrine, fluvial, and fluvioglacial, through which the Jhelum River meanders at 5200 ft. above sea-level before entering the deep gorge it has cut through the Pir Panjal.

From Nanga Parbat, immediately north of the Vale of Kashmir, the Great Himalaya sweep southeast and east for 1200 miles. Several major rivers rise on its southern flanks – the Jhelum, Ganga (Ganges), Chenab – while others rise in the high plateaus of Tibet to traverse the mountain ranges (e.g. the Sutlej) or like the Indus and Tsangpo (Brahmaputra) to flow parallel to them for hundreds of miles finally outflanking the Himalaya to reach the plains through deep gorges almost 1500 miles apart.

Generally the Indian frontier lies a little north of the line of the high peaks of the Central Himalaya, but in the west the state of Jammu and Kashmir extends far beyond the Great Himalaya, across the high open valley of the Upper Indus to include the Karakoram. This 250-mile stretch of almost uninhabited mountains contains the world's greatest concentration of high peaks, crowned by K2 (28,250 ft).

4. **The Eastern Himalaya.** Eastwards from Sikkim the character of the mountain system is different in several respects from that of the Western and Central Himalaya. The Siwalik belt is lacking or at best a very minor feature. Transverse rivers such as the Arun and the Tista break the Outer Himalayan belt into numerous spurs projecting from the main chain of mountains, and consequently prevent the structural strike from dominating the landforms. East of Kanchenjunga (28,146 ft.) high peaks become less frequent. The Tibetan peak Namcha Barwa (25,445, ft.) overlooking the bend of the Tsangpo (Brahmaputra) is the last of the great

2. *Western Himalaya:*
Kagan Valley, a tributary of the river Jhelum close to the borders of West Pakistan and Kashmir. The Middle Himalayan summits are here upwards of 12,000 ft. This photograph, taken in March, shows snow still lying within the high forest. The lower slopes are terraced to permit rain-fed cultivation of *rabi* wheat and oilseeds and *kharif* maize. The numerous flat-roofed homesteads on the ridge in the foreground are some indication of population pressure on this rugged terrain. The landslide scars and gully erosion could well be the consequence of deforestation in order to open up land for subsistence farming.

summits west of the river, beyond which the crest line falls progressively along the waterparting between tributaries of the Brahmaputra and the Salween.

5. **Hills of the Burma border.** Differing markedly from the Himalaya in the scale of their relief and in their morphology, the ranges which sweep southwest and south from the easternmost part of Assam none the less stem from the same orogeny. For the most part the Cretaceous and Tertiary strata of the region are relatively unresistant shales and sandstones arranged in simple anticlines and synclines. The trend of the close folds is clearly indicated in the parallelism of the elongated trellised drainage pattern, particularly well seen in the Chittagong Hill Tracts of East Pakistan and the adjacent hill country of southern Assam. In the north where the Patkai and Naga Hills form the Burma–India border the system reaches its highest elevation of 12,550 ft. in the Saramati peak. Generally, however, heights over 7000 ft. are exceptional and the level of ridges declines southward to average 2000–3000 ft. between the Chittagong coast and the Kaladan Valley.

6. **The Plains** which represent the present surface of the more or less deep alluvial fill of the trough marking the contact zone between the stable Peninsular Shield and the Himalayan fold system may be treated as a single physiographic unit despite the variation in detail there is within them. While alluviation in the floodplains of rivers great and small has been the common genesis of the regions' features, differences in age and scale are significant in characterising subregional divisions.

The plains are in the main the product of the larger rivers rising in the Himalaya – the Indus and its Punjab tributaries, the Ganga and its tributaries, and the Brahmaputra. Relatively speaking the tributaries from the Peninsular foreland, principal among them the Son, have contributed little by reason of their smaller scale, gentler gradient and the lesser precipitation in their catchments. The alluvial deposits of the great river systems may conveniently be differentiated on the basis of age and the consequent degree of obliteration of the features which distinguish an actively developing floodplain – levees, backswamp depressions, abandoned meander ox-bows, etc.

The *active floodplains* contain the usually braided and changing channels of the river separated by more or less temporary islands of young alluvium, sandy or clayey depending on distance from the channel responsible for their deposition. Low bluffs or levees mark the limits of the active floodplains. In the deltas particularly, the active floodplains are areas of frequent change which can affect a considerable breadth of country tens of miles in extent. Elsewhere as in the Middle Ganga Plain and Punjab the active floodplains are more permanently fixed between bluffs.

Meander floodplain and *cover floodplain* are terms suggested by recent Canadian surveyors of West Pakistan landforms to describe the still relatively young alluvium no longer subject to periodical

3.   *Western Ghats* south of Bombay, showing the horizon-
tally bedded lava exposed along the deeply dissected edge
of the Deccan Lava Plateau. In several locations similar to
this the abrupt slope has been utilised to generate hydroelectric power.

reworking by the rivers (see below, Fig. 4.2.5). In
the case of the meander floodplains, the levees,
meander belts, and backswamp features of the past
active stage may still be discerned, while in the
cover floodplain such features have been obscured
by the levelling effect of sheet flooding which has
gradually reduced the raised elements of the landscape and filled in the depressions.

A still older element of the alluvial landscape is
the *scalloped interfluve* or 'old alluvial' surface. The
term 'scalloped interfluve' is expressive of the way in
which the flanks of the older alluvial interfluve areas
have been cut into by the meandering of the active
rivers. These older surfaces, in some cases dated as
Pleistocene, are most widespread in the higher parts
of the Punjab and Ganga Plains, and in the latter are
found in quite extensive remnants in the Barind and
Madhupur Tract of the delta in Bengal. Benches of
similar age and material fringe the Tertiary hill
country of East Pakistan where they are valued as
relatively level but drainable land for tea plantations.
From the Upper Ganga Plain westwards into the
Punjab the interfluves may carry patches of sandy
soil sometimes wind blown and hummocky, while
their edges may be extensively fretted by gullies cut
back from the present river.

Independent of the great rivers, the plains increase
in slope as the mountain belt is approached. Here is

a zone of confluent alluvial fans constituting a continuous piedmont plain into which the short generally intermittent streams from the hills lose themselves. In Uttar Pradesh this belt of often gravelly,
porous alluvium is known as the *bhabar*, and is succeeded down-slope by the *terai*, a marshy zone
where the water-table reappears at the surface in a
spring-line of headward-sapping gullies. Bhabar and
terai are not found in this form throughout the piedmont belt, though comparable features with variations according to rainfall regime and local conditions are widespread. In the piedmont of Bengal and
the Assam Valley the terai is well developed in a
marshy zone known as the *duars*.

Because of its low relief continuous with the alluvial plains and its past links with former river systems in the Ganga–Sutlej interfluve, the **Thar Desert**
may conveniently be considered here. Much of the
surface is sand, arranged into dune formations and
in many areas 'fixed' by scanty vegetation. Clay
bands beneath the sand give rise to saline lakes towards the Indus in Khairpur. Peninsular Shield
rocks similar to those forming the Aravallis underlie
the whole area, outcropping in places as rocky inliers in the sandy waste. Similar scattered inliers
occur in the Punjab Plains near Sargodha, between
the Jhelum and Chenab rivers, forming the Kirana
Hills which rise 1000 ft. above the alluvial plain and
provide the most northerly surface evidence of the
projecting shield around which the Himalayan folds
have been wrapped.

7.   **Peninsular Foreland.** Under this term may
be grouped the areas made up of the geologically
'solid' stuctures which flank the plains on the south.

In the west, the Aravalli Hills (7a) consist of rugged
ridges of Pre-Cambrian rocks decreasing northwards from about 5600 ft. to disappear beneath the
alluvium of the plains around Delhi. A region of
lower relief (7b) developed on Vindhyan sandstones
and Archaean gneiss extends from the Aravallis to
the valley of the Son, east of which are the gently
rolling plateaus of Chota Nagpur (7c) where occasional isolated hills stand out abruptly as much as
3000 ft. above the general surface.

The Chota Nagpur Plateau slopes away to the
northeast, beneath the Ganges alluvium, but its
structures persist to form a foundered link to the
Shillong Plateau (7d) of Assam. This mass of
Archaean rock rising abruptly in a 5000-ft. wall

4. *Granite inselberg*, capped by a Hindu temple, Tiruchirapalli (Trichinopoly), Tamilnadu. One of many such outcrops which rise above the gneissic plateaus of South India. Robert Clive lived in one of the houses in the foreground.

towering over the delta plain of East Pakistan, marks the easternmost visible prong of the Peninsular Shield.

8. Plateaus, troughs and basins of the Peninsular Interior. The area physiographically most distinctive in this broad region is the Deccan Lava Plateau (8a) in the northwest, a countryside characterised by great expanses of nearly level plateau formed by the lava flows into which the rivers have cut a landscape of gently stepped broad valleys. From its high western edge, extensively over 2500 ft. above sea-level, the plateau slopes gently eastwards, its main area being drained by the Godavari, Bhima, and Krishna rivers. North of the Ajanta Hills the drainage is westwards along the structural troughs followed by the Tapti and Narmada, which separate the lava areas of the Satpura Hills and Malwa Plateau from the main mass.

The Eastern Hills (8b) comprise the plateaus of Bastar, mainly of Archaean rocks and extensively over 3000 ft. in the north, and the several ranges of Cuddapah and Vindhyan sedimentary rocks south of the Krishna.

The region of open plateaus and basins in the Archaean rocks (8c) lying between the Eastern Hills and the Deccan lava country is most clearly differentiated from the latter in Mysore State. The western edge of the plateau is here more than 5000 ft. high, but generally its peneplain surface lies at about 3000 ft., here and there studded with granite inselberge that tower sheer-sided 1000 ft. and more above the plateau. Northeastwards the plateau of granites and gneisses is esentially similar but at a lower general level of about 2000 ft. The limit of this Telangana Plateau to the northeast is the Godavari–Wainganga trough where a structural rift valley in the Archaean rocks preserves Gondwana coal measures.

Beyond the Wainganga, around Raipur, the Chhatisgarh Plain occupies a basin of Cuddapah sedimentary rocks overlooked by the Maikal scarp in Deccan lava to the north and enclosed on the south by the Bastar Plateau.

9. Upland blocks of Southern India and Ceylon.

The abruptness with which these Archaean blocks rise above the adjacent gneissic plateau surfaces set them apart physiographically though there is doubt about whether they are structurally separable.

The Nilgiri Hills rise to 8760 ft. and extensively over 6000 ft., below which level the block slopes steeply away on all sides; to the 3000-ft. Mysore Plateau to the north; most sharply towards the Coimbatore Plateau (about 1200 ft.) to the south-east; and to the west in a sinuous, much fretted edge, characteristic of the Western Ghats, tumbling 1200 ft. per mile over a bare five miles to the Malabar coastal lowland.

South of the Palghat Gap, the first clear break in the high western edge of the Peninsular plateaus south of the Tapti Valley, the highland blocks reappear. Unlike the Nilgiris, the blocks here present their steepest face to the north (where the Anaimalai and Palni Hills overlook the Palghat Gap) and southeast towards Madurai and Tirunelveli in the scarps of the Palni and Cardamom Hills. The highest summit is at 8841 ft. in the Anaimalais but the proportion exceeding 6000 ft. is less than in the Nilgiris. From the Cardamom Hills southwards the plateau belt narrows, losing height somewhat and culminating in a peak of about 5400 ft. within a score of miles of Cape Cormorin.

The high country of Ceylon is essentially similar to the southern mainland blocks though its limits, especially to the southwest, are not so distinct. A peak 8281 ft. high crowns the highest platform surface of the plateau. The relief of Ceylon is treated in more detail below (Chapter 5.2).

10. **The Lowlands of Eastern India and Ceylon.** From Orissa to Tamilnadu and Ceylon the lowlands comprise a number of distinctive repeating elements:

(i) Broad benchlands cut in the Archaean gneisses and Vindhyan sedimentary rocks back the younger sedimentary and alluvial features and represent the lowest of the series of plateau steps that mount into the interior of the Peninsula and Ceylon. This plateau element is well developed in Nellore (Southern Andhra Pradesh), Coimbatore (Tamilnadu), and lowland Ceylon.

(ii) Seemingly outliers of the next higher plateau step are a series of hill masses in Tamilnadu conveniently grouped under the collective Tamilnad Hills.

(iii) Low cuestas of Mesozoic and (more exten-sively) Tertiary marine sediments, standing up to 300 ft. above sea-level, cover a significant area south-wards from the Ponnaiyar River (inland from Cuddalore) and have their counterpart in the northern tip of Ceylon. This element, its red soil capping dating perhaps from Pleistocene times, may be linked genetically to the 'old alluvial' benchlands of Bengal and to similar features of the Kerala lowlands.

(iv) Young alluvial plains at their widest in the deltas of the major rivers Godavari, Krishna, and Cauvery, form an almost continuous belt from the Mahanadi to Cape Cormorin.

(v) The coastline itself shows ample evidence of progradation, both mainland and Ceylon coasts consisting frequently of actively silting lagoons behind off-shore bars which are being extended by long-shore drifting.

11. **The West coast lowlands** from Kutch to Cormorin may be seen as the product of marine erosion sawing into the steep western flank of the Peninsular plateaus, lava in the north, Archaean rocks in the south. The whole coast may be pictured as hinged about Goa, the Maharashtra–Gujarat shoreline often showing features of submergence, while that of Mysore–Kerala is emergent.

The Mysore–Kerala section of the coastal belt comprises three elements:

(i) A benchland with old leached soils along the foot of the plateau edge, often cut in Tertiary sediments.

(ii) A belt of alluvium along the larger transverse valleys and tending to fill in the lagoons cut off from the sea by

(iii) The line of multiple beach ridges.

The Maharashtra coast, or Konkan, as far as Bombay, is so cut up by spurs from the Ghats enclosing the basins of short rivers which terminate in drowned valleys as to deter longitudinal communications by land. The lateritic benchland element is present, but alluvium is restricted to the valley bottoms. North of Bombay a coastal plain becomes more evident, and although the rivers enter the sea through short estuaries, drowning has not been so severe as to prevent the active accumulation of silt and mud to form tidal marshes. The Western Ghats stand back from the coast in Gujarat, extending northward till the Tapti and Narmada valleys finally break their continuity.

Across the Gulf of Cambay the Kathiawar

Peninsula is a low plateau of Deccan lava fringed with a benchland above a coast no longer dominantly submergent. Kutch, which separates it from the Indus Delta, consists of a number of Mesozoic sedimentary and basaltic 'islands' in a 'sea' of mud-flats, perhaps once the estuaries of rivers which used to traverse and perhaps to drain the now arid Thar Desert.

2. CLIMATE

Climatologists now recognise that South Asia forms a more or less distinct climatic province whose weather systems have little connection to those of neighbouring provinces. No longer can one speak in terms of a single 'monsoon climate' affecting the southern and eastern margin of Asia. Ideas about the mechanisms controlling the climate of the sub-continent have changed greatly over the past decade or so with increasing knowledge of movements in the upper atmosphere and of their relationship to surface conditions. It is beyond the scope of this book to discuss the latest theories at length, but an attempt is made below to suggest how these theories may help our understanding of climate as it affects man in the region. Whatever the outcome of scientific debate, the winds, the temperatures, and the precipitation experienced by the inhabitants, suffered by them, and utilised by them in their struggle to survive will follow the same regimes and be subject to the same vagaries as in the past few thousand years. Our main concern is to present the realities of climate as one basis for the better understanding of the varied character of the geography of the region.

Most of us are now accustomed to the idea that excessive heat or cold or humidity in the outdoor environment of the place where we live can be effectively and inexpensively controlled indoors. The peasant farmer of South Asia is still a long way from that stage of economic and technological advance when he can escape from the actualities of climate and weather by taking refuge in an air-conditioned office or living-room. The European working in India in the nineteenth century enjoyed a slight advantage over the local peasant in being able to employ a servant to work the 'punkas' which kept the air in motion over his master's head, or to operate the primitive air-conditioners – grass screens in the doorways, on to which water is sprinkled, so humidifying and cooling the air passing through. Blanford* quotes extensively from a resident in the Punjab writing about its seasons. Although not ap-plicable in detail throughout South Asia, especially as far as the coldness of the cold season is concerned, the following extracts may help the 'denizen of the temperate zone' conceive the very different seasonal march of the monsoon climate.

'Like the rest of India, the Punjab has really but three seasons: the summer or hot season, the rains, and the winter . . . the cold season. The hot season begins in April. . . . The west wind holds sway and . . . is a veritable hot wind. A denizen of the temperate zone can hardly realise to himself the dessicating, truly scorching heat of this wind. When exposed to it one may imagine one is facing an open furnace. In order to enjoy fresh air at this season one must take exercise in the early dawn, between 4 and 5 in the morning; for no sooner has the sun risen than the heat sets in again. . . . At sunrise . . . houses must be closed, only a small door being left open for communication with the outside. . . . Man and beast languish and gasp for air. . . . Vegetation suffers equally: almost all green things wither; the grass seems burnt up to the roots; bushes and trees seem moribund; the earth is as hard as a paved highway; the ground is seamed with cracks; and the whole landscape wears an aspect of bareness and sadness. At length, in June, the hot winds cease to blow, and are followed by a calm; and now indeed the heat is truly fearful; all things pine for the rain. . . .

'The southerly and easterly winds bring first clouds and violent storms with heavy rain showers, which are repeated daily, or at all events every two or three days; and finally the rains. . . . In July the trees begin a second time to burst into leaf; grass springs up once more, and soon a vegetation is developed, that, fostered by warmth and moisture is scarce to be kept within due bounds. . . . After from four to six weeks of heavy rain, often falling unin-

* Blanford, Henry F., *A Practical Guide to the Climates and Weather of India, Ceylon and Burmah* (London, 1889), pp. 127–29.

terruptedly for 2 or 3 days in succession, it clears up, and sometimes some weeks pass without further rain; after which a week or two more of rainy weather bring the season to a close. Grateful as is the coolness brought by these showers, the more oppressively hot and sultry is it, when the rain ceases and holds off, if only for half a day. The atmosphere weighs on one like a heavy coverlet; and then comes the daily and nightly plague of mosquitoes. Insect and reptilian life is now active; of evenings it hums and buzzes and croaks all around. . . . Woodwork swells, and doors and windows can be fastened only with much difficulty. Shoes and all articles of leather become quickly coated with fungus, books become mouldy and worm-eaten, paper perishes, linen becomes damp. . . .

'The period which immediately follows the rains up to October is the most unhealthy season in the year. Decaying vegetation under an ardent sun generates miasma (pollution) the consequences being fever, dysentery, and not infrequently cholera. Towards the end of the rains one rejoices indeed to see the heavy dark clouds disappear, but the heat soon becomes once more so great, that one longs for the cold season . . . watching for some sign of the cool westerly and northerly winds. With the beginning of October these winds set in steadily, clearing the skies, and now the blue firmament appears in all its splendour. . . . From October to Christmas, as a rule, the weather is clear and fine, the air is pure and most delicious. . . . In December and January . . . the nights are positively cold. . . . During the second half of the cold season we have in the Punjab a good deal of rain. . . . In February we have a short spring; many trees unfold their leaves. . . . But this spring is of short duration, and in March it is already warm on the plains and the hot summer is at hand; an occasional dust storm, however, for a while keeps off the summer heat. . . .'

The Monsoon
Although the word has been applied to the climate of one-third of Asia, and has also been borrowed for use in other parts of the world, 'monsoon' rightly belongs to the Indian Ocean. It is derived from the Arabic (and thence Urdu) word 'mausim', denoting 'season', but was originally applied to the distinct seasonal winds blowing between Arabia and the East Indies, the winds which Arab traders used to drive their ships to and fro on their annual voyages in quest of spices, ivory, and fine fabrics. Through Portuguese and Dutch the word entered the vocabulary of the British merchants and rulers in India, and for these land-lubbers it came to mean the seasonal rhythm of wet and dry rather than the changing wind systems familiar to sailors. In fact the monsoon in common parlance tended to refer specifically to the wet–hot season, heralded by a fanfare of violent storms and torrential rain – the 'breaking of the monsoon'. However the word was used, its application to the climate of the area carried the sense of marked seasonality.

Two basic factors are strongly influential in the climate of the sub-continent: the mountain girt high plateaus which separate India–Pakistan from the rest of Asia on the north, and the great expanse of ocean washing the Peninsula and Ceylon and extending and widening southwards beyond the Equator. Only in Baluchistan and Kashmir does the region with which we are concerned extend appreciably beyond the mountain wall. The Himalaya, backed beyond the Brahmaputra (Tsangpo) and Indus valleys by the Kailas and Karakoram ranges, the latter with the Hindu Kush branching southwest to continue the rampart into Afghanistan, tower continuously over 12,000 ft. and for great distances over 18,000 ft. These ranges effectively bar the movement of air-streams at surface level between the subcontinent and 'inner' Asia and vice versa. By contrast, to the south no relief feature stands high enough to prevent the free flow of air-streams from the surrounding seas into the subcontinent when the pattern of air pressure permits. However, as will be seen below, the Himalaya play more than a merely passive and protective role in the climate of the region, and might be held to rank high among the factors involved.

The Mechanism of the Indian Monsoon*
The account which follows leans heavily on Pierre Pédelaborde, *The Monsoon* (London, 1963). In the present state of knowledge, many of its conclusions can be only tentative, but they probably represent a closer approximation to truth than do traditional explanations.

---

* Readers who are content to take the dynamics of the monsoon as read may turn to the descriptive treatment of climate which follows on p. 19.

In order to begin to understand the modern concept of the monsoon it is essential to discard most of the preconceptions deriving from traditional explanations founded upon a more or less purely thermal genesis of the seasonally reversing surface air-currents which characterise the system. Traditional accounts viewed the monsoons as land and sea breezes operating on a gigantic continental scale. Modern explanations of the monsoons have to take into account the vastly greater knowledge we now have of the atmosphere in depth, of the movements that take place in the upper atmosphere; of the influence of these movements on air-flow at or near the surface, and perhaps above all, of the dynamic qualities of the atmospheric circulation.

It is important to appreciate that there is a two-way interaction between air-flow and pressure pattern. Movement of air in a simple cyclonic depression (in the Northern Hemisphere) is in an anti-clockwise direction, while that in an anticyclonic system is in a clockwise direction. When air is forced by the relief of the land to flow along an anti-clockwise or cyclonic curve, there is a dynamic effect which tends to produce a pressure pattern characteristic of a depression – i.e. low pressure on the left of the path of the flow of air. Conversely air following a clockwise path will tend to produce anticyclonic conditions on the right of its path. Such dynamically induced pressure patterns appear in South Asia as a consequence of the manner in which the high mountain ranges influence the flow of the *jet-stream* which is discussed further below.

Not only does the relief of the land play a creative part in the dynamics of climate, but it also has a strong influence on cloudiness and rainfall. Air passing across abrupt changes of slope is caused to rise to elevations where temperatures may fall below dew point so provoking condensation and perhaps precipitation. The *orographic lifting* of air induced by the Himalaya, the Western Ghats, and the hills of Assam has a marked effect on rainfall in those areas. The other main process inducing air to rise in quantity is the *convergence* of streams of air leading to the increase in 'thickness' of the air-stream which finds an outlet in ascent from which cloudiness and precipitation can often result through cooling. Conversely, *subsiding* air is warming, and so becomes clearer as it descends, bringing dry weather. Such subsidence is generally associated with *diver-gence* of air-streams at the surface, but takes place also where air-flow is down a slope.

Meteorologically there are basically two seasons in the subcontinent:

(i) the season of the Northern Hemisphere's winter when the northern circumpolar circulation dominates the scene dynamically,

(ii) the season of the 'wet monsoon'. The north polar influences having withdrawn north of the mountain wall, equatorial maritime air is permitted to invade the region, bringing with it more or less heavy precipitation. The influence of the southern circumpolar circulation is felt in the strong surges of air of the southern 'trade winds' sweeping north of the Equator.

Winter. During the northern winter there is a general cyclonic circulation of air moving from west to east around a polar depression in the 'free air' of the troposphere. This depression overlies a high-pressure centre at the surface over the Arctic and is the result of the subsidence of very cold air refrigerated by radiation into space during the long polar winter night. Such subsidence in creating a surface 'high' tends to produce a 'low' in the free air above it, from which the air is subsiding.

Around the polar depression air is moving from west to east, the greatest velocities of flow being in the jet-streams which are normally located at the equatorward edge of the circumpolar whirl. The position of the jet-stream fluctuates between about 20° N. and 35° N. during winter, but in detail is considerably influenced by the Himalaya and high mountains to their west and north: the Tibetan Plateau, Karakoram, Pamirs, and the Hindu Kush (Fig. 2.2.1). This mass of high land, projecting upwards to altitudes sufficient to have a significant effect on air movements in the troposphere (the lower atmosphere to a height of 4–10 miles), causes the jet-stream of winter to bifurcate. The stronger branch of the jet follows a path which inscribes an anticyclonic (clockwise) arc across Afghanistan followed by a cyclonic (anticlockwise) arc along the southern flank of the Himalaya. A 'high' pressure system forms south of the jet-stream over Afghanistan and northwest Pakistan, from which air tends to subside over India, warming and stabilizing as it does so and bringing generally settled clear sunny conditions to South Asia.

While its main influence is to stabilize conditions

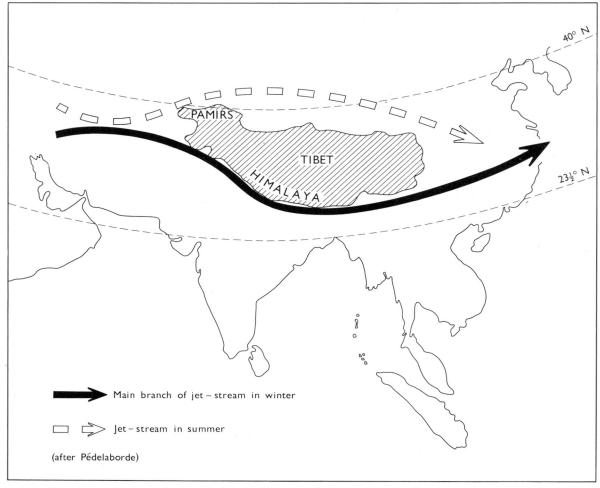

FIG. 2.2.1   Jet-stream: winter and summer

over the region, the jet-stream may be held responsible for periodical disturbances in the northwest of
the subcontinent.

Low-pressure systems in temperate latitudes tend
to follow paths immediately beneath the jet-stream.
Such disturbances are found to move along the
eastern Mediterranean and into northwestern
Pakistan – India, appearing here as perturbations or
waves, rather than as well formed frontal depressions. They occur as troughs of low pressure with
strongly convergent air in the westerly stream at
above 2000 metres. In South Asia they generally
overtop a gentle easterly (trade wind) flow of air at
the surface. Sharp cold rainstorms from towering
clouds and a drop in temperature accompany the
passage of such troughs, being followed soon by

clear weather. From October to April between four
and eight westerly perturbations occur each month.
The disturbances however are not intense and precipitation, while of useful quantity for agriculture
in the Punjab, Kashmir, and northwest Pakistan, is
not heavy, nor does it persist far down the Ganga
Valley, Patna being its extreme limit to the east. The
weakness of the disturbances is partly a function of
their being associated with an air-stream which is
subsiding as it enters the subcontinent, and has little
incentive to rise, being a cooler current overtopping
a warmer at the surface. Much of the precipitation
that does result is probably induced orographically
when the air is forced up along the flanks of the
Himalaya.

In winter the subcontinent can be regarded as·

divided into a wetter northwesterly and a drier southeasterly province, due to the limited effect on precipitation extended by the westerly waves. Over Peninsular India meteorological conditions combine to assure the constancy of the trade winds, generally light breezes in the stream of stable, warming, and so dry air. Drought is the expectation of most of the region throughout the winter.

A further factor among the meteorological influences of this season is the intertropical convergence, or I.T.C. Pushed south by the dominant influence of the circumpolar system of the northern winter the I.T.C. is none the less present in the latitude of Colombo, which consequently has no really dry month. The nature of the I.T.C. is further considered below.

Summer: the transition from winter. A distinctive characteristic of the Indian climate, sensibly if not strictly meteorologically, is its threefold division into (i) the cool and mainly dry winter, (ii) the hot and mainly dry season from about March or April into early June, and (iii) the wet monsoon, 'bursting' in June and lasting into September or later. A transitional autumnal period of various duration and weather, depending on latitude, links the 'wet' and the 'cool' seasons, but hardly ranks as a separate season. The meteorological elements in dispute for control over the subcontinent are those which dominate respectively, winter and summer. Through the hot–dry season between winter and the 'burst' of the wet monsoon there is a gradual change as the sun's apparent march towards the Tropic of Cancer brings with it a reduction in the dynamic power of the cold polar air-mass which has held the initiative throughout the long polar night of winter. As the circumpolar whirl diminishes in speed so does its power to send offshoots of polar air into low latitudes, including South Asia, and to maintain its branch of the jet-stream south of the Himalaya.

Solar heating over northwestern Pakistan–India gradually establishes a thermal 'low' at the surface, but while the jet-stream remains south of the Himalaya, it maintains its dynamic anticyclone aloft over Afghanistan and the plateau borderland of West Pakistan. This 'lid' of subsiding warming dry air prevents the surface thermal 'low' from having sufficient effect as a lifting agent to carry air aloft and so to bring about precipitation. While such conditions persist in the northwest into May, the monsoon has already broken in Burma. Here, beyond the eastern end of the Himalaya, the jet-stream's cyclonic path has produced a dynamic depression aloft which does nothing to inhibit the uplift of converging air-streams coming in from the south across Burma, where rains are heavy in May. These more unstable conditions affect the neighbouring parts of India and East Pakistan, where pre-monsoon rainfall is important to agriculture.

At this stage, in May, we see the subcontinent again divisible into two climatic provinces: a western one, now drier, and an eastern, now wetter. Even after the monsoon bursts more generally, the division remains true, and the same basic factors continue to operate though the comparative size of the two provinces alters in favour of the wetter region.

Summer: the wet monsoon. The 'break' or the 'burst' of the wet monsoon, has puzzled climatologists for many years, but it is only recently that our increased knowledge of upper air movements seems to open the way for an explanation to fit all the phenomena, though as yet no one theory has general acceptance. Fig. 2.2.2 of two cross-sections through the atmosphere along longitude 90° E. shows the strength of the resultant westerly and easterly air movements averaged for five-day periods.* The Tibetan Plateau and the Himalaya are represented by the shaded area. In the earlier section two branches of the jet can be seen, one lying just south of the Himalaya; light easterly winds blow at the surface over the Peninsula. By 6–10 June the southern branch of the jet-streams has gone and India is invaded by strong westerly currents at the surface, the southwest monsoon.

The removal of the jet-stream to north of the Tibetan Plateau leads to a reversal of the curvature of flow of free air to the north and northwest of the subcontinent (Fig. 2.2.1). Over northern Iran and Afghanistan the trajectory of free air takes on a cyclonic curve (anticlockwise), leading to a dynamic depression aloft where previously there was an anticyclone. Here then, to the northwest of Indo-Pakistan there develops a dynamic depression overlying

---

* The sections are adapted from Yeh Tu-Cheng, Dao Shih-Yen, and Li Mei-Ts'un, 'The Abrupt Change of Circulation over the Northern Hemisphere during June and October', in Bolin, Bert (Ed.) *The Atmosphere and the Sea in Motion* (New York, 1959).

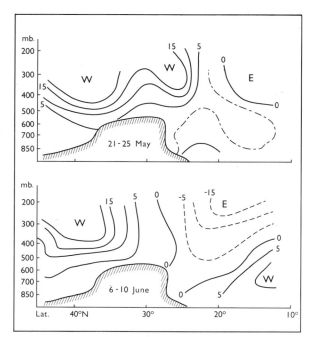

FIG. 2.2.2 Cross-sections through atmosphere along 90° E. Average wind speed in metres per second

the thermal depression already established at the surface, and it appears that this event may well be the trigger that sets off the 'burst' of the monsoon, allowing the vigorous inflow of equatorial air deep into India.

The intertropical convergence (I.T.C.), up till now situated between latitudes 10° N. and 20° N. is no longer prevented by polar air and the dynamic barrier of the jet-stream from moving north over India. There is, however, in the Antarctic circumpolar whirl a dynamic force from the Southern (now the winter) Hemisphere to give the trade winds their momentum, so that they cross the Equator, turning from southeast to southwest as they come under the contrary Coriolis force deflecting them to the right in the Northern Hemisphere. That it is a progression of surges of air from the south rather than suction into a fluctuating 'low' over northwest India–Pakistan that influences the movement of the I.T.C. seems to be demonstrated by the way in which the I.T.C. advances steadily north into the Ganga Valley (and can be observed so doing on the synoptic weather charts) and suddenly reappears near the Equator, to repeat its advance once again. There is no 'retreat' of the I.T.C. as one would expect if it were a simple frontal surface between contrasting surface air-masses.

The well-known 'pulsations' in the monsoon weather are due to waves of dynamic origin which develop in the I.T.C. (whose constituent air-streams are too homogeneous to give rise to frontal depressions of the type associated with the polar front in temperate latitudes). Over India such waves often develop into cyclonic vortices and the wet monsoon is punctuated by the cycle of their development as they pass westwards up the Ganga Valley. They bring periods of heavy rain, separated by more or less brief respites of clear weather, during which, however, the strong sunshine so raises temperatures and at the same time evaporates moisture from the sodden ground as to produce the unpleasantly sticky conditions which are harder to bear than the cooler if more thoroughly soaking weather of the rainy spells.

The amount of monsoon rainfall differs greatly from region to region over the subcontinent, and also is subject to considerable variability from year to year in the same region. Among the most important factors accounting for the distribution of rainfall is relief. The southwest air-streams when they strike the Western Ghats at right-angles rise abruptly to produce strong upcurrents and generally heavy precipitation along the crest of the Ghats. A little to the east air is tending to subside and a rain shadow effect is produced. The Himalaya play a dual role, stimulating uplift and also because of their great height channelling the monsoon air-flow northwestwards up the Ganga Valley. This channelling effect adds to the tendency to convergence and is probably responsible for carrying heavy rainfall much further into the northwest than might otherwise be the case. Relief has a strong effect in the northeast also, where currents coming in across the Bay of Bengal are funnelled over Sylhet and the Assam Hills, producing phenomenal rainfall at Cherrapunji as they rise abruptly against the Garo Hills.*

The northwestern corner of the subcontinent is relatively dry during summer despite the presence of the intense surface 'low' over the Thar Desert–Indus Valley, and the absence of relief barriers to the inflow of equatorial air. The primary reason for these dry conditions lies in the thinness of the monsoon

* Cherrapunji holds the world record for rainfall with an average annual fall of 425·1 inches; as much as 36·4 inches have fallen in twenty-four hours in the month of June, when the average fall is 106·1 inches.

flow towards its western flank, here only 500 metres thick, and furthermore, overlaid by a 'lid' of warm anticylonic air originating in the subtropical cell of high pressure standing over the Sahara and extending a ridge across Iran–Afghanistan. This lid limits the possibility for uplift of the surface air and so minimises precipitation.

Between these extremes of thickness the chance of convergent upflow and precipitation depends on the extent of the influence of the 'lid' which sometimes causes the spread of drought conditions far to the east of the normally arid areas of the Thar, Indus, and Punjab. Occasionally the 'lid' effect is withdrawn to the west and the monsoon air is allowed to escape upwards to bring torrential rain to the semi-desert.

A further cause of irregularity in monsoon rainfall is the occurrence of tropical cyclones particularly over the coasts of the Bay of Bengal, and especially in late summer. India averages thirteen tropical cyclones per annum. They are very destructive at the head of the Bay of Bengal when their impact may be combined with a 'hurricane wave' and wind-driven seas. The 'hurricane wave', which may be only 1 ft. in amplitude, is caused by the very low pressure in the eye of the cyclone, but other waves, driven by the violent winds may mount to 30 ft. and more when they are funnelled up a confined estuary. Hence the repeated calamitous cyclones that occur in the Meghna and other estuaries along the sea edge of the Ganges–Brahmaputra Delta. Tropical cyclones also affect the Coromandel coast of Tamilnadu and Andhra Pradesh. The late autumn (October–November) rainfall maximum of Madras is attributable in part to these cyclones, in part to the I.T.C.

In mid-October the southerly branch of the jet-stream returns to its winter position south of the Himalaya, indicating that once more Northern Hemisphere polar dynamics are in command of the situation. The return of the jet-stream to the Indian scene is accompanied by the restoration of light easterly air-streams to the surface, the trade winds. Drought conditions are re-established over northern India–Pakistan while the I.T.C., under the weakening dynamism of the southern circumpolar system with the end of winter, continues to allow a degree of convergence to bring rain to a progressively smaller area of South India and Ceylon.

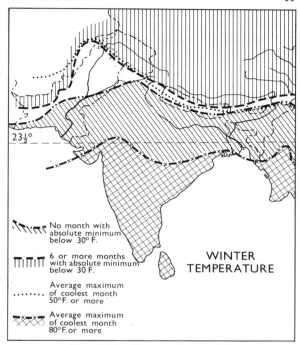

FIG. 2.2.3 Temperature: winter

Temperature and Rainfall

Whatever the dynamics and pressure patterns that ultimately control atmospheric movements over the subcontinent, the climatic elements to which man, animals, and plants are most sensitive are temperature and rainfall.

Winter temperature. Thanks to the protective influence of the mountain systems to the north and northwest, India and Pakistan enjoy higher winter temperatures north of the tropic than are experienced in comparable latitudes elsewhere in Asia. Fig. 2.2.3 shows a number of winter isotherms, three of which indicate clearly the influence of the mountain wall.

(i) *The isotherm for six or more months with an absolute minimum temperature of below 30° F.* avoids entirely the Indo–Gangetic Plains, and follows the mountains, entering the region only in Kashmir and the high northerly third of Baluchistan.

(ii) That for the *average maximum for the coolest month at 50° F.* follows a very similar path along the Himalaya–Hindu Kush.

(iii) The isotherm for the *absolute minimum temperature at or below 30° F.* follows essentially the same course east of the River Sutlej's traverse of the

Himalaya, but west of this it enters the plains to
follow the course of the Sutlej downstream to its
junction with the Indus, and so west to skirt the
mountain edge and run parallel to the Makran coast.
Thus the plains of the Punjab, in West Pakistan and
India, and the foothills lying to the northwest
experience occasional frosts, these becoming more
regular northwestwards across the Indus into the
Vale of Peshawar and beyond. But temperatures in
the plains fall very little below freezing; the absolute minimum recorded at Jacobabad is 30° F.,
Multan 29° F., Lahore 28° F., Delhi 31° F., Agra
28° F.

This corner of the subcontinent, furthest from the
sea, enjoys a modest degree of continentality, which
gives it a more invigorating cool season (except
perhaps for the ill-clad and the underfed) than is
found elsewhere. Close to the hills, in Peshawar and
Rawalpindi for example, light snowfalls occur but
the temperature never falls below 26° F. at Peshawar. The plains here stand at over 1000 ft., a fact
which accentuates the effect of the continentality
and northerly latitude as far as temperature is concerned.

It will be noted that none of the three isothermal
lines discussed above suffers any deflection from its
west–east orientation within the borders of north-
eastern India. Not until immediately beyond India's
most eastern limits do two of the lines swing
abruptly south to parallel the watershed between
the Salween and the northernmost tributaries of the
Irrawaddy.

The fourth isotherm shown on Fig. 2.2.3 is that
for the *average maximum temperature of 80° F.
or more in the coolest month*. It is seen to lie mainly
just south of the Tropic of Cancer, and runs from
Kathiawar to close to the mouth of the Ganga,
almost precisely delimiting 'peninsular' from 'continental' India and suggesting by its position the combined effect of latitude and marine influence.

With the sole exception of Chitral and the adjacent areas of montane and intermontane Kashmir,
no part of the subcontinent has an average maximum of less than 50° F. in the coolest month. Although this is rather a crude measure, it is an indication that as far as temperature is concerned plant
growth can continue to some extent throughout the
cool season. In the Peninsula and Ceylon conditions
are pleasantly warm. At Bangalore (3021 ft. above

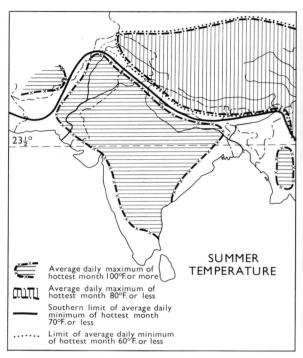

FIG. 2.2.4   Temperature: summer

sea-level) the absolute minimum is 52° F.; at
Madras 57° F. Infrequent disturbances bring occasional cloudy skies to the northwest, but these seldom persist beyond western Uttar Pradesh. Otherwise the cool season is generally one of clear blue
skies, warm days, with calm or light breezes.

Summer Temperature. Fig. 2.2.4 depicts certain
summer isotherms, all of which suggest more nearly
homogeneous conditions than in winter. The
greater part of the subcontinent is contained within
the isotherm for the average daily maximum of
100° F. or more in the hottest month. The mountain
fringe and all but a small section of the coastal zone
escapes such sustained extremes of heat. The unfor-
tunate stretch of coastal lowland is in northern
Tamilnadu and southern Andhra Pradesh, an area
with an anomalous rainfall regime. While elsewhere
midsummer temperatures in the coastal zone are
moderated by on-shore breezes and at latest from
June by the monsoon rains, the Carnatic then lies
on a lee-shore and in the extended rain shadow
of the Western Ghats.

The annual regime of temperature for fourteen

FIG. 2.2.5 Temperature regimes (for location of stations see Fig. 2.2.9)

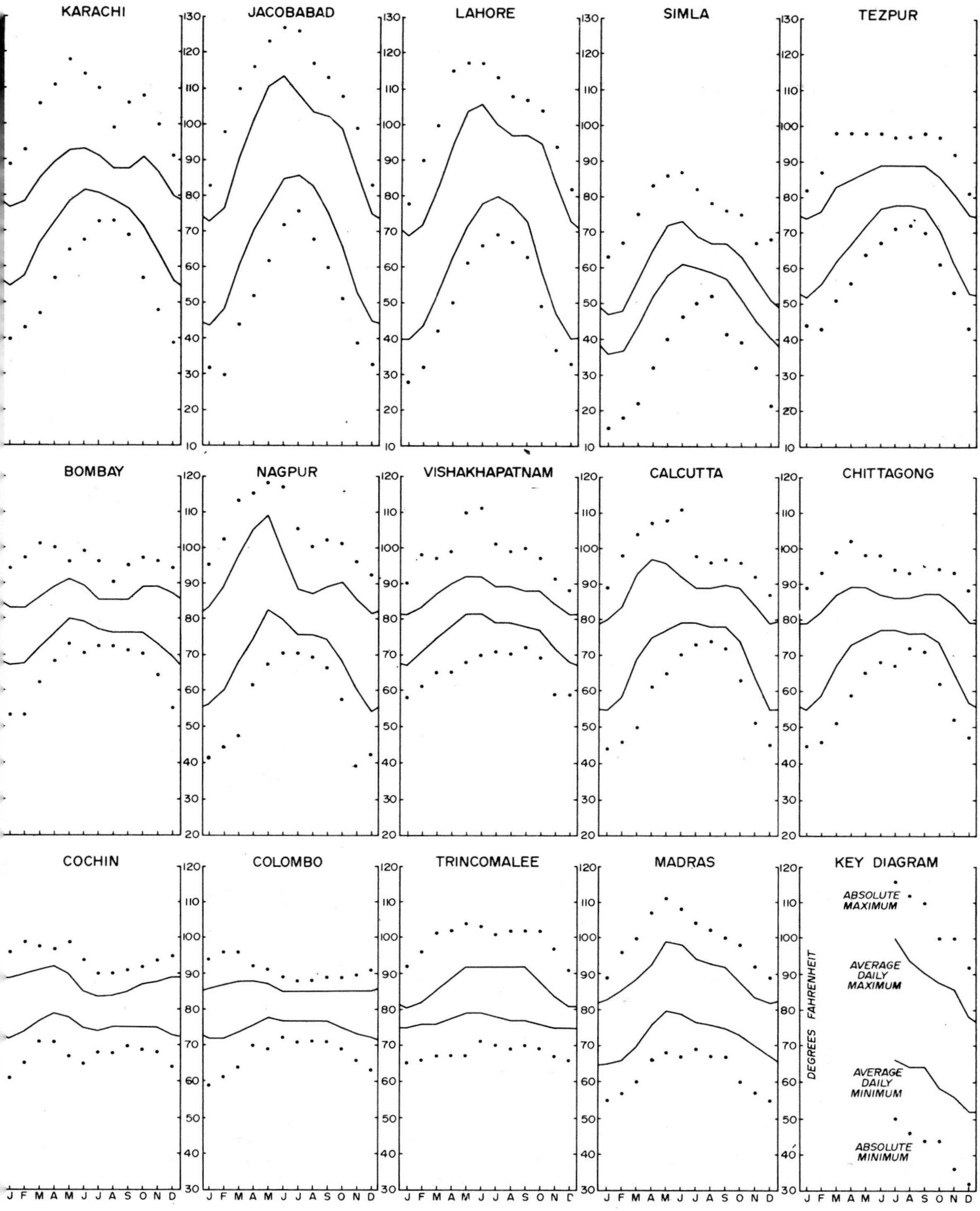

5. *Farmer's house at Chhor near Mirpur Khas*, Hyderabad, West Pakistan. This area is particularly hot in summer so the houses are designed to minimise the amount of sunshine and heat admitted, and to introduce any breeze that blows (from the southwest) through the fixed ventilators on the roof. The thick walls are of sun-dried brick finished with mud plaster.

selected stations is shown in Fig. 2.2.5. The graphs are for the average daily maxima and minima, month by month; the unconnected points represent the absolute maximum and minimum temperature for each month (i.e. the highest and lowest readings ever recorded).

From an examination of the graphs the following salient features emerge:

1. The characteristic regime shows a relatively steep climb in temperature from a midwinter minimum (December or January) to a maximum in May or June, the peak of the hot dry weather.

2. With the break of the monsoon, bringing fairly general cloud if not rain the temperature drops less abruptly through July–August–September. In some cases this falling-off takes the form of a trough on the graph, as temperatures rise again to a secondary maximum in September–October, reflecting the reduction in frequency of rainfall and in cloud cover.

3. Generally temperatures fall more steeply again from October to December, marking the change in meteorological conditions following the re-establishment of the jet-stream south of the Himalaya.

4. In winter the diurnal range of temperature is greater than in summer at most stations, a consequence of lower minima resulting from night radiation in clear weather.

5. Diurnal and seasonal range tends to increase with latitude and with continentality of position:

compare Bombay and Nagpur, Karachi and Jacobabad.

Several progressions may be noted. Colombo's near equatorial equability, is modified in Trincomalee where rainfall is mainly in winter, the associated cloudiness reducing temperatures. The progression Colombo–Cochin–Bombay–Karachi illustrates the transition into a thoroughly monsoonal regime, the ranges of absolute and average diurnal and annual temperatures increasing polewards.

Nagpur, in the heart of South Asia, may be taken as illustrating the typical monsoon regime. Compared with Bombay its range is greater on each count. Towards Calcutta there is again some modification, but that its regime is rather less equable than Bombay's may be attributable to its position inland, some sixty miles from the open sea. The graphs of Chittagong on the East Pakistan coast and more clearly still, Tezpur in the Assam Valley show the moderating influence exerted on temperature by the pre-monsoonal rainy weather of March–April–May referred to on p. 17 above. Such rains are appreciably less significant in West Bengal.

The contrast between the temperature regimes of Calcutta and Vishakhapatnam could be explained in terms of the latter's closer proximity to the sea, which reduces absolute, diurnal, and annual ranges. Madras has much the same regime as Vishakhaptnam but suffers higher temperatures in May–June–

July when it receives little or no rainfall from the southwest monsoon whose air-stream is subsiding and so clearing as it flows down from the Western Ghats and the Mysore Plateau.

Northwestwards from Nagpur the monsoon rains arrive later and last a shorter time, consequently their cooling influence is less clearly felt. Winters however are quite cool, and here one sees the combined effect of latitude continentality and occasional cloudiness. Lahore and Jacobabad have essentially similar regimes, but that of the latter is more extreme. It has been included as being notorious for having one of the highest absolute maxima recorded for an inhabited place: 127° F. As has been mentioned above, winter temperature minima in the plains of the northwest are only exceptionally low enough to inhibit plant growth. Summer maxima, however, *averaging* over 100° F. for six months at a time, and over 110° F. for two of these are wilting to plants and extremely enervating to animals including man.

Lastly, Simla is included as typical of the Himalayan hill-stations to which British rulers in India used to flee to escape from the stifling heat of the plains. Its regime is in general closely parallel to that of Lahore. Although at 7224 ft. above sea-level (cf. Lahore 702 ft.) Simla's average minima in winter are only three to four degrees below that of the plains city, though its absolute minima are much lower. Its average maxima march ten degrees or so above its minima, keeping a good thirty degrees below the maxima at Lahore.

Rainfall

Of all the climatic elements rainfall plays the most significant role in the life of South Asia. While temperatures are rarely so extreme as to arrest plant growth, deficiencies of moisture due to the vagaries of rainfall are accepted as a normal hazard in agriculture. Most parts of the region experience complete drought for several weeks each year, and in many areas rainfall frequently varies so considerably from 'normal' as to affect farming adversely.

The map of *rainfall incidence* (Fig. 2.2.6) summarises the comments on precipitation made above in the section on climatic dynamics. In this map the subcontinent is divided into regions having similar rainfall regimes (though not similar rainfall totals). A rainy month is regarded as one during which

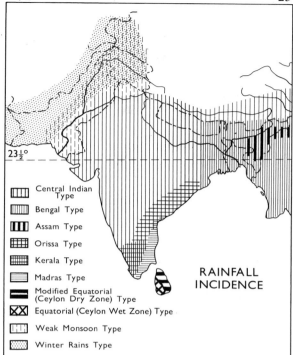

FIG. 2.2.6 Rainfall incidence

more than one-twelfth of the mean annual rainfall is normally received. Other maps and diagrams are essential to a full appreciation of rainfall, and it must be stressed that this map attempts to express only one aspect of it. While the formula used brings out well the significant differences in proportion of wet to dry months in characteristically monsoonal areas, it tends to mask the inadequacies of monthly means. Ten types of rainfall incidence are distinguished on the basis of the occurrence of the rainy months throughout the calendar year.

1. The basic type to which others can be regarded as modifications, is the *central Indian type* in which the rains begin in earnest in June, and continue for four months. None of the remaining eight months of the year receives one-twelfth of the annual rainfall, but this is not to say that no significant amount of rain occurs. The discussion of the rainfall dispersion diagrams below will bring out the importance of rainfall outside the main rainy season. The central Indian type of rainfall incidence is seen to extend over almost the whole of northwestern India, east to include Uttar Pradesh and most of Madhya Pradesh, south to include Maharashtra and the

interior and northern parts of Mysore and Andhra Pradesh.

2. In the *Bengal type*, which covers Bihar, West Bengal, East Pakistan, and the adjacent tips of Orissa and Assam, substantial rains begin earlier giving a five-month rainy season from May to September.

3. In the *Assam type* there are earlier rains still, and the season extends to six months, from April to September. The influence on the Bengal and Assam types of the somewhat different mechanism of the monsoon experienced in Burma was referred to above.

4. Southwards of the central Indian type the influence of the intertropical convergence (I.T.C.) in its late season position is felt on the east coast, being augmented by tropical cyclones in late summer and autumn. The *Orissa type*, of Orissa, almost all except southern Andhra Pradesh, and western Mysore is one in which the rains start in June (as in the central Indian type) but persist into October or November, giving five or six months with more than one-twelfth of the annual rainfall.

5. In the *Kerala type* of the southwest coast and plateaus the rains come earlier (May) and last six months in the specified amount.

6. The *Madras type* is one of the subcontinent's 'anomalies'. Deprived of the main onset of monsoon rains by the sheltering effect of the Ghats, the Coromandel coast has to wait until August or September for the start of appreciable rains, and the rainy season lasts only four to five months.

7. The *Ceylon dry zone type* of the northern and eastern parts of the island has not more than a month or two with less than one inch. Such a statement although statistically supportable, may give the impression of less droughty conditions than actually obtain all too frequently in the dry zone. Maximum rainfall (over one-twelfth the annual average) occurs from October to January.

8. The *Ceylon wet zone* of southwest Ceylon has a regime approximating to equatorial with no pronounced dry season and a double maximum from April–June and October–November.

9–10. At the other end of the subcontinent, the central Indian type degenerates into the *weak monsoon type* which overlaps with the *winter rains type* in the Western Mountains and northern Punjab Plains.

Areas shaded as the weak monsoon fringe receive

rains in the three months from July to September. Winter rainfall begins in December or January, and persists into April or May.

The rainfall dispersion diagram set out in Fig. 2.2.7 illustrates the gradational nature of the regional boundaries shown on the map of rainfall incidence. Variability of rainfall – in any month from year to year, and in annual total from year to year is characteristic of the region. Each graph is based upon a run of statistics, covering usually twenty years (ten years in the case of a few stations). The graph is constructed as follows. The highest figure for each month forms the uppermost line; the lowest forms the bottom line (often this line fails to appear above zero). Between the top line and the next (the upper quartile) are the highest quarter of the recordings, while the lowest quarter of readings lie below the next lower line (the lower quartile). The shaded area, the interquartile range (I.Q.R.), thus contains half the readings and in a sense can be read to mean that as often as not the rainfall will fall within this range. Fig. 2.2.8 showing the annual totals of rainfall treated in like manner will be discussed along with each station's pattern of monthly rainfall.

The reader is warned against reading the diagrams to mean that, for example, the monthly totals shown by the uppermost line all occurred in the same year! The graph for any single year might well show an erratic progress within the limits of the maximum and minimum values shown.

The rainfall dispersion diagrams will be discussed station by station, grouped according to regional type of rainfall incidence to which they belong.

1. *Central Indian type* (Stations: Jaipur, Ahmadabad, Bombay, Allahabad, Nagpur, Bellary).

Nagpur may be taken as our starting-point, since it represents the mean situation for the type region. The monsoon rains start here in June. From this month throughout July, August, and September the rains are normally heavy, but their range of variability is not inconsiderable. June has brought as little as 2.3 inches, or as much as 19.7 inches, but this could be attributed to the vagaries in the date of the break of the monsoon. By July the wet monsoon is firmly established, and the total ranges between a minimum of 8 inches and a maximum of 22 inches: the I.Q.R. for this peak month is between 14.4 and 20 inches. From the July maximum the

FIG. 2.2.7 Rainfall: monthly dispersion diagrams

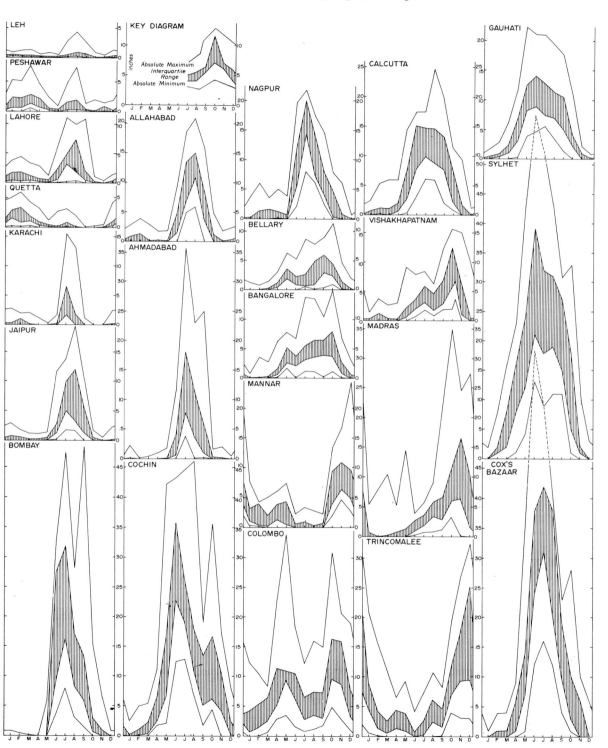

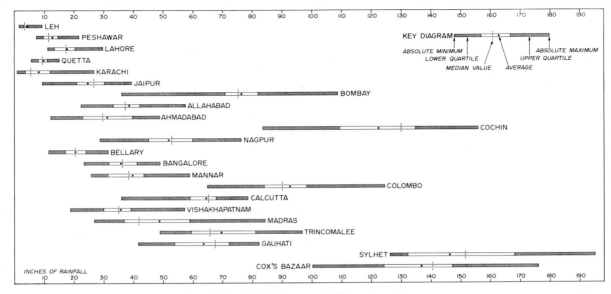

FIG. 2.2.8   Rainfall: annual dispersion diagrams

The unshaded portion of each bar is the interquartile range for annual rainfall, within which the dot indicates the *mean* (average) and the pecked line the *median* (the central point above and below which half the readings fall). In the case of most stations in the subcontinent where the rainfall is concentrated in three to five months of the year, the pattern of annual variation closely resembles that of the few rainy months.

totals fall off in August and September. In the latter month it is noteworthy that the minimum is about 2·5 inches, and even the I.Q.R. begins at 4 inches, little enough when a single twenty-four-hour spell has been known to bring almost 7 inches of rain. By October the minimum expectation has plunged to nil where it remains throughout the eight months ending in June. Appreciable rain may come in October, but the chances are that the rainfall will be between 0·5 and 4·8 inches, most of which might come in a single storm!

The narrowing of the I.Q.R. from November to May is a measure of the real drought of the cool–dry and hot–dry seasons. While the highest rainfalls recorded throughout the dry season range from 1 inch to over 6 inches, the mean expectancy of rain is very low, and negligible in December and January. Throughout the pre-monsoon period of February to May the mean expectancy is between nil and 1·6 inches, and so may be discounted as far as agriculture is concerned. In Fig. 2.2.8 Nagpur is seen to represent a fairly central tendency for all the stations. The extreme range of its annual rainfall is between 28·5 and 76 inches, the I.Q.R. being 45 to almost 60 inches. Thus despite a mean annual rainfall of about

52 inches, in one year out of four less than 45 inches may be received.

The other stations in the central Indian type may now be compared with Nagpur to bring out any significant differences.

Allahabad, lying further north, differs mainly in the later incidence of heavy rain. June has been known to bring 9·3 inches but the mean expectation is of between 1·5 and 5 inches and in some years no rain at all has been recorded. July sees the minimum at 5 inches, the maximum 18·6 inches, but the highest rainfalls belong to August (maximum 21 inches: interquartile range (I.Q.R.) 11–15 inches). Compared with Nagpur, the rains come later and end sooner. For ten months (September–June) the monthly minimum can be nil and by October the best that can be expected is 5 inches, and on balance not more than 1·5 inches. The dry season is a little drier than at Nagpur.

In the range of its annual rainfall Allahabad shows a rather narrower and lower range of variation round an I.Q.R. of 33–42 inches. With 40 inches regarded in a very general sense as the minimum annual rainfall capable of supporting rain-fed agriculture, it is interesting to note the occurrence of this liability in rather more than 50 per cent of years, as far down the Ganga Plain as Allahabad.

Lying further west and a little north, Jaipur's pattern is very close to that of Allahabad, differing only in having a rather lower expectation of rainfall throughout the year, and naturally in the annual totals.

Lahore marks the transition between the 'central Indian' and 'winter rainfall' types, but belongs rather to the former. Marking its westerly position in relation to the main monsoon air-stream flowing up the Ganga Plain from the southeast, Lahore has its maximum rainfall in August (more often than not) though its *mean* maximum is in July. Although winter rainfall is slight, a secondary maximum is recorded in January–February. There is, however, a risk of little or no rain one year in four in every month of the cool–dry and hot–dry seasons.

In *Ahmadabad* and *Bombay* the basic patterns of Nagpur, Allahabad, and Jaipur are seen again but in exaggerated form. Ahmadabad is the drier of the two, not achieving quite such high totals in July–August–September as does Bombay, and tending to end its rains conclusively in October, whereas Bombay's I.Q.R. for that month lies between 1·5 and 3 inches. Both stations show extreme variability in September when the maximum rainfalls diverge widely from the I.Q.R., and both agree in their sustained drought from November to May during which seven-month period the I.Q.R. scarcely rises from its zero level! This is in some contrast with the more easterly stations of Nagpur and Allahabad where the pre-monsoon showers, unreliable though they are, invite comparison with Bengal and East Pakistan.

In Fig. 2.2.8 Ahmadabad and Bombay show more pronounced differences in the amount and degree of variation in their annual rainfalls. Ahmadabad's total ranges between 12 and 49 inches, with the I.Q.R. 23 (almost) to 39·5 inches. Bombay's extreme range is between 36 and 108·5 inches, but its I.Q.R. is less wide than that of Ahmadabad, 71–81·5 inches.

2. The *Bengal type* of rainfall incidence is represented by *Calcutta* which differs from Nagpur in two ways: the rains begin earlier (so that May normally expects between 2·5 and 7·5 inches, and can receive almost 15 inches) and maintain a higher total steadily throughout the four months June–September, with October, like May, likely to have

reasonable falls. As at Nagpur, December is dry, with the I.Q.R. at *nil*. Within the same incidence-type, *Cox's Bazar* on the eastern side of the Bay of Bengal shows a similar pattern at the much higher rainfall total of 140 inches on average. Here the pre-monsoon fall (the 'little rains') are significant as early as April.

3. *Assam type.* Further east and northeast the fact that the April rains exceed one-twelfth of the annual rainfall justifies separating this region from Bengal. *Sylhet* and *Gauhati*, immediately south and north of the Shillong Plateau, show basically similar patterns, but contrast strongly in the total rainfall in the main rainy season. Sylhet with a mean rainfall of 146 inches (extreme maximum 195 inches) suffers the full onslaught of the monsoon air-streams while Gauhati (mean rainfall 63 inches, extreme maximum 82 inches) enjoys a measure of protection in the lee of the plateau. Compared with central India the dry season, though quite as severe while it lasts is of shorter duration; December and January are extremely dry, November and February–March may be so but normally receive an inch or two, all of it may be in a single downpour.

4. *Orissa type.* Southwards from the central Indian type, the principal change is in the duration of the rainy season into September and October, with the maximum in the latter month. The pattern is clearly seen in the graph for *Vishakhapatnam* where the rains generally persist into November, which however may sometimes mark the start of the dry season. On the Orissa coast cyclones probably contribute to the late season rains, but an important influence at this time is the I.T.C.

5. *Bangalore* and *Cochin* both qualify for inclusion in the *Kerala type*, having a six-month rainy season, but they differ in detail. Cochin, on the west coast is open to the early vigour of the inflowing monsoon in May–June, and receives its maximum rainfall then, with a secondary peak in October. At Bangalore, with a much lower total, the wet season is of similar length but the I.Q.R. lies between 2–4 inches (June) and 4–8 inches (October). Bangalore seems to benefit from the northward march of the I.T.C. in May, but once the southwest monsoon sets in during June, its interior position in the rain shadow of the Western Ghats leads to definite reduction in rainfall. The influence of the 'retreating' I.T.C. at both stations is seen best perhaps in the

October–November rainfall, and the less pronounced drought of December.

6. *Madras* has a quite anomalous regime. The southwest monsoon has little effect, and though there is a steady increase in rainfall from April to September the amount averages less than 5 inches in any month, and less than 2 inches in April to June. Late in the year the retreating I.T.C. is strongly supplemented by cyclones on the coast. Maximum falls of over 8 inches in twenty-four-hour periods are recorded for October to January. Madras suffers badly from unreliability of rainfall. Even in November–December, when rainfalls average 14 and 5·5 inches, and the I.Q.R. is 6·5–16·5 inches, and 2·3–7 inches respectively, the monthly totals may occasionally touch zero. Contrariwise, in the dry season from January to June, occasional monthly totals of 22, 5·5, 10·5, 5·5, 14·5 and 4 inches have been known.

7. The *dry zone of Ceylon*, represented by *Mannar* and *Trincomalee*, may be regarded as a region transitional in type between Madras and Colombo. The late season maximum is found here, and Trincomalee has a run of four months (October–January) with over one-twelfth of the annual average rainfall of almost 65 inches. Mannar whose average rainfall is just under 40 inches, has a similar overall pattern of incidence. Both stations show a minor maximum in April–May and some tendency for the January rains to persist into February, and in both (but particularly in Mannar) can be seen the risk of absolute drought occurring in *any* month between February and September.

8. *Colombo* in the *wet zone of Ceylon* has a more nearly equatorial regime, showing a double maximum following the equinoxes. Applying the formula used here to define the rainy season, we find here the first example of a station having two well defined rainy seasons: April–June and October–November, when each month has more than one-twelfth of the annual total. It should be noted, however, that no month has a mean rainfall of less than 2·7 inches, though the extreme minima of January and February may occasionally be nil.

9–10. *Weak monsoon and winter rains types.* The remaining stations, in the northwest of the subcontinent all demonstrate semi-arid to arid conditions, with low and very variable annual totals. The four stations while indicating the regime characteristic of the region are not fully representative as to the amount of rainfall received. Along the outer side of the Himalaya, in the Vale of Kashmir and the submontane belt immediately east of the Indus, rainfall totals are generally rather higher than in any of these four stations. Thus Srinagar averages 26 inches annually.

The double origin of rainfall in the northwest is seen in each graph, though barely so in the case of *Leh* where the monthly totals are so very low on account of this town's sheltered location north of the Indus and the main Himalaya. *Peshawar* and *Quetta* show the pattern well, both favouring slightly the late winter and spring as the wetter season of the year. At *Karachi* the summer monsoon brings most of what little rainfall is received. No month, however, is without risk of complete drought in this city of notorious variability of rainfall, and the probability of no rain is very high in April–May and September–November, when the I.Q.R. fails to rise above zero. The annual total shows great variation also (Fig. 2.2.8). As is typical of semi-arid climates, precipitation when it comes may be torrential and in July and September falls in twenty-four hours greater than the annual average total have been recorded.

Fig. 2.2.9 shows the location of the several climatic stations mentioned and the distribution of mean annual rainfall. Selected climatic data for these stations is tabulated (Table 2.2.1) on p. 31.

Climatic Regions

The preceding sections have demonstrated the gradualness of changes from place to place in the amount and seasonal distribution of rainfall and temperature. Perhaps the only exceptions to this generalisation are found in the way rainfall decreases more or less abruptly in the lee of the Western Ghats, and the sharpness of climatic change within and beyond the Himalaya, a characteristic of high mountain regions. Apart from these orographically determined zones of abrupt gradation, 'progression' and 'transition' are the terms most appropriate in describing climatic realities. A number of climatic 'types', characteristic of the core of particular regions may be identified, but lines drawn to separate climatic regions should be regarded in most cases as indicating broad zones of transitional conditions.

The map of climatic regions (Fig. 2.2.10) draws

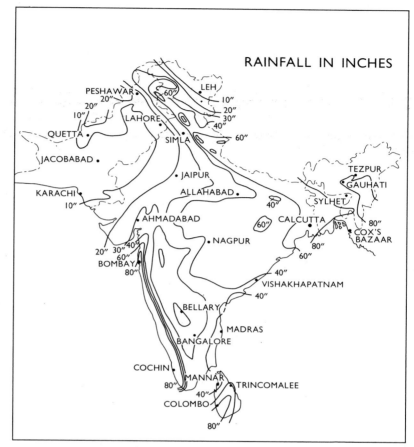

RAINFALL IN INCHES

FIG. 2.2.9 Rainfall: mean annual isohyets and location of climatic stations

upon several climatologists and geographers who have attempted to classify climate, in two cases on a world-wide basis, in one instance with monsoon Asia as the objective. Although he does not map his climatic types, Pédelaborde's approach to the problem from the viewpoint of causes rather than in the consequences of climate for man has influenced the scheme put forward here.* Among other authorities consulted are the works of the classical climatologists Köppen and Thornthwaite.†

The Type Regions
  I. Ceylon type
    (a) Wet zone
    (b) Dry zone

---

* Pédelaborde, P., *The Monsoon* (London, 1963).
† For Köppen and Thornthwaite's classifications a readily available source is Trewartha, G. T., *Introduction to Climate* (London, 1954).

  II. Kerala–Assam–East Pakistan type
  III. Coromandel coast (Madras) type
  IV. Central India–Malabar type
    (a) Malabar coast
    (b) East central India
    (c) West central India
    (d) Rain shadow belt
    (e) Semi-desert (of Gujarat–Rajasthan)
  V. Lahore type
  VI. Karachi type
  VII. Himalayan type

  I. *Ceylon type*: equable with a low range of temperature. Only on this ground can it be regarded as approximating to an equatorial climate. Aspect in relation to moisture-bearing air-streams controls the very significant local differences in the amount of seasonal rainfall. It is essential to distinguish:
  I (a) Wet zone (see diagrams for Colombo).
  I (b) Dry zone (see Trincomalee).

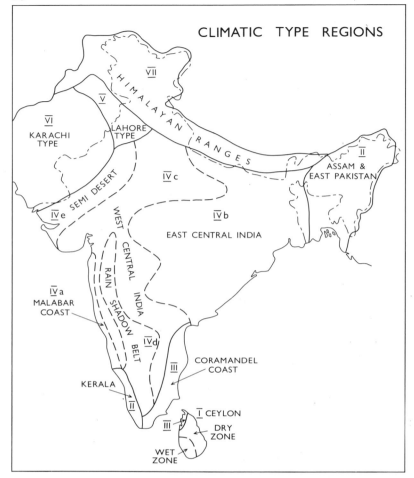

FIG. 2.2.10 Climatic-type regions

II. *Kerala–Assam–East Pakistan type*: compared with Ceylon there is a distinct but brief dry season, two months generally receiving less than an inch of rain. The range of temperature is slightly greater than in Ceylon, though (to quote Pédelaborde) 'there is no true winter'.

III. *Coromandel coast* (*Madras*) *type*: the main rains come in October–November, in large part from tropical cyclones, which helps explain the coastal nature of this type region. The southwest monsoon air-stream is subsiding as it passes over the region in June–July. Consequently little or no rain falls, and temperatures remain high throughout the summer.

IV. *Central India–Malabar type*: this covers the greater part of India and can be regarded as representative of the 'standard' monsoon regime and its minor variants. The march of seasons characteristic

of the South Asian monsoon climate is found throughout the region with slight variations in the duration of the several periods.

(i) Winter (December–February) is generally quite dry with warm clear days and cool nights.
(ii) Early spring (March–April) is still generally dry but temperatures rise and may be uncomfortable by day.
(iii) Late spring (May–mid-June) brings humid air and in southern Malabar and West Bengal appreciable rainfall occurs.
(iv) From mid-June to mid-September the wet monsoon brings heavy rains and reduced temperatures.
(v) Autumn (mid-September–November) is marked by a fall in temperature as air begins to flow from the east and north. Gradually

drought conditions are established throughout the region.

Subdivision of this type region is on the basis of rainfall amount.

(a) *Malabar coast*: northwards from Kerala to the Gulf of Cambay the length of the dry season increases, though total rainfall averages generally not less than 70 inches. In the south, Mangalore has four months with less than 1 inch of rain. Goa and Ratnagiri have five, and Bombay seven months.

(b) *East central India* comprises most of Madhya Pradesh, Bihar, Orissa, and West Bengal, with a part of Andhra Pradesh and the submontane plains of eastern Uttar Pradesh. The 40-inch annual isohyet arbitrarily separates the area from a drier

(c) *West central India*: rainfall totals 25 to 40 inches (and with these lower amounts variability increases).

(d) *The rain shadow belt* parallels the length of the Western Ghats through Maharashtra, Mysore, and Tamilnadu, widening at its centre into Andhra Pradesh. Over about half the belt rainfall is less than 25 inches. It is rather better distributed in the south where the influence of the 'retreating' I.T.C. is felt.

(e) *The semi-desert* of Gujarat–Rajasthan has the highest variability of annual rainfall of any part of India. With a total of less than 25 inches (e.g.

Jodhpur 14 inches) a variability of over 30 per cent makes agriculture hazardous indeed in this region which deteriorates westwards into the wastes of the Thar or Great Indian Desert.

V. *Lahore type* of the Punjab Plains is an extreme continental version of the central India type, modified by having some useful winter rainfall, more valuable (inch for inch) than the modest falls of the summer monsoon since it is less subject to evaporation. Summers are very hot, winters cool with rare night frosts. The proportion of winter rainfall in the total increases northwestwards.

VI. *Karachi type* extends from the Thar Desert into the plateaus of Baluchistan. The mountain ranges intercept a certain amount of moisture but the region as a whole is the eastern extremity of the Afro-Asian deserts in the belt of subtropical high pressures. A meteorological 'lid' generally inhibits rain-producing uplift of any moisture-bearing air-streams which may penetrate the region.

VII. *Himalayan type* (including the northwestern hill country): orographically induced rain or snowfall occurs at all seasons to some extent. Summers are mild, winters not excessively cold (except beyond the main Himalayan ranges).

TABLE 2.2.1

Climatic Data

| | Temperature °F. | | | | | Rainfall in inches | | | | | | | |
	Jan.	Feb.	Mar.	Apr.	May	June	July	Aug.	Sept.	Oct.	Nov.	Dec.	Year
JACOBABAD													
Av. Daily Max. Temp.	73	77	91	102	111	114	109	104	103	99	87	75	95
,, ,, Min. ,,	44	49	61	71	78	85	86	83	76	66	53	45	66
,, ,, Temp.	58·5	63	86·5	86·5	94·5	99·5	97·5	93·5	89·5	82·5	70	60	80·5
,, Rainfall	0·2	0·3	0·2	0·2	0·1	0·3	0·9	0·9	0·2	<0·1	<0·1	0·2	3·5
KARACHI													
Av. Daily Max. Temp.	77	79	85	90	93	93	91	88	88	91	87	80	84
,, ,, Min. ,,	55	58	67	73	79	82	81	79	77	72	64	57	72
,, ,, Temp.	66	68·5	76	81·5	86	87·5	86	83·5	82·5	81·5	75·5	68·5	78
,, Rainfall	0·5	0·4	0·3	0·1	0·1	0·7	3·2	1·6	0·5	<0·1	0·1	0·2	7·7
LAHORE													
Av. Daily Max. Temp.	69	72	83	95	104	106	100	97	97	95	83	73	89
,, ,, Min. ,,	40	44	53	63	72	95	80	78	73	59	47	40	61
,, ,, Temp.	54·5	58	68	79	88	92·5	90	87·5	85	77	65	56·5	75
,, Rainfall	1·1	0·9	0·9	0·5	0·7	1·7	5·5	5·3	2·4	0·3	0·1	0·4	19·8
PESHAWAR													
Av. Daily Max. Temp.	63	66	75	85	98	106	103	99	96	88	77	67	85
,, ,, Min. ,,	40	43	52	60	70	77	79	78	71	58	46	39	59
,, ,, Temp.	51·5	54·5	63·5	72·5	84	91·5	91	88·5	83·5	73	61·5	53	72
,, Rainfall	1·4	1·5	2·4	1·8	0·8	0·3	1·3	2·0	0·8	0·2	0·3	0·7	13·5
	Jan.	Feb.	Mar.	Apr.	May	June	July	Aug.	Sept.	Oct.	Nov.	Dec.	Year

	Jan.	Feb.	Mar.	Apr.	May	June	July	Aug.	Sept.	Oct.	Nov.	Dec.	Year
QUETTA													
Av. Daily Max. Temp.	50	54	64	74	84	93	95	93	87	77	65	55	74
,, ,, Min. ,,	27	30	38	45	52	59	65	62	50	39	31	27	44
,, ,, Temp.	38·5	42	51	59·5	68	76	80	77·5	68·5	58	48	41	59
,, Rainfall	1·9	2·0	1·7	1·0	0·4	0·2	0·5	0·3	<0·1	0·1	0·3	1·0	9·4
AHMADABAD													
Av. Daily Max. Temp.	85	88	97	104	107	101	93	90	93	97	93	86	95
,, ,, Min. ,,	58	59	67	74	79	81	79	77	76	72	65	59	71
,, ,, Temp.	71·5	73·5	82	89	93	91	86	83·5	84·5	84·5	79	72·5	83
,, Rainfall	<0·1	0·1	0·1	0·1	0·4	4·3	11·2	8·1	3·7	0·6	0·1	0·1	28·6
ALLAHABAD													
Av. Daily Max. Temp.	75	79	92	103	107	103	92	89	91	90	83	76	90
,, ,, Min. ,,	47	51	61	71	80	83	80	79	77	67	54	47	66
,, ,, Temp.	61	65	76·5	87	93·5	93	86	84	84	78·5	68·5	61·5	78
,, Rainfall	0·9	0·6	0·6	0·2	0·6	5·0	12·6	10·0	8·4	2·3	0·3	0·3	41·8
BANGALORE													
Av. Daily Max. Temp.	81	86	91	93	92	85	82	82	82	82	80	79	85
,, ,, Min. ,,	57	60	65	69	69	67	66	66	65	65	62	59	64
,, ,, Temp.	69	73	78	81	80·5	76	74	74	73·5	73·5	71	69	74·5
,, Rainfall	0·2	0·3	0·4	1·6	4·2	2·9	3·9	5·0	6·7	5·9	2·7	0·4	34·2
BELLARY													
Av. Daily Max. Temp.	87	93	99	102	102	94	90	90	90	89	87	85	92
,, ,, Min. ,,	63	67	73	78	78	76	75	74	73	71	67	63	71
,, ,, Temp.	75	80	86	90	90	85	82·5	82	81·5	80	77	74	81·5
,, Rainfall	0·1	0·2	0·2	0·8	1·9	1·7	1·6	2·4	4·9	4·2	2·0	0·1	20·1
BOMBAY													
Av. Daily Max. Temp.	83	83	86	89	91	89	85	85	85	89	89	87	87
,, ,, Min. ,,	67	67	72	76	80	79	77	74	76	76	73	63	74
,, ,, Temp.	75	75	79	82·5	85·5	84	81	80·5	80·5	82·5	81	75	80·5
,, Rainfall	0·1	0·1	0·1	0·1	0·7	19·1	24·3	13·4	10·4	2·5	0·5	0·1	71·2
CALCUTTA													
Av. Daily Max. Temp.	80	84	93	97	96	92	89	89	90	89	84	79	89
,, ,, Min. ,,	55	59	69	75	77	79	79	78	78	74	64	55	70
,, ,, Temp.	67·5	71·5	81	86	86·5	85·5	84	83·5	84	81·5	74	67	79·5
,, Rainfall	0·4	1·2	1·4	1·7	5·5	11·7	12·8	12·9	9·9	4·5	0·8	0·2	63·0
COCHIN													
Av. Daily Max. Temp.	89	90	91	92	90	85	84	84	85	87	88	89	88
,, ,, Min. ,,	72	74	77	79	78	75	74	75	75	75	75	73	75
,, ,, Temp.	80·5	82	84	85·5	84	80	79	79·5	80	81	81·5	81	81·5
,, Rainfall	0·9	0·8	2·0	4·9	11·7	28·5	23·3	13·9	7·7	13·4	6·7	1·6	115·3
JAIPUR													
Av. Daily Max. Temp.	74	78	89	99	105	103	94	90	93	94	85	76	91
,, ,, Min. ,,	47	51	60	70	78	81	78	76	73	65	54	48	65
,, ,, Temp.	60·5	64·5	74·5	84·5	91·5	92	86	83	83	79·5	69·5	62	78
,, Rainfall	0·4	0·3	0·3	0·2	0·6	2·2	7·7	8·1	3·2	0·5	0·1	0·3	23·9
MADRAS													
Av. Daily Max. Temp.	85	88	91	95	101	100	96	95	94	90	85	84	92
,, ,, Min. ,,	67	68	72	78	82	81	79	78	77	75	72	69	75
,, ,, Temp.	76	78	81·5	86·5	91·5	90·5	87·5	86·5	85·5	82·5	78·5	76·5	83·5
,, Rainfall	1·4	0·4	0·3	0·6	1·0	1·9	3·6	4·6	4·7	12·0	14·0	5·5	50·0
NAGPUR													
Av. Daily Max. Temp.	83	89	98	105	109	98	88	87	89	90	85	81	92
,, ,, Min. ,,	56	60	68	76	82	79	75	75	74	68	60	54	69
,, ,, Temp.	69·5	74·5	83	90·5	95·5	88·5	81·5	81	81·5	79·0	72·5	67·5	80·5
,, Rainfall	0·4	0·7	0·6	0·6	0·8	8·8	14·6	11·4	8·0	2·2	0·8	0·5	49·4
SIMLA													
Av. Daily Max. Temp.	47	48	57	65	72	73	69	67	67	63	57	51	61
,, ,, Min. ,,	36	37	44	52	58	61	60	59	57	51	45	40	50
,, ,, Temp.	41·5	42·5	50·5	58·5	65	67	64·5	63	62	57	51	45·5	55·5
,, Rainfall	2·4	2·7	2·4	2·1	2·6	6·9	16·7	17·1	6·3	1·3	0·5	1·1	62·1
TEZPUR													
Av. Daily Max. Temp.	74	76	83	83	87	89	89	89	89	86	81	75	83
,, ,, Min. ,,	52	56	62	67	72	77	78	78	77	71	61	53	67
,, ,, Temp.	63	66	72·5	75	79·5	83	83·5	83·5	83	78·5	71	64	75
,, Rainfall	0·5	1·1	2·3	6·2	9·9	12·0	14·4	14·4	8·2	4·2	0·7	0·2	74·1

	Jan.	Feb.	Mar.	Apr.	May	June	July	Aug.	Sept.	Oct.	Nov.	Dec.	Year

	Jan.	Feb.	Mar.	Apr.	May	June	July	Aug.	Sept.	Oct.	Nov.	Dec.	Year
COLOMBO													
Av. Daily Max. Temp.	86	87	88	88	87	85	85	85	85	85	85	85	86
„ „ Min. „	72	72	74	76	78	77	77	77	77	75	73	72	75
„ „ Temp.	79	79·5	81	82	82·5	81	81	81	81	80	79	78·5	80·5
„ Rainfall	3·5	2·7	5·8	9·1	14·6	8·8	5·3	4·3	6·3	13·7	12·4	5·8	93·1
TRINCOMALEE													
Av. Daily Max. Temp.	80	82	85	89	92	92	92	92	92	88	84	81	87
„ „ Min. „	75	76	76	78	79	79	78	77	77	76	75	75	77
„ „ Temp.	77·5	79	80·5	83·5	85·5	85·5	85	84·5	84·5	82	79·5	78	82
„ Rainfall	6·8	2·6	1·9	2·3	2·7	1·1	2·0	4·2	4·2	8·7	14·1	14·3	64·9
	Jan.	Feb.	Mar.	Apr.	May	June	July	Aug.	Sept.	Oct.	Nov.	Dec.	Year

CHAPTER THREE

INDIA

1. INDIA: THE POLITICAL MAP

Constitutionally India is a federation of seventeen states together with a number of Union territories administered by the Central Government. The states and territories as in 1967 are shown in Fig. 3.1.1. The pattern of India's political geography reflects a number of different forces at work.

Brought into being by the partition of the former British Indian Empire into two sovereign states, India and Pakistan, India's external boundaries are a product of the treaties and conventions predating independence and of the act of partition itself. For the most part the boundary with Pakistan, as set by the arbitration of Lord Ratcliffe, ensured that districts with a majority of Moslems went to Pakistan. Partition therefore had a mainly religious basis, although very large minorities of Moslems remained in India, and of Hindus in Pakistan.*

There remain several small areas in dispute between India and Pakistan along the boundaries with both West and East wings of the latter, but these are of little significance to either country when compared with the issue of Jammu and Kashmir which has embittered Indo–Paskistan relations throughout their separate existence and has on several occasions led to the outbreak of hostilities between them. Both sides can ill afford to divert to defence as much of their resources as they do. Put at its simplest, the 'rights' of the Kashmir issue are confused by the conflict between what one side holds to be its moral claims to rule in a Moslem majority region and the other its legal entitlement to rule an area ceded to it by its former ruler, the Maharaja of Kashmir. The issue seems unlikely to be resolved to the satisfaction of both sides in the near future. Meanwhile the State is in effect partitioned, the western part being under Pakistan's rule (following occupation of the area in an attempt to take over the State in 1947) while the larger part including the Vale of Kashmir is administered by India as a state within the Union.

At the time of independence India contained within her territory a number of enclaves of foreign soil, French and Portuguese, dating from the early days of European mercantile contact with the country. The French retired gracefully from the scene, handing over to India the sovereignty of Pondicherry where they maintain a valuable research institute. The Portuguese held on to their possessions till India forced the issue by the military occupation of the principal area, Goa, and so ended European suzerainty. (See Fig. 3.1.3.)

As to the internal boundaries of the Indian states two factors have been uppermost. The British had in the course of two hundred years of political influence divided the subcontinent up into eleven provinces (in which the process of introducing self-government had progressed with varying degrees of success) and a patchwork of Indian or princely states in which a form of indirect rule through hereditary Maharajas, Rajas, etc. obtained. Until the East India Company handed over political control to the British Government after the Indian Mutiny of 1857, the British had been gradually extending the area of their direct control. British Government rule put a stop to this process, and effectively froze the pattern of princely states as of

* In 1961 47 million Moslems constituting 10·7 per cent of India's population were enumerated in the census. They were widely distributed: Uttar Pradesh had 11 million, West Bengal 7 million, Bihar 6 million, and Maharashtra, Andhra Pradesh, Assam, about 3 million each; Jammu and Kashmir, Mysore, over 2 million each; Gujarat, Madras, Madhya Pradesh, and Rajasthan, over 1 million each. Very large migrations following partition account for Punjab's low figure of about 400,000.

6. *Char Minar (the 'four minarets') Hyderabad*, Andhra Pradesh, with the private palace of the Nizam of Hyderabad on the right. Both buildings are in the Moghul-Islamic tradition. The Char Minar was built as a monumental arch to commemorate the conclusion of a battle against plague in 1591. Before independence the Nizam was the most powerful of the Princes, a Moslem ruler over the large mainly Hindu Native State of Hyderabad. The City of Hyderabad is now capital of Andhra Pradesh.

1857, each becoming a protectorate of the British Crown.

The coming of independence in 1947 enabled this pattern to be unfrozen, and indeed threw the whole political system into the melting-pot, from which was cast (after several modifications) the present situation. In this last phase of state-making a powerful new factor has operated, that of language. A comparison of the map of states with that of the distribution of major languages (Figs. 3.1.1 and 3.1.2) shows some significant correlations. Where language is not a differentiating factor, the boundaries of the former British Indian provinces (Fig. 3.1.3) can often be traced, but substantial alterations have been made to the pattern of the former princely states. Democratic, often linguistic states have replaced the latter, some of which like Hyderabad leave scarcely a trace on the map today; others, like

Mysore live on with altered boundaries as well as altered constitutions.

Several hundred languages and dialects were recorded by the census (1652 'mother-tongues' were enumerated in 1961) but only thirteen are spoken by populations of upwards of six million. The languages which have real importance politically in the sense that they form a basis for the differentiation of states are as follows:

TABLE 3.1.1

Principal Languages

	(millions)		(millions)
Hindi	133	Malayalam	17
Telugu	38	Bihari	17
Bengali	34	Oriya	16
Marathi	33	Rajasthani	15
Tamil	31	Punjabi	11
Gujarati	20	Assamese	7
Kannada	17	Kashmiri	2

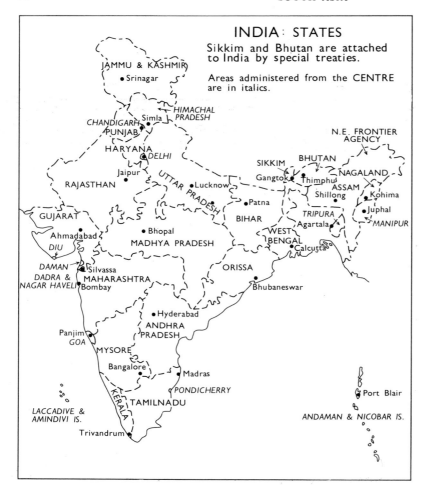

FIG. 3.1.1   India political

NOTE: Tamilnadu was formerly **Madras** State

These languages belong to two distinct language families. Most of them are Indo-Aryan languages and many of their speakers find it relatively easy to communicate across language barriers in Hindustani or 'bazaar Hindi'. Four tongues belong to the Dravidian group of languages: Telugu, Tamil, Kannada, and Malayalam. Their speakers would look to English rather than Hindi for a lingua franca, and through their representatives in the Central Government have repeatedly expressed a strong opposition to proposals that Hindi become the single national language of India.

The predominance of Hindi is even stronger than the above figures suggest. As is shown in Fig. 3.1.2 Hindi is the language of education across Northern India. To the Hindi speakers may be added those who speak Urdu, Bihari, and Rajasthani. A major

language, Urdu, spoken by 23 million is not listed in Table 3.1.1 since no Urdu-speaking Indian state is in existence or in question. Urdu is the principal language of West Pakistan, and is spoken by many Indian Moslems. At its simplest it is closely akin to basic Hindi, and its speakers could be added to the Hindi total. The main differences lie in their scripts and in the vocabulary and style of literary expression. Bihari's 17 million speakers can probably with even greater justification be regarded as Hindi speakers, as might also Rajasthani's 15 million.

The close fit of the pattern of states with that of linguistic regions is plain from the maps. Each of the four Dravidian languages has its state, as also have Bengali, Marathi, Gujarati, Bihari, Oriya, Rajasthani, Punjabi, Assamese, and Kashmiri. Not all the inhabitants of the 'linguistic states' adhere to the

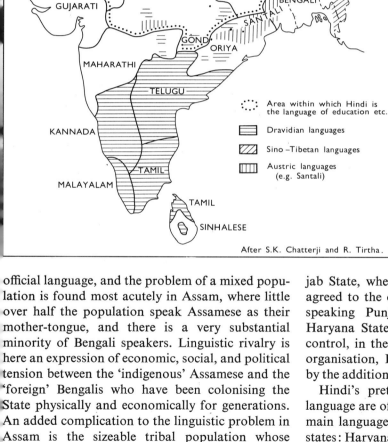

FIG. 3.1.2 India: languages

official language, and the problem of a mixed population is found most acutely in Assam, where little over half the population speak Assamese as their mother-tongue, and there is a very substantial minority of Bengali speakers. Linguistic rivalry is here an expression of economic, social, and political tension between the 'indigenous' Assamese and the 'foreign' Bengalis who have been colonising the State physically and economically for generations. An added complication to the linguistic problem in Assam is the sizeable tribal population whose several languages belong to the Tibeto–Chinese family. There is some prospect of Assam being reorganised on a federal basis, to include a number of units such as Nagaland State, Manipur, Tripura, and the Northeast Frontier Agency.

Another area of liguistic rivalry has been in Pun-

jab State, where in 1966 the Central Government agreed to the creation of a new, smaller, Punjabi-speaking Punjab State, and a Hindi-speaking Haryana State, with a joint capital under Union control, in the new city of Chandigarh. In the reorganisation, Himachal Pradesh was strengthened by the addition of four formerly Punjab districts.

Hindi's pretensions to becoming the national language are of course strengthened by its being the main language in a block of four centrally placed states: Haryana, Uttar Pradesh, Bihar, and Madhya Pradesh. The boundaries of Uttar Pradesh are almost coincident with those of pre-independence United Provinces and there have been few changes to Bihar.

Madhya Pradesh, however, is a new creation, comprising the Hindi-speaking parts of the former

7. *New Delhi*, Central Secretariat Buildings. The grand scale of the capital's design produces magnificent vistas such as this, but means also that the humble office worker has a long journey on foot, bicycle or bus, to get to work.

Central Provinces, and the princely states of the Central Indian Agency, plus the Bastar region where tribal languages, e.g. Gond of the Dravidian group survive.*

Table 3.1.2 summarises the states of the Indian Union (in order of population) and their principal languages. The size range as measured by population is considerable. Leaving aside the special cases of Jammu and Kashmir and Nagaland (the latter recently promoted to statehood as a gesture of good faith on the part of the Central Government towards the dissident tribal population on the Assam–Burma border) the largest state, Uttar Pradesh, has six times the population of the smallest Assam. Uttar Pradesh is in a size class of its own, being separated from the next in rank, Bihar, by 28 million. At most eight, more generally one or two million separate ranks below Bihar. In terms of numbers all the states from Assam upwards are of 'world class' exceeding in population countries such as Australia, Belgium, and the Netherlands; Uttar Pradesh is more populous than any European country outside the U.S.S.R.

---

* Other tribal languages in central India include some belonging to the Austric family of languages, probably the most ancient in the region.

TABLE 3.1.2
Administrative Divisions of India

State	Population (nearest million)	Main languages
Uttar Pradesh	74	Hindi, Urdu
Bihar	46	Hindi, Bihari
Maharashtra	40	Marathi
Andhra Pradesh	36	Telugu
West Bengal	35	Bengali
Tamilnadu	34	Tamil
Madhya Pradesh	32	Hindi
Mysore	24	Kannada
Gujarat	21	Gujarati
Rajasthan	20	Rajasthani, Hindi
Orissa	18	Oriya
Kerala	17	Malayalam
Assam	12	Assamese, Bengali
Punjab	11	Punjabi, Urdu
Haryana	8	Hindi, Urdu
Jammu and Kashmir	4	Kashmiri
Nagaland	0·4	Various tribal

Union territories	Population (thousands)	Main languages
Himachal Pradesh	2800	Hindi, Pahari
Delhi	2658	Hindi, Urdu, Punjabi
Tripura	1142	Bengali
Manipur	780	Bengali
Goa, Daman, Diu (formerly Portuguese)	627	Marathi, Kannada
Pondicherry (formerly French)	369	Tamil, French
Andaman and Nicobar Islands	64	Andamanese, Nicobarese.
Dadra and Nagar Haveli (formerly Portuguese)	58	Gujarati, Marathi
Laccadive, Minicoy, and Amindivi Islands	24	Malayalam.

Fig. 3.1.3   British India

D. Diu; Da. Daman; M. Mahé;
K. Karikal; P. Pondicherry
Y. Yanam; Ch. Chandernagore.

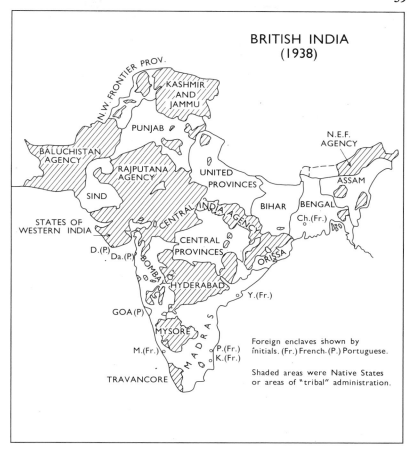

BRITISH INDIA
(1938)

Foreign enclaves shown by
initials. (Fr.) French. (P.) Portuguese.

Shaded areas were Native States
or areas of "tribal" administration.

Government

The two Houses of the Indian Parliament, the Upper House or Council of States and the House of the People meet in Delhi and form the Central Government. The House of the People is elected by universal adult franchise, its membership being approximately proportionate to the population of the states. Universal adult suffrage is a significant achievement in a country where only 24 per cent of the population (28 per cent of those over five years old) were recorded as literate in 1961. The Council of States has a 'rotating' membership mostly elected by the members of the State Legislative Assembly of each state. In each state there is a Legislative Assembly directly elected by the people, and a Legislative Council, composed partly of elected members of the Assembly, partly of non-members representative of local government, educational and cultural interests. Most revenue is collected by the Centre which distributes funds to the States, which, within the plans approved by the Centre, are responsible for executing schemes of development, etc. The Centre is directly responsible for the administration of the Union territories in most of which there are Legislative Assemblies with powers less wide than those of the State Legislatures.

India's system of government is thus a federal one, similar in many respects to that of other federal nations such as Australia and Canada. Its strength lies in its broadly democratic basis. Among its weaknesses is the risk that development finance may be directed to areas where political pressures arising from local loyalties are strongest rather than to those where capital might be used most efficiently.

Difficulties have arisen during periods of food shortage. States with reserves of food have sealed their borders with less fortunate states, preventing the free flow of food grains in order to protect themselves against the price inflation that would inevitably follow the reduction of their reserves.

8. *Village Panchayat*, Tamilnadu.
The constitution of the Panchayat
requires that there be at least two
women members and that two members be from the Harijan or 'untouch-
able' castes.

At the village and district levels within states, while the framework of democratic government is present, inequalities of wealth and differentiation of opinion of the basis of caste are probably even stronger influences than at the State or Centre. Efforts are being made through the re-establishment on democratic lines of the traditional system of village government, known as Panchayat Raj, to engender among the populace a greater sense of involvement in their own government, and an appreciation of how much they can achieve by their own efforts in the way of economic and social development.

The problem of caste remains a very real one in India today, entering strongly into the day to day life of the mass of the population.* Although the former rigidities of the caste system are breaking down in the urban areas and among the westernised middle-class, much of the inertia and reluctance to change commonly exhibited by the rural dweller may be traced to his religious traditions central to which is the belief in caste. In this context the most serious aspect of the caste system is the acceptance of economic and social status within the community as determined by birth. The peasant farmer or farm labourer can do little to improve his lot if his 'betters' (often in caste as well as economic terms) control the generally conservative public opinion of the village. This is just one, but not the least, among the many problems facing agricultural development which is more fully discussed below.

2. INDIA: FOOD AND JOBS FOR THE PEOPLE

India's Population

The census of 1961 recorded the population of India (with Jammu and Kashmir) as 439 million, an increase of 21·5 per cent over that of 1951. There seems no immediate prospect, short of disastrous famines, of the rate of increase diminishing; it may in fact become greater for a time, as the death-rate is reduced through improved health measures extending the life-span. India in common with other countries in South and Southeast Asia is experiencing in an acute form demographic events through which the Western countries and Japan have already been. The main difference lies in the greater speed of these events at the present time. In the West

* For an excellent discussion see Zinkin, Taya, *Caste Today* (London, 1962).

during the nineteenth century, populations began to increase significantly, as standards of living as measured by housing conditions, diet, and public sanitation improved. Medical science had little to do with the early reduction in death-rates. More recently, particularly since World War I, the mass application of preventive medicine through vaccination and the increase of understanding of disease have brought death-rates down and extended the life-span to nearly seventy years in several countries.

Fig. 3.2.1 shows the movement of the birth- and death-rates in India compared with those of the United Kingdom and Japan over the past 80–100 years. It will be noted that in the United Kingdom birth- and death-rates showed a progressive decline over most of the period, the birth-rate falling faster than the death-rate, so that the two converge. After World War II the death-rate has remained fairly stable while the birth-rate has risen slightly to stabilise at a level a little above the death-rate. In the United Kingdom industrialisation and urbanisation were far advanced by 1870 when the graph begins. Japan's industrialisation started later, and although death-rates began to fall from the 1920s, birth-rates remained high until the abrupt change following the war. It is likely that Japanese rates will now stabilise at parallel levels approximating to those of the United Kingdom. In the case of India, the birth-rate remains high while the death-rate has been

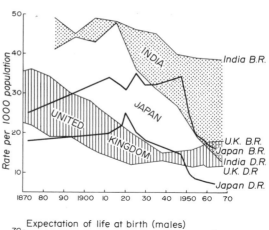

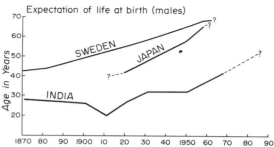

FIG. 3.2.1   India: birth- and death-rates; expectation of life

9. *Village women drawing water at a South Indian well.* The brass pots full of water will be carried home on the women's heads or on their hips. The scene typifies the traditional social and technical level of village life which is a hard one for the average peasant.

falling, so that the rates continue to diverge, which means an increasing rate of natural increase in population.

In India public health measures and medical science are operating simultaneously to reduce the death-rate very rapidly and before measures to reduce the birth-rate have begun to have an effect. It is officially claimed that malaria has been well-nigh eliminated, and that smallpox innoculation of the whole population has been achieved. Thus the average expectation of life at birth of an Indian infant has risen from 20 years in 1921 to 32 in 1941 and 45 in 1960, and can be expected to continue to rise towards the level attained in the advanced countries. The death-rate has been falling quite independently of economic development, but eventually demographic and economic conditions must interact. Unless food and other necessities can be produced to support the increasing population, recurrent famine is inevitable. Not only is more food needed but, as every famine has shown, the means to purchase food. India needs most of all a stronger economy, producing more jobs, so that people can buy more food, and raise themselves to the level of living where the restriction of the size of family becomes both desirable and practicable.

It has been calculated that about 100 million new jobs must be created by 1981 to absorb the workless and the increased adult population by that time. The land already has to support too many in an overcrowded and under-employed countryside, so the jobs need to be created in the towns. Some authorities hold that it is through urbanisation that birth-rates have been brought down in the advanced countries. The key to urbanisation is industrialisation, for which vast amounts of capital and great inputs of energy and knowledge are going to be needed.

Famine and the Food Supply

While the long-term solution to the problem of raising standards of living almost certainly lies in industrialisation and urbanisation, there is a more immediate problem of feeding the hungry millions whose numbers are increasing at little short of ten million every year. Regional shortage of food is no new phenomenon in India. Several times during the nineteenth century there occurred disastrous famines with the loss of hundreds of thousands of lives from starvation, or more usually from epidemic diseases to which starving bodies could offer little resistance. India is by nature exposed to the risk of famine. The monsoon rainfall regime is not only highly seasonal but also highly variable. In regions where rainfall is always low, as in much of West Pakistan, man adjusts to the conditions either by accepting semi-aridity as a limitation on his economic activity or by creating through irrigation schemes a man-made environment in which he can to a large extent control the supply of life-giving moisture. In either case, the famine risk is small.

Much of India, however, is in the position of *normally* receiving rainfall timely enough and adequate enough to support agriculture. Irrigation in many areas is not essential in most years. It is in such regions that famine has been most prone to occur. Subsistence agriculture practised in an over-crowded countryside and in a climate permitting only seasonal production allows little scope for the accumulation of food reserves sufficient to tide the family over a bad season, let alone a run of bad seasons. The most devastating famines, in terms of the numbers who died in them, have happened in regions where the normally adequate rainfall has permitted agriculture to support quite high densities of population. Bengal, United Provinces (Uttar Pradesh), and Orissa have suffered severely. Maybe ten million people, one-third of the population, are believed to have died of a famine in Bengal in 1770; 800,000 died of famine in the United Provinces in 1836; one million in Orissa in 1865–66; $5\frac{1}{2}$ million in Bombay (Maharashtra–Gujarat) and Madras (Tamilnadu–Andhra Pradesh) in 1876–78.

Several factors combined to reduce the severity of famine by the beginning of the present century. The construction of railways meant that regions hit by famine could now import foodstuffs from more fortunate regions with a surplus. Extensive canal irrigation schemes were converting semi-deserts (in particular the Punjab) into regions producing a reliable surplus of food. That economic destitution was a major factor in most famines was recognised by the authorities in British India. Starvation could occur in the sight of plenty if people had not the means to earn money with which to purchase food. Governments set up 'famine relief works' to help provide work, and so money to buy food.

As recently as 1966–67 Bihar has been in the grip

of famine. Failure of the monsoon rains of 1966 meant that the main food crop could not be raised. As in every Indian famine the worst hit are the landless labourers. When the rains fail their labour is no longer needed on the land. They are the first to feel the economic pinch, and having little or no property or possessions are soonest brought to destitution and starvation. Without alternative means of earning a living, first the landless labourer then the share cropper and the tenant farmer are threatened. Under the traditional farming and landholding system too many villages live from hand to mouth at the best of times and in the face of calamity the economy proves quite inadequate to provide for those in the community who lack reserves of food or money.

The Bengal famine of 1943, which killed three million or more, occurred when, as the commission set up to inquire into it reported, 'Famine on a catastrophic scale had indeed faded from memory.' No single factor could be blamed for the disaster; partial crop failure, wartime dislocation of communications, the loss to the Japanese armies of Burma, for long a ready source of rice for India, hoarding and exploitation of shortage by profiteers – all these factors combined to convert into catastrophe a difficulty which might well have been mitigated had there been an administrative machine adequate to the problem.

Despite man's technological advances, the possibility of famine has not been banished, and it would seem that its removal depends on the creation at the village, regional, and national level of an economy sufficiently broadly based and an agricultural sector well enough provided with reserves as not to be threatened by fluctuations in production brought about by natural causes. The ability of the Central and State governments to meet the immediate needs of famine-threatened areas for food will for some time continue to depend on their capacity to find surplus food grains elsewhere within India, and their willingness to redistribute such supplies, or to bring in supplies from outside.

Food Needs

In discussing food shortages and the measures necessary to meet them it is important to distinguish between two kinds of food need: a quantitative need, failure to meet which results in under-nutrition, and a qualitative need, which if not met produces malnutrition. Under-nutrition is the more readily observable and can be met by simply filling the hungry stomach. Malnutrition is more insidious, for simply feeding the hungry will not necessarily cure it, and its debilitating effect on the working adult reduces the productive efficiency of the population.

P. V. Sukhatme in *Feeding India's Growing Millions* (Asia Publishing House, London, 1965) makes an exhaustive analysis of India's food needs by measuring the extent of under-nutrition and malnutrition. He assessses the scale and kind of agricultural development necessary to meet the demands determined by population increase and by a quite modest change in diet to provide minimum nutritional levels. The discussion which follows is based largely on Sukhatme's work.

TABLE 3.2.1

Current Consumption Levels for India with Western countries*

	INDIA		WESTERN COUNTRIES	
	Grams per person per day	Percentage of total calories	Grams per person per day	Percentage of total calories
Cereals	375	67·2	328	38·2
Starchy roots	30	1·4	316	7·4
Sugar	45	8·0	88	11·4
Pulses and nuts	65	10·3	16	2·0
Fruits and vegetables	80	1·5	362	3·9
Meat	4	0·3	152	10·5
Fish	7	0·2	34	0·9
Eggs	1	0·1	33	1·4
Milk, milk products	140	6·0	573	11·3
Fats and oils	11	4·9	47	13·0
Calories	1970	100	3060	100
Percentage of calories from:				
Carbohydrates		79		58
Proteins		9		11
Fats		12		31
Total protein	51		90	
Animal protein	6		44	

Under-nutrition. Table 3.2.1 allows a close comparison to be made of the diet of the average Indian with that of the average westerner. The much greater importance of cereals and pulses for the supply of calories (a measure of the energy-giving fuel the body requires) in the Indian diet is immediately apparent, as is also the disparity between the total calorie intake of the two groups. It is estimated that

* Europe, North America, Oceania, and River Plate countries.

the average Indian, typically of lighter build than the European, and requiring less 'fuel' to keep himself warm, needs 2300 calories per day. At present he gets less than 2000 or 87 per cent of the requirements. On the other hand the Westerner's needs are 2600 calories, and his present diet provides 17 per cent in excess of this. In India, as elsewhere, there is of course a wide range of consumption levels from which the average is compounded. Studies in Maharashtra show calorie intakes ranging from 1120 for the poorest agricultural labourers up to over 3000 for the wealthiest people. Sukhatme considers that over India as a whole, between one-third and one-quarter of the population are under-nourished.

Malnutrition is thought to affect at least half the population. A lack of a properly balanced diet is a major factor in reducing resistance to disease. A deficiency of iron causes anaemia and several diseases may be traced to the lack of some vitamin or mineral in the diet. Commonly, retarded growth in children is due to protein deficiency. Not only is the Indian diet deficient in protein (51 grams per day compared with 90 grams in Western countries) but what protein there is comes largely from vegetable sources, the pulses being important in this regard. Experts differ on the significance of animal protein to health, but it is generally thought that children in particular need to obtain protein in foods in which it is more concentrated than in cereals or pulses, so that the protein requirements will be satisfied without an excessive intake of calories.

The scale of agricultural development needed up to the year A.D. 2000 if food is to be adequate in both quantity and quality is indicated by two estimates linked to different projections of population. If population increases to 1000 million, total food needs will be 4½ times those of 1960 and the need for animal products 8 times greater. At a lower estimate of 836 million people, the increases are 4 times and 6½ times respectively. For the larger population total food supply would have to increase at the rate of 3·7 per cent per annum and for the lower projection 3·3 per cent, throughout the period. Table 3.2.2 shows the scale and nature of change which would have been necessary in 1960 to bring the diets to minimum nutritional standards. Projecting these minimum needs forward to 1981 Sukhatme concluded that India had the capacity to meet the needs for cereals and pulses but would

have greater difficulty in supplying animal products, particularly milk, in sufficient quantity.

The necessity to spend on capital equipment such as machinery what foreign exchange can be earned, forces India to strive for self-sufficiency in food supply. The prospects for bringing uncultivated land into production are poor. Already 48 per cent of the surface is cultivated, and maybe 6 per cent more might conceivably be used but at excessively high cost. A better prospect of increasing the cropped area is by irrigation which can often permit double cropping where formerly only a single crop could be taken. Of about 160 million hectares cropped about 25 million are at present double cropped, a figure which could be doubled. The 30–35 million hectares now irrigated might be increased eventually to 70 million.

In the shorter run, very sizeable increases in yield from existing fields can be achieved by using fertilisers. India lags far behind Japan or Britain in this respect as figures for the decade 1950–60 show (Table 3.2.3).

TABLE 3.2.2

Food Available and Needed (in 1960)

(This table compares per caput and total food available with that needed to meet **minimum** nutritional standards)

	Per caput (grams per day) Available (A)	Needed (B)	Per cent B/A	Total (million tons per yr.) Available	Needed
Cereals	375	403	107	58·9	63·3
Starchy roots	30	46	153	4·7	7·2
Sugar	45	50	111	7·1	7·8
Pulses and nuts	65	104	160	10·2	16·3
Fruits and vegetables	80	137	171	12·6	21·5
Meat	4	7	175	0·6	1·1
Fish	7	17	243	1·1	2·7
Eggs	1	2	200	0·2	0·3
Milk and milk products	140	201	144	22·0	31·5
Fats and oils	11	18	164	1·7	2·8
Calories	(1970)	(2370)	120		
Animal protein	6·4	10	159		
Vegetable protein	44·9	55·6	115		
Fats	27·8	41·1	148		
Per cent calories from cereals, roots, sugar	79	69			
Per cent calories from protein	10·4	11·1			
Per cent animal of total proteins	12·4	15·2			
Total foods				119·1	154·5

TABLE 3.2.3

Cereal Yields and Fertiliser Consumption

	Cereal yield 100 kg./hectare 1950/51	1960/61	Fertiliser consumption kg./hectare 1950/51	1960/61
India	6·5	8·3	0·5	2·5
Japan	29·3	41·1	153·0	303·7
United Kingdom	23·9	31·3	111·6	180·2

That India can expect considerable improvements in yields as cultivation techniques improve is suggested by the comparative yields obtained on experimental farms as compared with the average for the State (Table 3.2.4).

TABLE 3.2.4
Comparative Crop Yields

	Experimental farms	State average
Madras (rice)	1836 kg./ha.	969 kg./ha.
Mysore (*jowar* millet)	1019	384
Punjab (wheat)	1741	942
Uttar Pradesh (maize)	2173	772

Even more convincing are the results of controlled experiments in fertilising the farmers' own fields. These have been carried out in many places and the average improvement can be taken to indicate the scale of increase of yield which may be expected from applying fertilisers, provided water is adequately available. Thus nitrogen (ammonium sulphate) applied at 22·4 kg./ha. brings an average improvement of 250 kg. of rice, 230 kg. of wheat; P_2O_5 (superphosphate) improves rice yields by 210 kg., wheat 170 kg. per hectare. Together such doses give an average improvement of 450 kg. in rice yield.

So far attention has been paid to increasing calorie output by increasing cereal yields. A less desirable way of achieving a similar end is to extend the use of tuber and root crops such as tapioca, potatoes (sweet and 'Irish'). While such crops yield more abundantly of carbohydrate per unit of area than either rice or wheat (7000–13,000 lb. of dehydrated tapioca per acre compared with averages of about 2100 lb. of rice or wheat) they are deficient in protein as compared with cereals. Kuriyan suggests that such crops have value where alternative sources of protein are available as in Kerala where fish is widely eaten.*

Pest control, seed selection, and breeding can further enhance yields. By 1965–66 almost 5000 seed farms were expected to be in production, providing improved strains to about half the farm land. There is no doubt that an increase in cereal production of from 20–35 per cent could be achieved by using quantities of fertiliser well below those employed in Japan.

Pulses present more of a problem. They are rarely irrigated, generally being grown as a dry rabi crop.

* Kuriyan, G., 'The Food Problem in India – a continuing crisis', *Indian Geographical Journal*, XL (1965), pp. 51–71.

10. *Food shop* in Hyderabad, Andhra Pradesh. Potatoes, various pulses and condiments (chillies, ginger, turmeric, etc.) are for sale. Garlands and tinsel for festive wear hang above the stallkeepers' heads.

For this reason they respond less to fertilisers than do cereals. To produce enough pulses will require allocating more land and water to them and cultivating them in rotation with grain crops to their mutual benefit.

The production of animal products, particularly milk, in the quantity required presents the greatest problems, despite the enormous number of India's cattle. The yield of milk is incredibly low – 1½ lb. per day for cows, 3 lb for buffaloes – since the animals are kept to breed draught cattle. Many fewer cattle could produce more milk if properly fed on fodder crops, straw, oil-seed cake, etc.; yet oil-seed cake ranks sixth among India's exports, accounting for 4 per cent of their value between 1960–66. Mechanisation can eventually remove the need for plough teams, but some change in the popular and prohibitive attitude to cattle slaughter may have to come before effective rationalisation of mixed farming practice can occur.

Planning for Food

Most of the changes outlined require action by administrators in the provision of capital works such as
irrigation systems and grain stores, seed multiplication farms, fertiliser works, and so on. Farmers
need short-term loans to purchase improved seed,
fertilisers, and better cattle. Above all farmers need
incentives to change their traditional methods and
maybe to accept change in their social system where
it militates against the redistribution or consolidation of holdings in the public interest. The education of farmers to the point where they press for
these changes is a colossal problem in mass communication, but without many millions of farmers
undertaking the agricultural revolution described
above, India cannot hope to progress.

To date, India's five year plans have achieved a
good deal in terms of increased agricultural production. The vagaries of climate, however, continue as a major hazard. After a run of moderately
good years, 1965–66 and 1966–67 were years of
severe and widespread drought. Production of food
grains in 1965–66 was 72·0 million metric tons
against a target of over 100 million, a disaster which
together with that of the renewed hostilities with
Pakistan went a long way to explain the fall in per
capita income back to levels of 1960–61. Table 3.2.5
summarises the trends in agricultural production
since the First Plan.

TABLE 3.2.5

Trends in Agricultural Production

	1950/51 (beginning of 1st plan)	1960/61 (beginning of 3rd plan)	1964/65	1966/67
Food grains (million metric tons)	54·9	82·0	89·0	75·0
Oil-seeds (million metric tons)	5·1	7·0	8·3	6·5
Cotton (million bales)	2·6	5·3	5·4	4·9
Jute (million bales)	3·5	4·1	6·0	5·3

In order to fill the gap left by the short fall in production, increased quantities of cereals had to be
imported to a total of about 10·4 million tons in 1966,
the highest of a run of progressively rising figures
since the start of the Third Plan when (1961) imports were 3·5 million tons. For a country whose
most important assets are land and people this is a
depressing state of affairs, but one which may perhaps ensure a greater effort in the agricultural sector of the economy during the Fourth Plan which
has yet to be published in detail. The draft outline
for this plan stresses the need to put more capital

into agriculture and those industries, particularly
the fertiliser, pesticide, and agricultural equipment
industries, which are a main support of agricultural
development. It is recognised that the production of
these ancillary commodities and goods is not
enough and that attention must be given to the economic and social framework within which the cultivator has to operate so that he has the incentive and
the means to improve his efficiency. Some of the
specific problems to be overcome have been mentioned above. Among them is one of crucial importance which at the same time illustrates a fundamental contradiction in India's socio-economic
fabric. It is comprehended in the phrases 'land to
the tiller' and 'security of tenure'.

Commentators such as Ronald Segal in *The Crisis
of India* (Penguin Books) and the Planning Commission itself point out the need to assure the cultivator security of tenure as a first step to persuading
him to borrow in order to invest in increased agricultural output from his land. At the level of Central Government planning, the attitude to production generally is a socialistic one, and the plans have
reiterated the aim to reduce the discrepancies in
wealth within the Indian community. Laws have
been passed abolishing the numerous intermediaries
who used to stand between the cultivator as the
payer of land revenue and the State as collector of
revenue. Legislation has also been provided to enable states in their turn to set an upper limit on the
amount of land which an individual could hold, and
although the states have so enacted, there has been
little implementation of the law and much evasion
of its intention. Tenant farmers still lack adequate
protection against eviction, and where rents are a
fixed proportion of the crop (25–50%) there is
little incentive to improve yields. Segal considers
the landowners are more powerful in the State
legislatures than at the Centre, and so are able to
weaken if not to frustrate the good intentions of the
Centre towards the tenant cultivator

Planning in General

In planning for economic development no country
can expect to be able to 'pull itself up by its own
bootlaces'. No country in the developed world is
completely self-sufficient. The economist's concept
of 'self-sustaining' growth does not imply growth
within a closed economy, but rather continuing

development, the capital for which is generated by the country's own efforts internally and through external trade. All countries have a measure of dependence on others through the economies of division of labour operating on an international level. A country seeking to develop has to decide what pattern of economy is capable of achievement, what factors among its own resources can best be advanced both to increase national wealth internally and to provide goods or services for sale to others in order to earn the foreign exchange with which to import the goods or services that others are better able to provide.

India's planners have at their disposal vast resources of land, materials, and manpower, but a minimum of capital and technology. At its simplest, in any economy, capital is generated when the productive capacity of the country is geared to yield more than immediate consumption demands. The savings that accumulate are potentially capital for investment in new expanded productive capacity. India's mainly traditionalist and locally self-sufficient agricultural population is terribly poor. Production barely feeds the local people since there are many more rural dwellers than are needed to produce the crops. Only a small part of production enters the channels of trade, and consequently the people's ability to earn money (let alone to accumulate capital reserves) is very small.

The problems facing India's planners are formidable: to activate the human resources to produce what the nation needs in the way of food and other raw materials from the land and to produce a surplus of such commodities as can profitably be exported; to establish and expand industries upon which future economic growth can be erected; to raise the general level of economic life so that people can have more money with which to buy more of the necessities of a better life; and at the same time to bring about agricultural and industrial revolutions as quickly as possible so that the population explosion does not devour the whole substance of whatever increases in production can be achieved. No other country of comparable size has attempted so much within a largely free and democratic society. China has faced problems of similar scale and kind, and has achieved more in the same time, but in a society far from free or democratic. Herein lies the dilemma for the 'free' Western world. India looks mainly to the West for capital and technological help, and for markets for her exportable surplus. Many sympathetic observers of the Indian scene, both Indian and Western, wonder whether the present spirit of Indian democracy is adequately determined and resolute for the task before it. Ultimately the solution to India's problems must be worked out by India herself, no matter what help and advice is forthcoming from her friends.

Planning for Jobs

India's planners have the unenviable task of trying to design a pattern of development to cope with present problems as well as establishing foundations upon which future expansion can take place. Meanwhile the population continues to grow, giving the planners no sign of a respite.

The three five-year plans which have run their course since 1950–51 have done rather more than keep the economy abreast of the increase in population. The First Plan (1950/51–1955/56) was a period of recovery from the neglect of the economic fabric during wartime and the early uncertainties of independence. Industrial development was mainly responsible for creating $4\frac{1}{2}$ million new jobs, but 5·3 million were still jobless at the end of the plan.

In the Second (1955/56–1960/61) and Third (1960/61–1965/66) Plans more attention was paid to industrial development, but much of it was capital-intensive rather than labour-intensive, and cost great sums of foreign capital. Development of this kind was probably inevitable over some years if India was to create within her own control the industries which would at some future date be able to make the machines for manufacturing enterprises of a more labour-intensive character.

Official estimates are that over the period of the First and Second Plans (1951–61) the labour force increased by 21 million: non-agricultural employment increased by 12 million jobs and maybe a further 5 million found jobs in agriculture. Unemployment at the start of the Third Plan amounted to about 7 million, and despite the creation of 14·5 million jobs (10·5 non-agricultural) the number of unemployed had risen to about 10 million by 1966, three-quarters of whom are probably rural dwellers.

These figures of unemployment do not, however, tell the whole story, for in the rural areas there is among agricultural labourers and small farmers a considerable measure of under-employment due to the seasonal nature of much of their work. The planners estimate the number of under-employed 'willing and able to take up additional work' at 16 million, but the total could be much greater. A start has been made to utilise some of this seasonal surplus of labour in Rural Works Programmes.

In the long run, however, and for the bulk of the increasing population that will be seeking work, jobs have to be created in occupations other than agriculture. Already there is a surplus of people on the land, estimated at 20–25 per cent of the agricultural population, and as the agricultural revolution progresses greater production from the land will require fewer people still than now work it. Thus the massive need is for jobs in manufacturing and service industry. The extent and basis of India's industrial development are discussed below in Chapter Three, Section 4.

3. INDIA: AGRICULTURE

The wide variety of physiographic and climatic environments contained within India is reflected in the diversity of its agricultural geography. The Indian peasant farmer operates still predominantly within a subsistence economy. His first aim is to feed himself and his family and then maybe produce some saleable surplus to pay for the necessities and small luxuries he cannot produce himself. His mode of economic life has changed relatively little over many centuries, so that within any particular region the pattern of agricultural activity follows well-tried traditional lines. The crops grown, the methods of tilling the soil and tending the crops, the way farming activity adjusts to the climatic calendar, and the manner of exploiting local variations in site – such as floodplains, slopes, and upland interfluves – all owe much to tradition built up over millenia of trial and error.

Over the past hundred years or so, and with accelerating effect in recent decades, a number of factors have been operating to bring about change in the agricultural scene. The development of manufacturing industry and overseas trade, and the growth of cities stimulated a demand for agricultural commodities which has increased the farmers' interest in growing crops for cash. This factor affects regions in different ways according to their physical suitability for cultivating the commodities

11. *A farmer's house in Tamilnadu:* Mudbrick walls and tiled roof. Wood frame string beds are seen on the porch and outside, near the rice-straw stack. Cow dung is drying in the forecourt. A light wooden plough is leaning against the house.

12. *Transplanting paddy* by the "Japanese Method", i.e. in lines to facilitate subsequent weeding. The women do the work while a foreman supervises and two assistants hold the line. A farmer in the background is preparing another paddy field. (Tamilnadu)

in demand and, of course, affects farmers in different degrees according to their accessibility to markets (through costs of transportation), their technical skill and their economic capability. A common problem facing the individual farmer who might wish to change his cropping system in response to a new demand is how to obtain financial credit on which to feed his family while a cash crop occupies the fields which formerly produced food. Another widespread difficulty results from the way in which a farmer generally holds his lands in many separate 'parcels' scattered among the lands of his fellow villagers. Some of his fields almost inevitably lie in various directions and distances from his homestead, making access to work wasteful in time and close supervision of all fields difficult. To be able to farm each plot to his own plan, especially if this involves a crop growing when other farmers have their fields fallow and are grazing them with cattle, the farmer must fence his fields, an excessively expensive proposition when they are widely scattered. The persistence of traditional techniques of agriculture may in part be due to the persistence of traditional landholding systems. It is difficult indeed for the individual farmer, however enlightened, to act independently of his fellow villagers.

Within particular regions great changes in agriculture have been made possible by governmental action in providing irrigation water from large-scale works. These have in many areas radically changed the physical environment of farming, but have not generally had much effect on the traditional socio-economic environment within which the farmer operates.

India's size compels us to take a rather generalised view of its agricultural geography, but the foregoing comments should warn us not to overlook the diversity in pattern and economic objectives which may be masked by the generalisation. After the discussion of crops and crop associations a number of sample studies are presented as a corrective to over-generalisation.

TABLE 3.3.1

Area Under Principal Crops, 1966–67

Crop	Area (m. hectares)
Rice	35·6
Jowar	18·0
Wheat	13·1
Bajra	12·5
Maize	5·1
Small millets	4·7
Barley	2·9
Ragi	2·4
Total cereals	94·2
Gram	8·0
Other pulses	14·2
Total food-grains	116·5
Cotton	7·8
Ground-nuts	7·3
Other oil-seeds	7·6 (castor, sesamum, rape-seed, mustard, linseed)
Sugar-cane	2·3
Jute	0·8
Tree crops (estimate)	1·5 (coconut, 0·9; tea, 0·3; rubber, 0·2; coffee, 0·1)

13. *Mechanical reapers* such as this seen cutting wheat in the Ganga Plain are relatively uncommon. Until there is alternative work for the landless agricultural labour force extensive mechanisation could aggravate their economic situation.

The Crops (see Table 3.3.1)

The preferred cereals in India are rice and wheat. **Rice** occupies almost twice the area of the next most extensive crop, jowar. East of longitude 80° E., and along the west coast of the Peninsula south from latitude 20° N. rice dominates the agricultural scene. In southern India generally, as in Ceylon, rice tends to be grown wherever irrigation water can be brought to suitable alluvial soils, but since such lands interdigitate with cultivable areas unsuited to rice the regional pattern tends to be more complex than in the rice-dominant regions. Rice is grown mainly as a rain-fed, and so a *kharif* crop occupying land in the wet summer season and harvested in November–December after the rains.

Wheat is particularly favoured in the Punjab Plains where, as a *rabi* crop (i.e. sown after the rains and harvested before the end of the dry season), it can use what winter rains there may be to supplement the residual soil moisture from the monsoon rains or late season irrigation. It is grown widely throughout the Ganga Plain in Uttar Pradesh, diminishing in importance into Bihar. In the Central Ganga Plains, *rabi* wheat (and the pulse gram) and *kharif* rice constitute a well defined crop

association type. South from the alluvial plains, wheat maintains its importance into Madhya Pradesh, often in association with gram as a *rabi* crop, and the millets, jowar or bajra as the *kharif* cereal. On the Deccan lava black soil cotton appears as a *kharif* cash crop in the same association.

Jowar, the most acceptable of the millets, used both as a food grain and a fodder crop, is grown as a 'dry' crop, rain-fed in the kharif season. Its distribution is seen to be generally complementary to that of rice in the Peninsular Interior where it thrives on the heavier soils.

Bajra comes into its own as the kharif millet where soils are lighter and the rainfall low and precarious. Thus it dominates the western half of Rajasthan and northern Gujarat, and is important in drier parts of the Punjab and in the rain shadow belt east of the Western Ghats in Maharashtra. In Mysore, Tamilnadu and southern Andhra Pradesh, the three millets, jowar, bajra, and ragi are the major food grains on heavier, lighter, and poorest soils respectively where rice cannot be grown. **Ragi** is of particular importance in thin soils of the high plateau country of Mysore west of Bangalore, and ranks as the second most important crop in the Uttar Pradesh Himalaya and parts of the Eastern Hills complex of Bihar and Orissa.

Maize and **barley** are relatively minor crops viewed in the all-India context, but become important in some hilly districts such as the Aravallis, the lower slopes of the Himalayan Ranges in Himachal Pradesh, the Chota Nagpur Plateau, and the sub-Himalayan belt in Bihar. Maize is grown as a kharif crop, barley as a rabi crop. The latter is more tolerant of droughty conditions than is wheat, and being also less expensive to cultivate is popular in areas of light soils and other areas where the risk of crop failure is high.

The importance of **pulses** to India is not adequately measured by the area they occupy. Since religious beliefs prevent many Hindus from eating meat, and economic restraints and tradition limit its consumption by others, pulses represent one of the major sources of protein in the diet. **Gram** is the principal pulse and does well as a rabi crop on the poorer soils in areas of wheat and jowar cultivation. The pulses are valuable not only as food for man and beast, but also for their ability to fix atmospheric nitrogen in the soil.

Cotton, because of the predominantly subsistence basis of Indian agriculture generally plays a role in the farming programme secondary to that of the food grains. Apart from the irrigated cotton areas of the Punjab most of the land under this crop is in the Peninsula, the major block of cotton-growing districts extending through the Deccan lava country in central Maharashtra, northern Mysore, western Madhya Pradesh, and the lands in Gujarat surrounding the head of the Gulf of Cambay. A smaller and separate cotton region in west-central Tamilnadu extends southwards from Coimbatore to the coastal districts of Ramnathapuram (Ramnad) and Tirunelveli (Tinnevelly).

mills especially in the Ganga Plain in Uttar Pradesh. Productive soils and an assured supply of rainfall or irrigation are needed to produce good returns.

Jute although a minor crop in terms of total area, is of considerable significance in the rural economy of the alluvial districts of West Bengal, eastern Bihar, and the Assam Valley. Like cotton it is grown for sale to the urban manufacturing centres. Having lost its former sources of raw jute at partition in 1947 (the Pakistan jute regions) India has made considerable efforts to increase production. She is hampered in this by her lack of the richest alluvial soils (which are in the delta in East Pakistan) and by the necessity to use as much land as

14. *Harvesting* crops by hand is still the general rule throughout South Asia. Here bearded wheat is being reaped in the Ganga Plain.

Ground-nuts are the most extensively grown of a group of miscellaneous crops (including castor, sesamum, rape-seed, mustard, linseed, etc.) producing *vegetable oils* for cooking purposes and industrial use. Ground-nuts are particularly important in South India in the lighter lands of Tamilnadu and Andhra Pradesh but are grown in many districts of the plateau country of the Deccan. **Mustard** and **rape-seed** are widely grown in the Ganga Plains.

Sugar-cane is grown on a small scale for domestic consumption in most parts of India, but assumes major importance within areas tributary to sugar

possible for growing food. Mesta (or kenaf), a crop similar to jute but tolerant of drier growing conditions is becoming important as a source of a coarser fibre suitable for manufacturing into gunny bags.

Tree crops have in common a heavy demand on water and a need for good drainage. **Coconuts** are grown particularly in coastal Kerala and Mysore, for their fibre (coir) and their flesh (copra) from which coconut-oil is pressed. Unlike the other tree crops discussed here, coconut groves are managed as smallholdings and not on the lines of specialised plantations.

Tea leads as a plantation crop grown on large specialised estates often retaining British capital and management, though the foreign element in both is being progressively reduced. The main tea gardens are in Darjeeling and submontane Duars of West Bengal, in Assam (along the Assam railway and the north flank of the Brahmaputra Valley) and in the Nilgiri and Cardamom Hills of Tamilnadu–Kerala.

The area under **rubber** has almost trebled since partition, and is confined to the western flanks of the Nilgiri and Cardamom Hills.

Coffee is grown mainly north of the Palghat Gap on the Nilgiri Hills and the slopes of the Western Ghats in Mysore State.

Crop Associations

Granted this range of major crops, differing widely in their optimum requirements, one may attempt to define the characteristic types of Indian farming on the basis of crop associations.

Two types of agriculturally productive land use, representing opposite extremes in their level of commercialisation may be disposed of first.

Shifting cultivation or 'swidden farming' is practised widely in Assam on much the same system as is used in the adjacent areas of East Pakistan's Chittagong Hill Tracts (see below, Chapter Four, Section 3). *Jhum* land is cleared of bamboo jungle of several years' growth, the slashed vegetation is fired, and a mixture of seeds planted. Hill rice, maize, millets, cotton, vegetables, and bananas are typical crops. In some of the more remote parts of the Western Ghats of Mysore, in upland Orissa and elsewhere a similar system is practised.

Plantation agriculture involving large estates planted to tea, rubber, or coffee (or, in some South Indian examples to combinations of these) represent an exotic element in the cultural landscape even if they have been taken over by Indian management and/or ownership. The estates are characterised by the estate village for the work force, the manager's home and headquarters, the processing plant and a high level of development of communications. Although insignificant in the total picture as far as area occupied is concerned, plantation agriculture makes a most valuable contribution to India's trade, tea accounting for 16 per cent of exports during the Third Plan.

The remaining and overwhelmingly predominant

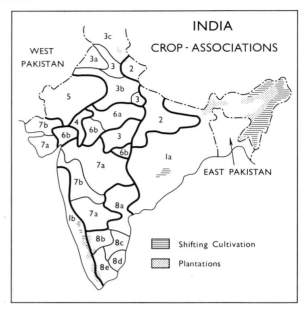

FIG. 3.3.1   India: crop association regions

part of Indian agriculture can be defined as *peasant* or *subsistence farming* (in the sense that most production is for family consumption) with some margin of commercial involvement. The map (Fig. 3.3.1) is an attempt to show the basis for regional divisions by crop associations. The major divisions are as follows:

1. Regions tending to *monoculture or dominance of rice*:

   (1*a*) Eastern India: the minor position occupied by crops other than rice is more fully examined in the study of East Pakistan (Chapter Four, Section 3). Gram is of some importance as a rabi crop in the Ganga Plain, the Damodar and Lower Mahanadi valleys. Jute is grown in the alluvial areas of higher rainfall in West Bengal, the Assam Valley, northern Orissa, and the easternmost districts of Bihar.

   In the hill and plateau country maize or ragi, as an alternative kharif cereal, and various oil-seeds either as rabi crops (rapeseed, mustard, linseed) or kharif crops (sesamum, castor) rank after rice.

   (1*b*) The west coast of the Peninsula in Maharashtra, Mysore, and Kerala is dominated by rice cultivation. Northwards of Panjim (Goa) where rainfall becomes more variable ragi is found as second crop to rice, while southwards coconuts assume the second rank. The importance of the latter crop is related in part to the extensive stretches of sand bars developed on the prograding coast south of Panjim. On the more elevated interfluves and benchlands cassava is locally important as a food crop, yielding tapioca flour from its tubers. Wherever possible, however, rice is grown as the preferred food.

2. *Rice–wheat* region (with gram often present as a secondary rabi crop and barley displacing wheat in some marginal areas on lighter soils): the Middle Ganga Plain and a projection southwards onto the plateau towards Jabalpur; Himachal Pradesh.

3. Regions with *wheat dominant* or at least important, occupy the Ganga Plains in Punjab and western Uttar Pradesh and extend in a broad belt southwards, bounded on the west by a line running roughly from Delhi to the Gulf of Cambay, and on the east by the 80° E. meridian. Southwards wheat gives place to jowar as the major food grain and is of little importance south of the Tapti Valley.

This wheat-growing region may be subdivided on the basis of the crops, other than gram (grown almost everywhere in the wheat region), which are associated with it. Undifferentiated *wheat–gram* areas are shown on the map (Fig. 3.3.1) as 3.

(3a) The *wheat–cotton* districts of the Punjab Plains form a distinctive region where irrigated kharif cotton is the cash crop, though it fails to exceed either wheat or gram in the area it occupies.

(3b) A *wheat–bajra* region extends from western Uttar Pradesh northwestwards to include Delhi and to form a transitional zone in the drier districts of Punjab and Haryana bordering Rajasthan. Northeast of Delhi sugar-cane is the second crop in several canal-irrigated districts of the Ganga–Jumna interfluve. Barley holds a similar position in the drier districts flanking Delhi on the south.

(3c) A *wheat–maize* region can be distinguished in the Himalayan foothills where maize is a kharif crop, often grown on terraced slopes as in the mountains of northern West Pakistan.

4. *Maize–barley* as an association with wheat as a minor crop is seen in the group of hilly districts in the highest parts of the Aravallis of Rajasthan, a region of highly unreliable rainfall.

5. *Bajra*, the cereal most tolerant of drought is understandably dominant west of the Aravallis in the semi-arid lands on the border of the Thar Desert. Some wheat is grown on the meagre winter rains, especially towards the north, while as summer rains improve southwards in Kutch, where also some heavier soils are found on lavas, jowar becomes important.

6. The *wheat–jowar* region reflects well the agricultural transition between the northern wheat-growing plains and the millet-growing Peninsular Interior.

(6a) From south of Delhi, extending through much of eastern Rajasthan and western Madhya Pradesh, wheat's supremacy is challenged as winter rainfall diminishes and irrigation is no longer widely available.

(6b) Jowar as a rain-fed kharif crop begins to take precedence, and cotton, also a summer crop, appears on the black soils of the Deccan lavas.

7. *Jowar* gives a measure of agricultural unity to a region extending from Kathiawar and the Narmada Valley southwards through the drier centre of the Peninsula as far as the Tungabhadra Valley. Within this region is enclosed most of the Deccan Lava Plateau famous for its black cotton soils (regur) in some parts.

(7a) *Jowar and cotton* are associated particularly on the heaviest deep regur soils of the Deccan lavas in north-central Maharashtra. Even beyond the southern edge of the lavas, in northern Mysore, cotton is still found in conjunction with jowar in the alluvial valley floors where black soils occur despite the absence of lavas, but the increasing importance of ground-nuts reflects in this area the lighter soils derived from Archaean rocks.

(7b) *Jowar–bajra*. In the immediate rain shadow belt of the Western Ghats bajra rather than cotton stands second to jowar, and on the thin black-red soils of the higher interfluves may take first place. The transitional area of

Kutch lying between regions of bajra and jowar dominance may be included in this association type.

8. The remaining agricultural regions of South India are characterised by the varied interplay of soils, rainfall, and water storage facilities. On the drier lands millets and ground-nuts, on irrigated land rice provide the principal ingredients of crop associations, with cotton a localised element in southern Tamilnadu. Since the proportion of alluvial lands in the total agricultural area, and with it the importance of rice tends to increase down valley and towards the coast, a small-scale map can only suggest a direction of change in the relative importance of crops.

(8a) The better watered areas of the Middle Krishna basin and the Nellore coast in Andhra Pradesh may be described as a *jowar–rice* transition zone on the fringe of the rice-dominant region of higher and more reliable summer rainfall that stretches north and east from about the line of the Godavari River.

(8b) A *ragi–rice* association characterises the plateau lands of Mysore, with their generally light shallow red soils. Rice growing here depends on tank irrigation. The dominance of ragi over jowar which is also grown, indicates the farmers' need to insure against drought.

(8c) *Bajra–rice–ground-nuts*. As the plateau steps down eastwards towards Tamilnadu, bajra tends to supplant ragi as the 'dry' cereal, complementary to 'wet' rice where irrigation water is available for the latter. Ground-nuts, favouring sandy soils, are the first or second ranking crop in this region.

(8d) The alluvium of the Cauvery (Kaveri) Delta and the greater extent of coastal plain sedimentary materials in central Tamilnadu may explain the fact that jowar is preferred to bajra in this *jowar–rice–ground-nuts* variant of the previous region's crop association.

(8e) In a belt of districts running south from Coimbatore to the coast, *cotton*, grown on black soils, is added to an association of *rice–jowar–ground-nuts*. Rainfall is low, but tank irrigation is highly developed.

Irrigation

In a country of such a markedly seasonal rainfall regime and with many areas of only moderate or low rainfall suffering from great variability of the total received, it is not surprising that man's ingenuity has long been exercised to reduce his direct dependence on capricious Nature. Upwards of one fifth of the cultivated area is now irrigated, canal systems accounting for 40 per cent of this, wells for 28 per cent, tanks for 18 per cent, and miscellaneous methods (such as minor river diversions) the rest. By the end of the Third Plan almost 35 million hectares would have been brought under irrigation, 16 million in major and medium schemes, 19 million in minor schemes. Some of the largest canal irrigation schemes were established under British rule in the last quarter of the nineteenth century. These schemes understandably undertook the development of the most immediately economical water resources, leaving only more expensive projects for development in the present century. Since independence the need to provide food for a rapidly increasing population has been a spur to the survey and development of what water resources remained unharnessed. The situation may best be summed up by a quotation from a recent Indian Government source (*India – a Reference Annual*, 1966). 'The possibilities of diverting the normal flow of rivers into irrigation canals have been almost exhausted. The plans for the future development of irrigation, therefore, increasingly aim at impounding by dams the surplus river flow during the monsoon for use in dry weather.' By the end of the Third Plan it was anticipated that about 36 per cent of the usable flow in India's rivers would be utilised for irrigation.

Significant as the recent engineering achievements in irrigation have been, it is important to remember that it is the farmer using water on his fields who ultimately determines the efficiency of the investment of land, capital, and skill. The Planning Commission in its draft outline of the Fourth Five Year Plan* suggests that the current practice of spreading water thinly so as to give some benefit and protection against drought to as 'large an area as feasible should be changed in the direction of providing water in quantities which will permit of intensive farming with the object of raising yields.

---

* *Fourth Five Year Plan, a Draft Outline* (1966), p. 173.

Canal Irrigation

Plans for the utilisation of several of the major resources remaining were in process of execution during the Third Five Year Plan. Table 3.3.2 lists the principal canal irrigation schemes completed, under construction or for the planning and preliminary development of which funds were allocated under the Third Plan. Only schemes benefiting at least 100,000 hectares (247,000 acres) are included here. The location of the schemes is shown in Figs. 3.3.2 and 4.2.7.

Before independence, little attempt was made to provide for water storage in irrigation schemes. The major works were on the rivers of the Indus and Ganga systems fed in part from the Himalayan snowfields. In these rivers although there is considerable seasonal fluctuation in discharge a moderate flow continues throughout the year. Peninsular India lacks snowfield reservoirs and the regime of its rivers reflects the high degree of seasonality of rainfall. The effect is accentuated in that several of the larger rivers flow eastwards rising in the dry rain shadow belt of the Western Ghats. The southern plateaus between Kerala and Tamilnadu enjoy a longer rainy season, but their rivers are relatively small. Thus in the Peninsula effective irrigation depends on storage.

The very numerous small *tanks* of South India are, of course, storage dams in miniature. Since they control only small catchments they are very susceptible to variations in rainfall, and are rarely capable of providing a carry-over of water from one season to the next. They may best be regarded as local measures taken to guarantee water for rice cultivation in a limited area in the valley floor immediately below the tank *bund*, in districts where direct rainfall is normally inadequate. Tanks are a common feature of the landscape in Tamilnadu, Mysore, and Andhra Pradesh. The engineering techniques available to local villagers limited their ability to control strong flows of water and restricted the scale of tank construction. Tank bunds are low earth embankments – sometimes rockfaced – of up to a score or so feet high at their maximum. In the broad depressions of the South Indian plateaus such embankments could hold back a body of water very shallow in relation to its surface area, and so very prone to loss of water by evaporation. Commonly the area irrigated is less than that of the

15. *Bhakra Dam:* one of the spillways in action at this 740 ft. high dam on the river Sutlej which stores water for power and irrigation.

tank! However, the existence of a tank exercises an influence on the level of the water-table in its vicinity, and it is usual to find well irrigation as a by-product of tank irrigation. The floor of the tank itself may also be cultivated or used for grass cutting for fodder or for grazing as the water-level recedes.

The use of more advanced techniques of construction and control of water storages was limited to a few multipurpose schemes aimed at providing hydroelectric power as well as irrigation water. The *Krishnaraja Sagar Dam* on the Upper Cauvery in Mysore, completed in 1930, irrigates 48,560 hectares and through its storage capacity regulates the flow to the Sivasamudram Power Station (installed capacity 42,000 kW.).

Since independence several factors have combined to multiply multipurpose storage schemes in the Peninsula. Economic development generally has led to an increased demand for power; population pressure has made increased food production a matter of urgency, and in this irrigation plays an important part; advances in the technology of earth-moving and earth-dam construction have made technically and economically feasible schemes which were engineers' pipe-dreams thirty years ago.

TABLE 3.3.2

Major Canal Irrigation Schemes

Source: *India, a Reference Annual*, 1967 and 1968

(Schemes established before Independence are shown with date in brackets. Some of these have been expanded. Schemes in italics are in early stages of development or planning.)

(A) *Ganga Plains: using rivers rising in the Himalaya*

		'000 hectares on completion
Haryana–Punjab:	Upper Bari Doab (1878)	335
	Western Yamuna (1886; 1944)	248
	Sirhind (1886) (R. Sutlej)	600
	Gurgaon Canal	102
	(River Yamuna)	
Haryana–Punjab–Rajasthan:	*Beas Project* (Beas–Sutlej link)	324
	(Beas Dam at Pong)	2100
	Rajasthan Canal	1163
	(linked to the Beas Project and Harike Barrage on Sutlej)	
	Bhakra–Nangal	1460
	(River Sutlej)	
Uttar Pradesh:	Upper Ganga (1884)	696
	Lower Ganga (1878)	465
	Sarda (1926)	795
	Sarju Canal	254
	Ram Ganga	690
	Mata Tila	165
U.P.–Bihar:	Gandak Canals	1439
Bihar:	Kosi	569
	Western Kosi	325
	Rajpur	161

(B) *Ganga Plains: using rivers rising in the Peninsular Plateaus*

Rajasthan–Madhya Pradesh:	Chambal	566
Bihar:	Sone (1891)	347
	Sone Barrage	124
	Sone High Level C.	172
West Bengal–Bihar:	Damodar Valley	437
	Mayurakshi	247
West Bengal:	Kangsabati	384

(C) *Peninsula* (proceeding southwards)

Madhya Pradesh:	*Tawa* (River Tapti)	304
Gujarat:	Kakrapara Canal	228
	(River Tapti)	
	Ukai (River Tapti)	155
	Narmada	403
	Mahi	203
Orissa:	Hirakud (Stage I)	243
	(River Mahanadi)	
	Mahanadi Delta	651
Andhra Pradesh:	Godavari Delta (1890)	449
	Nizam Sagar	111
	(River Manjra) (1931)	
	Nagarjunasagar	833
	(River Krishna)	
	Vamsadhara	135
	K.C. Canal	122
	Pochampad	231
Maharashtra:	*Krishna*	106
	Bhima	190
	Jayakwadi	142
Andhra Pradesh–Mysore:	Tungabhadra	517
Tamilnadu:	Kaveri (Cauvery) Mettur (1934)	134
Mysore:	*Malaprabha*	121
	Ghataprabha	121
	Upper Krishna	243
Kerala:	*Kallada*	105

Independence brought political changes which have had a bearing on the accomplishment and geographical distribution of great multipurpose schemes. Within the federal budgeting system each state seeks financial support from the Central Government for developments within its area and is able also to spend its own resources for such purposes. There is therefore a tendency for capital made available by the Centre to be spread over all the states. Another political factor has been the substitution of a more unified system of states for the irregular pattern and uneven system of British Indian provinces and native states. With fewer and now equal political units to bring to terms, schemes involving the sharing of water resources have been easier to plan and to execute.

The *Tungabhadra* scheme on a main tributary of the Krishna had a long history of political frustration owing to the fact that the river formed the boundary between the native state of Hyderabad (the Nizam's Dominions) and the province (or presidency) of Madras, under more direct British control.

For more than forty years after the scheme to dam the Tungabhadra was first mooted in 1901, Hyderabad declined to co-operate on the grounds that the state would lose fifty-four square miles of land beneath the proposed lake. Even after agreement had been reached in 1944 progress was held up by disputes as to which side should control the construction of the project, and the dam was finally built to a common design by separate teams working from either bank. The redrawing of state boundaries after independence eventually placed the dam in Mysore, though problems still remained in the areas to be irrigated which lay in both Mysore and Andhra Pradesh, their boundary crossing the lines of some of the feeder canals. In addition to irrigating 517,000 hectares when canals are completed, the scheme is planned to support hydro-electric stations most of which have been established, with an ultimate installed capacity of 108,000 kW.

The *Hirakud Dam* on the Mahanadi River in Orissa involved the construction of the world's largest earth dam to irrigate in stage one (com-

FIG. 3.3.2 India: canal irrigation

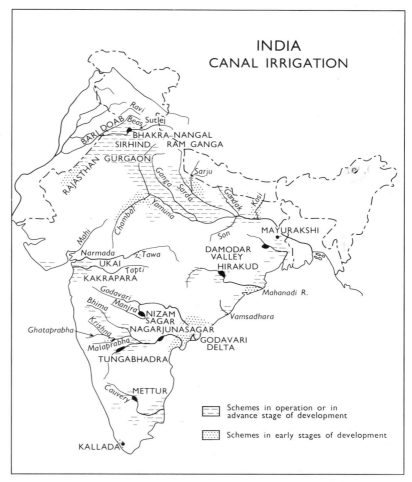

pleted) 243,000 hectares, and eventually (by 1970) a further 650,000 hectares and raise 270,000 kW. of power. Less than one third of the area to be brought under irrigation lies in districts immediately below the dam. Most of the advantage will be felt in the Mahanadi Delta where a diversion dam will control the distribution of water into existing and new channels.

The complex of dams and power-stations that make up the *Damodar Valley Corporation* are examined more fully in a later section. Irrigation of 437,000 hectares, flood control, navigation, and the development of power (104,000 kW.) are involved.

In the *Mayurakshi* project in West Bengal, consisting of the Canada Dam, irrigation of 247,000 hectares, mainly of *rabi* crops, is the principal objective, though a small amount of power (4000 kW.) is to be developed also. The provision by these several schemes of more certain supplies of irrigation water to the cultivators of the Orissa Deltas and the West Bengal Plains will make possible more intensive utilisation of land, particularly by guaranteeing water to allow the preparation of fields for early rice crops sown in the pre-monsoon period (cf. the *aus* paddy crop of East Pakistan) and by allowing for dry-season cropping. Where schemes are required to produce a sure output of power, they cannot always be operated to the complete satisfaction of both farming and industrial interests. In all these schemes, located in areas where traditional agricultural practices have adjusted to a reasonably reliable monsoon rainfall and an equally certain dry season, difficulty is being experienced in persuading farmers to adapt to the new availability of water, especially if the (to them) uncertain advantages of irrigation are accompanied by the more certain increase in costs which in turn will force a higher input of effort to justify the expense.

The *Bhakra–Nangal* project (see Fig. 4.2.7) harnesses the River Sutlej before it issues on to the Punjab Plains, from the Outer Himalaya. In the scale of its irrigation command – 1,460,000 ha. in Punjab, Haryana and Rajasthan will benefit – the project will rank with the great epic feats of the British period in the Punjab and Sind. Dams have been built at Bhakra (225 metres high) and Nangal (27 m.), and 1049 km. (over 650 miles) of main canal takes the water across the Punjab and into Rajasthan, into increasingly arid country. A power-station at Bhakra and two utilising the fall on the canals carry an installed capacity of 604,000 kW. Storage and power production of this scale are quite new concepts in the development of the Himalayan rivers. For long it was thought that seismic instability would militate against such schemes, but advances in engineering have made them possible.

The use of the waters of the Ravi, Beas, and Sutlej is to be effectively integrated through a system of storages on each river and linking canals. The Ravi is linked to the Beas by a canal which takes off the Ravi at Madhopur. A barrage at *Harike* just below the confluence of the Beas and Sutlej will take water across the Punjab into the *Rajasthan Canal* which is being constructed to water 1,163,000 ha. in the Thar Desert in Bikaner. Near Mandi tunnels will link the Beas to the Sutlej to generate 660,000 kW, irrigate 320,000 ha. and augment Bhakra Dam. On the Beas at Pong a dam will yield 240,000 kW. and ensure perennial irrigation to 2,100,000 ha. in Punjab, Haryana and Rajasthan.

In the Ganga River system British irrigation engineers concentrated their attention on the more westerly rivers whose waters could be channelled to areas of only moderate rainfall. Thus the waters of the *Yamuna* and *Ganga* were among the first to be diverted in the last decades of the nineteenth century. Later the Sarda was controlled, and since independence, schemes on the *Ramganga, Gandak*, and *Kosi* are under construction. As with the projects in Orissa and West Bengal, the immediate need for irrigation water is less apparent than in the drier Punjab, Rajasthan, and western Uttar Pradesh. None the less famines have occurred as far east as Bihar and Orissa, and the normal rainfall regime leaves scope for irrigation as a means to more reliable and higher yielding agriculture. The eventual irrigation command of these three Ganga tributaries is shown in Table 3.3.2. Each scheme will also produce power, those on the Gandak and Kosi sharing the output with Nepal.

Well irrigation is traditional in almost every state of India but reaches its greatest importance in the alluvial plains of the Punjab rivers and the Ganga. The time-honoured methods used to raise water vary from place to place but rural electrification is making possible the introduction of power pumps. The hand-excavated well has limitations as to the depth it is economic to dig to find a good aquifer. The increasingly general availability of electricity and oil-engines to power deep wells has made popular the tube well which can be sunk to and operated at much greater depths. Such wells are

16. Electrically driven *tube wells* such as this one in Madras (another in the right background) have been made possible by modern drilling methods and rural electrification. Water is discharged first into concrete channels whence it is led to the paddy fields beyond.

especially important in Uttar Pradesh where some are powered by small generating stations which utilise the fall in the Upper Ganga Canal.

Sample Studies of Village Agriculture

The village studies have been selected to illustrate the characteristic agricultural landscapes and the varied nature of the relationship between crops, terrain, and climate in a few of the crop association regions.* That by no means do all of the studies fit neatly into the generalised scheme of crop associations is one justification for their inclusion as a reminder that the generalisation is a gross simplification of a very complex situation.

The studies are of:

(a) Chhapra Tarukha and (b) Patna Ahiyai in the so-called rice–wheat region of Uttar Pradesh;

(c) Hehal, near Ranchi, in the rice-growing region of the Chota Nagpur Plateau;

(d) Changapur, in the heart of the jowar–cotton region of Maharashtra;

(e) Shiruru, on the coast of Mysore State;

(f) Bekud, in the southern edge of the Deccan Lava Plateau in Mysore;

(g) Hadadi, in the gneissic plateau of central Mysore.

Although these villages will not appear on most atlas maps, indication of their location is given in each study.

(a) Chhapra Tarukha and (b) Patna Ahiyai

The two village studies refer to a region which (on district data) would fall into the eastern part of the rice–wheat region of the Middle Ganga Plain. They represent contrasting conditions found in the area, one an area of low lying young sandy alluvium, the other an area of older alluvium typical of interfluves in the region. The fact that the crop association situation in neither village can properly be termed

---

* The author acknowledges with gratitude permission to use studies from the following sources:
(a) and (b) from Shafi, Mohd., *Land Utilization in Eastern Uttar Pradesh* (Aligarh, 1960).
(c) from Karan, P. P., 'Land Utilization and Agriculture in an Indian Village', *Land Economics*, xxxiii (1957), pp. 55–64.
(d) Personal communication via Dr. C. D. Deshpande, from Mr. V. H. Deodhar.
(e), (f), and (g) from Learmonth, A. T. A., *Sample Villages in Mysore State*, University of Liverpool, 1962.

17. *The 'Persian Wheel'* in its twentieth-century version, a very common means of raising irrigation water from wells in the Indus Plains of West Pakistan and north western India. The masked bullock provides the motive power to turn the gear wheels which drive the bucket wheel round which is a long chain of metal cans. These scoop water from the well and pour it into a trough leading to an irrigation channel.

'rice–wheat' is a warning against assuming that the generalised type obtains everywhere within its defined region. On the evidence of these two villages a sub-type association of rice with gram and barley would be indicated

(a) *Chhapra Tarukha* (Fig. 3.3.3) a village in Varanasi District, Uttar Pradesh, is sited close to the Ganga on young sandy alluvium (*khadar*). Quality of soil is judged by coarseness of sand, the best being silty sand, the poorest coarse sand. Fields of the best quality land tend to be small and long, indicating more fragmentation of the more desirable areas. A few wells give water for irrigation of a small area in the rabi season; wells are difficult to build and maintain in the sandy soil. There are two cropping seasons; kharif (summer) and rabi (winter). Rainfall is highly concentrated in the monsoon months, June to October. Of an average total of about 40 inches, 24 inches (57 per cent) falls in two months, July–August. From November to May no month averages more than one inch, and (as in Bengal) the rabi season rainfall is negligible as far as agriculture is concerned. The rainfall regime approximates to that of Allahabad (see Fig. 2.2.7).

Kharif cropping. Millets (bajra) and pulses

18(a), (b). The *dauri* method of raising water is one of many simple but labour consuming means of bringing irrigation water to the fields. In these photos, taken in Uttar Pradesh, a team of four work rhythmically to swing a pair of baskets from the lower ditch to a higher channel commanding the fields to be irrigated. The straw matting is to protect the mud bank from being washed away.

(pigeon-pea) are sown together on almost half the kharif sown area, the millets being harvested in September, after which the pulses grow through the rabi season to be harvested in March. A third of the sown area is under small millets sometimes mixed with rice – in the expectation that if early (August) floods destroy the millets, the rice will survive, while if September floods come the rice may suffer but a harvest of millets will have been taken. Mixing of crops is common practice in India as an insurance against the failure of one. A Hindi proverb runs 'Cultivate mixed crops and be content with whichever comes up'.

About a quarter of the cultivated area lies fallow in the kharif season. Altogether the kharif cropping programme is adjusted to the difficulty of raising hot-weather crops on 'droughty' light soils, hence the importance of drought tolerant millets.

Rabi cropping. The pulses continuing from the kharif season and others, gram and peas, occupy nearly 90 per cent of the cultivated land, with a small acreage of barley and wheat intermixed with gram, peas, or each other. The importance of the pulses is due to the light sandy soils which suit these

crops and in which they can put down long root systems to reach ground-water.

Table 3.3.3

Chhapra Tarukha

Total cultivated area 351 acres.
Percentage of total cultivated area under crops in *kharif season:*

Bajra and pulses (mixed)	36
Small millets and rice (mixed)	12
Small millets	8
Other crops and mixtures of crops*	20
Fallow during kharif	24
Total	100

Percentage of total cultivated area under crops in *rabi season:*

Pulses (carried forward from bajra-pulse mixture)	36
Gram	45
Gram and barley (mixed)	6
Peas	6
Gram and peas (mixed)	3
Potatoes	2
Other crops and mixtures of crops†	2
Total	100

* Millets, sun-hemp, rice, fodder, maize: no single crop or mixture exceeding 3 per cent.
† Wheat, barley, peas, gram.

FIG. 3.3.3 (a), (b), (c): Chhapra Tarukha

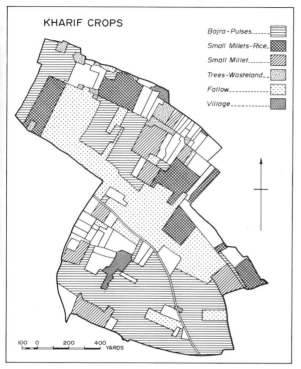

KHARIF CROPS

Bajra-Pulses_____
Small Millets-Rice__
Small Millet_____
Trees-Wasteland____
Fallow_____
Village_____

100 0   200   400
                YARDS

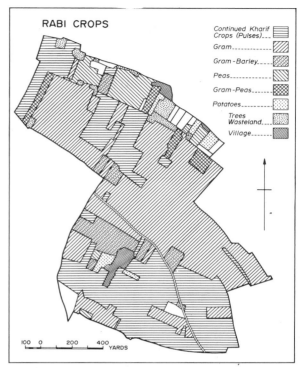

RABI CROPS

Continued Kharif
Crops (Pulses)___
Gram_____
Gram-Barley_____
Peas_____
Gram-Peas_____
Potatoes_____
Trees
Wasteland____
Village_____

100 0   200   400
                YARDS

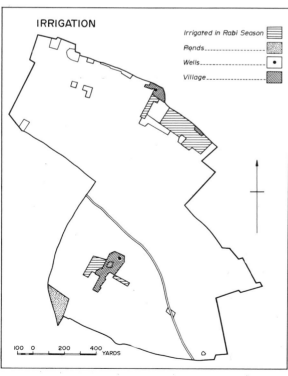

IRRIGATION

Irrigated in Rabi Season
Ponds_____
Wells_____
Village_____

100 0   200   400
                YARDS

(b) *Patna Ahiyai* (Fig. 3.3.4) a village in Azamgarh District, Uttar Pradesh, lies on the old alluvium (*bhangar*) of the interfluve between the Ganga (thirty miles south) and the Ghagra (thirty miles north). The best land is clay-loam. Lighter soils carry crops in alternate seasons, or the pulse pigeon-pea; heavier moisture-retentive soils carry a kharif crop of transplanted rice. Well irrigation is important for watering rabi crops. In the 230 acres of the village there are twelve wells and several ponds.

Kharif cropping. Rice is the main crop, followed by sugar-cane, maize, and millets. The contrast between the cropping patterns of this village on clay soils and Chhapra Tarukha only thirty miles away but on sandy soils is very marked.

In both villages nearly a quarter of the land lies fallow during the summer season, the explanation given being to restore fertility. That almost no land is left fallow in the rabi season indicates that despite the drought of winter, the virtue of pulses as nitrogen-fixing and food-giving crops is well appreciated by the peasant farmer.

Rabi cropping depends on irrigation from wells and on moisture carried over from the rainy season.

Fig. 3.3.4 (a), (b), (c): Patna Ahiyai

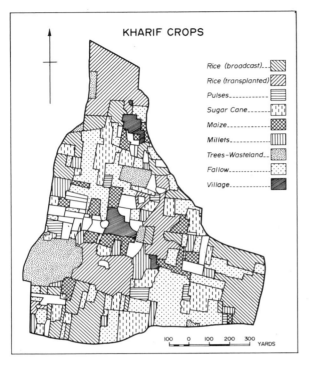

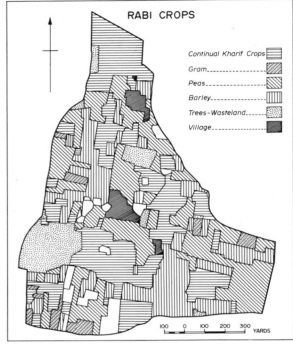

Peas and barley predominate, but neither exceeds the area of crops remaining in the ground from the kharif season: sugar-cane, transplanted rice, and pigeon-pea.

Table 3.3.4

Land Use: Patna Ahiyai

Percentage of total cultivated area under crops in *kharif season:*

Rice (broadcast)	20
Rice (transplanted)	18
Sugar-cane	14
Maize	8
Millets	6
Pigeon-pea	2
Mixed crops (of the above, plus fodder, vegetables, sun-hemp)	8
Fallow	24
Total	100

Percentage of total cultivated area under crops in *rabi season:*

Continued kharif crops (transplanted rice, sugar, pigeon-pea)	35
Peas	33
Barley	25
Gram	4
Mixed crops (of the above, plus wheat, barley) and others (vegetables, potatoes)	3
Total	100

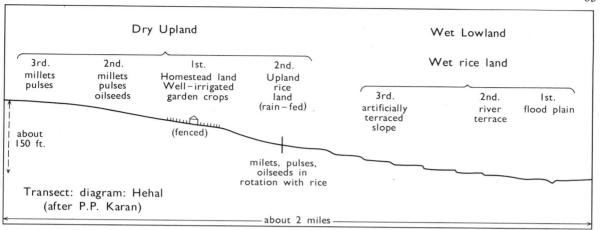

FIG. 3.3.5 Hehal (transect diagram)

(c) Hehal, near Ranchi, on the Chota Nagpur
Plateau was selected by P. P. Karan for study, as
representative of its region. It lies at 2200 ft. on a
gently dissected plateau of gneiss and granite, with
a relative relief of the order of 100–200 ft. between
valley floor and hill crest. With a total of about 60
inches of rainfall its regime is similar to that of
Nagpur (Fig. 2.2.7): rainfall is concentrated in July–
August and there is a very marked dry season. The
uplands are areas of dry thin red soils, poor in
nitrogen and phosphates, while lowlands are regarded as wet and have dark grey sticky soils, rich in
organic matter. Land is classified according to
productivity in three grades within each of the two
main divisions of dry upland and wet lowland (Fig.
3.3.5, and Table 3.3.5). First-class upland is homestead land used mainly for vegetables and carefully
manured, watered from wells and fenced. Second-
class upland lies relatively close to the homesteads
but is unfenced and little manured for crops of

TABLE 3.3.5

Hehal

Site	Dry Upland			Wet Lowland		
	Upper slopes of plateau			Valley side with artificial terraces	River terraces	Valley bottom
Class	3rd Most remote from homestead	2nd	1st Homestead land	3rd	2nd	1st
Irrigation	None	None	Well (for vegetables and rabi crops)	Tank (for rice)	Tank (for rice)	River
Bhadoi crops (32 per cent) (June–Nov.)	Millets, pulses	Millets, upland rice, pulses (in rotation)	Vegetables	Rice (mainly rain fed)	—	Rice
Aghani crops (57 per cent) (June–Dec.)	—	Oil-seeds (small area)	Vegetables	Oil-seeds (small area	Transplanted rice	Trans-planted rice
Rabi crops (11 per cent) (Nov.–March)	—	—	Oil-seeds, pulses	—	—	—

Based on Karan, P. P., 'Land Utilization and Agriculture in an Indian Village', *Land Economics*, xxxiii (1957), pp. 55–64.

millets and pulses. Further from the homesteads, third-class land is even less well cared for, carries similar dry crops, and periodically has to be left fallow for from two to five years. The lowlands are the areas to which soil wash from the uplands has gravitated over the centuries. The deeper valley bottom soils tend to collect and hold moisture, and these are the first-class lowland areas. Above them river benches form natural terraced lands, constituting second-class lowland, and above them again man has cut broad terraces out of the slopes. Rice cultivation is the rule on all these lowland areas, yields, as might be expected, being highest in the valley bottom land where plants can be assured of water for the longest period. Double cropping of rice is practised on the first-class lowland areas.

The cropping calendar is closely similar to that characteristic of lowland Bengal, the main difference being the extensive cultivation of millets. The salient characteristics of land utilisation at Hehal are shown in Table 3.3.5.

(*d*) *Changapur* lies close to Amraoti (Amravati) about eighty miles west of Nagpur, in a region of black cotton soils developed on Deccan lava. The area stands about 1050 ft. above sea-level and is one of gentle relief, rising only 35 ft. within a distance of half a mile either side of a perennial stream. Soils are coarse-grained alluvium derived from the lavas, but have the tendency characteristic of the black lava soils to become water-logged very quickly where there is poor drainage; and may remain so for a week after heavy rain.

The rainfall regime of Nagpur (Fig. 2.2.7) may be taken as approximating to that of Changapur: strongly seasonal, but with reasonable reliability from June to September. Its variation is, however, enough to encourage the practice of mixed cropping of kharif crops by way of insurance. With cotton as a dominant crop are mixed jowar and/or *tur* pulse; with jowar dominant *mung* pulse is grown; with *tur* pulse dominant, bajra. Only a small area is devoted to rabi crops of gram, wheat, and linseed. Double cropping within the calendar year is uncommon and can only be practiced when an early maturing crop of ground-nuts can be cleared from the field in time for sowing the rabi crop, or when the kharif crops fails and time is available for rabi cultivation. Crop areas can therefore be expressed adequately as per-

centages of the total area sown which approximates closely to the net sown area. Table 3.3.6 shows the relative importance of different crops, and the land use in the village.

The reason given for the area shown as 'not sown' is that capital was lacking. This may be related to the fact that the village, as a settlement, is a deserted one, there being only a temple and an inn within its present boundaries. Farm workers have to travel at least two miles from their homes to work the Changapur fields, which probably explains several indications noted by the land-use surveyor of the lack of intensive cultivation: farmers never seen in the fields after 1 p.m.; little or no systematic manuring of fields. He comments that education of the farmer and the provision of loans with which to buy fertilisers and seed would certainly raise production.

TABLE 3.3.6

Changapur – Crops and Land Use

Crop	Percentage of area sown	
Cotton	51·2	
Jowar	28·7	
Tur pulse	6·7	kharif crops *c.* 93·5
Mung pulse	1·3	
Ground-nuts	4·6	
Bajra	1	
Chillies	1	
Til (oil-seed)	1	
Gram	2·8	rabi crops 6·5
Linseed	2·3	
Wheat	1·4	

Land Use
(total area about 791 acres)

	Per cent
Sown area	87·9
Arable, but not sown	7·1
Waste and fallow	2·5
Grazing	2·1
Other uses	0·4

(*e*) *Shiruru* (Fig. 3.3.6) is a large village (over 5000 population) in the middle of the coast of Mysore State. Its rainfall regime is comparable to that of Cochin (see Fig. 2.2.7). It is typical of much of the Mysore–Kerala coast, having long beach ridges backed by low wet lands, inland of which rises the dissected lateritic low plateau. Settlement is mainly on the beach ridges where homesteads with their gardens and fruit trees are strung out beneath the continuous belt of coconut-palms or cluster on the sandy rises which represent former islets in the one-time lagoon. Fishing, boat building, and the making of coir are industries which supplement the near monoculture of rice. The low-lying lagoonal allu-

19. Fishing provides an important supplementary source of protein in many South Asian homes, and is an important village activity in many coastal areas of India, Pakistan and Ceylon. This view in Kerala shows *fishermen preparing their nets* beneath coconut palms. Much cordage used is made from coir fibre obtained from the coconut husk. Behind the nearest boat a crew can be seen pulling their boat ashore. Their village houses shelter among the palms in the background.

vial lands carry a single crop of rice during the monsoon. A small amount of sugar-cane is irrigated along the banks of a minor stream. The lateritic plateau is here under scrub and rough grass. The overall population density is about 1300 per square mile. Fortunately non-agricultural employment supports nearly a third of the population, and a few hundred more spend most of the year working away from home on coffee plantations.

(*f*) *Bekud* (Fig. 3.3.7) is near the southern edge of the Deccan Lava Plateau between the towns of Bijapur and Dharwar. The landscape is the typical stepped surface of lava flows. The uppermost levels are about 2500 ft. above sea-level, and stand 500–600 ft. above the valley into which streams are incised. In rainfall regime it is comparable to Bellary (see Fig. 2.2.7) though perhaps not quite so dry.

The upland surface is mainly grazing land for cattle and sheep, the latter providing an important export of wool. Animal manure is valued for crop land. Cultivated land is in the valley, the best areas being on alluvium irrigated from wells and small dams for sugar-cane, vegetables, chillies, bananas, etc. Dry crops dominate on the thin black soils however, bajra being by far the chief, followed by jowar. Maize, pulses, ground-nuts, cotton, and Deccan hemp are minor crops.

Population density is 110 per square mile overall, 230 per square mile of cultivated land.

(*g*) *Hadadi* (Fig. 3.3.8) in Chitaldrug District lies on the plateau developed on Archaean gneiss at about 2000 ft. above sea-level. The rainfall regime is similar to that of Bekud (above) with a total averaging about 22 inches. The village is typicl of the 'tank'

irrigated country. A tank is held behind a low dam thrown across a shallow valley and supports a small area of irrigated rice and sugar-cane immediately below the dam. Grass upstream of the tank probably indicates the area periodically flooded when the tank is full. Such areas are used as a source of cut

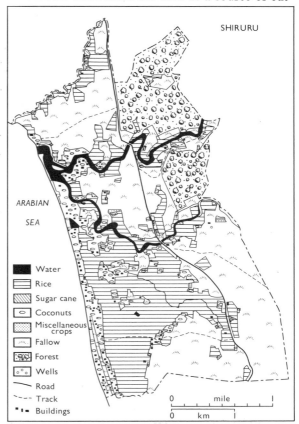

Fig. 3.3.6 Shiruru

grass for feeding to cattle, or for grazing tethered animals. Apart from the small irrigated area, the crops depend on rainfall and the characteristic association is of millets (especially jowar and ragi), oil-seeds (especially ground-nuts), pulses, and cotton.

FIG. 3.3.7 Bekud

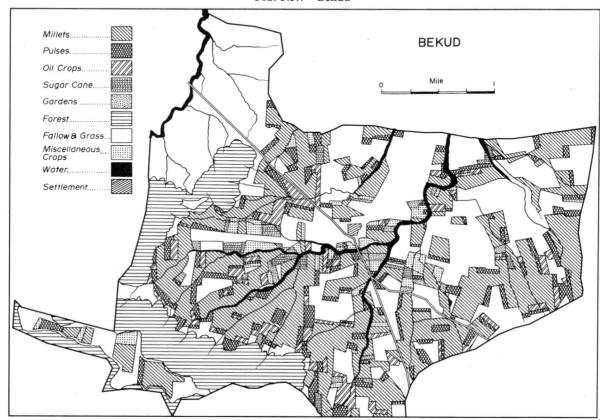

BEKUD

Millets
Pulses
Oil Crops
Sugar Cane
Gardens
Forest
Fallow & Grass
Miscellaneous Crops
Water
Settlement

20. *Agricultural landscape* near Bangalore, Mysore State. The undulating plateau of gneiss and granite is punctuated with rocky rises such as that from which the photograph was taken, and another on the other side of the shallow valley. A small tank is seen in the left middle distance, its bund picked out with trees and grass. Beyond (and below) the bund are rice fields watered from the tank. Above the tank oilseeds and groundnuts are cultivated without irrigation. Note the great length of the bund in relation to the water area stored, a typical feature of South Indian tanks.

Fig. 3.3.8   Hadadi

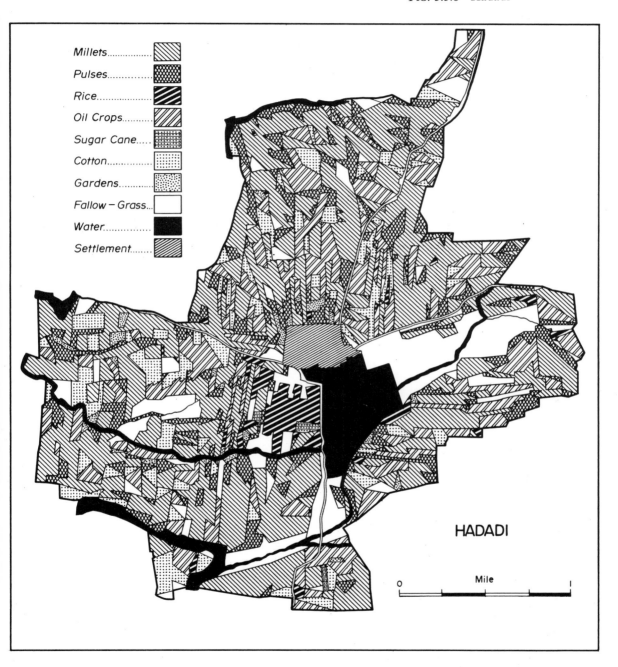

Millets
Pulses
Rice
Oil Crops
Sugar Cane
Cotton
Gardens
Fallow – Grass
Water
Settlement

HADADI

0   Mile   1

4. INDIA: INDUSTRY

Demographers place high among the priorities in the struggle both to reduce the rate of population increase and to improve living standards, the related objectives of urbanisation and industrialisation. Modern large-scale industry is expanding rapidly in India and now employs about 4·6 million people in factories.* In addition, half a million are employed in mining and about a million on plantations. A less certain number, estimated at about 20 million, engage in small-scale 'cottage' industries, a quarter of them operating handlooms, but not all of these can be regarded as full-time industrial workers. Cottage industry, particularly the domestic spinning and weaving of cotton into *khadi* cloth, has a respected place in Indian culture reinforced by Gandhi's insistence on the dignity of creative craftsmanship in village life. Although it is recognised as less efficient than factory industry, cottage industry has been protected and encouraged. It is labour-intensive, rather than capital-intensive, and so can for a modest investment of capital provide some additional income to the under-employed rural population especially during periods of seasonal slackness in agriculture. Government support of

21.   *Village industry, Tamilnadu:* Skeins of newly dyed cotton yarn drying. There is a considerable production of 'home-spun' yarn and hand-loom woven cloth in India, protected from factory competition by Government regulation.

small-scale and cottage industries through the organisation of marketing both at home and overseas, the supply of raw materials, and the development of improved techniques and equipment is aimed at increasing the employment potential of such industries and improving the prospects of their competing with, or in some cases being integrated with, large-scale industry.

The scale of the problem of creating industrial employment for an expanding labour force has been referred to in Chapter Three, Section 2 above. Although the rate of provision of new jobs has not so far kept pace with the rate of growth of population, let alone provided for the much needed transfer of surplus labour from agriculture to industry, there has been a considerable advance in Indian manufacturing since independence. Table 3.4.1 summarises the production trends of certain key raw materials and manufactured goods.

Three figures are given: that for 1950/51 shows the situation before the start of the First Plan; that for 1960/61 the end of the Second Plan; that for 1966/67 the year following the end of the Third Plan.

Due to difficulties resulting from the conflict with Pakistan, as a result of which some foreign credits were suspended and import restrictions had to be introduced, there was some short fall in production in 1965/66 compared with Third Plan targets.

The relative importance of the major industries as employers of labour may be gauged from Table 3.4.2 which compares data for 1950 and 1960.†

Another measure of the relative importance of different groups of industries is the 'value added' by those industries to the materials or semi-finished goods they process. In 1950/51 consumer goods made up 69 per cent of the total value added by manufacturing, and machinery only 8 per cent. By 1965/66, in a total value almost three times as great, consumer goods accounted for 34 per cent, machinery for 22 per cent.

In attempting to plan for the creation of a pattern and scale of economic activity that will become self-generating, the planners have had to balance the competing demands of the present, seen in terms of

---

* A factory is defined as an enterprise employing ten or more workers (using power), or twenty or more workers (not using power).

† Based on Karan, P. P., 'Indian Industrial Change', *Annals Association of American Geographers*, 54 (1964), p. 336.

TABLE 3.4.1

Industrial Production

(Sources: *India, a Reference Annual 1968; Fourth Five Year Plan – Draft Outline; U.N. Monthly Bulletin of Statistics;
Economic Bulletin for Asia and the Far East*

Item	Unit	1950/51	1960/61	1966/67
Coal	million metric tons	32·8	55·5	70·9
Petroleum (crude)	,,　　,,		0·4	5·6
Petroleum products	,,　　,,	0·2	5·8	11·9
Electricity generated	'000 million kWh.	5·3	17·0	35·0
Iron ore	million metric tons	3·0	11·0	19·3
Steel ingots	,,　　,,	1·5	3·5	6·6
Aluminium	'000 metric tons	4·0	18·3	72·9
Copper	,,　　,,	7·1	8·5	9·1
Zinc concentrates	,,　　,,	—	—	10·0
Automobiles	'000	16·5	55·0	75·2
Diesel engines (stationary)	,,	5·5	43·2	112·2
Electric motors	'000 h.p.	0·1	0·7	2·1
Radio receivers	'000	54	282	761
Power pumps (agric.)	,,	?	128	311
Tractors	,,	—	0·6	11·0
Nitrogenous fertiliser	'000 metric tons N	9	99	293
Phosphatic fertiliser	'000 metric tons P_2O_5	9	54	144
Sulphuric acid	'000 metric tons	101	361	702
Caustic soda	,,　　,,	12	99	233
Paper, paper board	,,　　,,	116	350	580
Cement	million metric tons	2·7	7·9	11·1
Cotton textiles, cloth (mill made)	million metres	3401	4649	4202
(small and cottage industry)	,,　　,,	814	2089	3102
Jute textiles	'000 metric tons	800	1022	1117
Rayon yarn	,,　　,,	2·1	43·1	80·8
Sugar	million metric tons	1·1	3·0	2·2
Tea	million kg.	277	320	369
Coffee	'000 metric tons	21·0	54·1	71·0
Vanspati (cooking oil)	,,　　,,	170	340	366

the demand for food, clothing, and jobs, and the future, in terms of the needs to establish a strong industrial base of heavily capital-intensive enterprises upon which industries more productive of

TABLE 3.4.2

Workers in Major Industries

Industry	Workers (thousands)	Percentage change since 1950
Cotton	1043	+16
Food processing	586	+47
Engineering	537	+32
Jute	259	−21
Chemicals	185	+34
Mining and metals	124	+11
Total	2734	+20

employment in relation to the investment required can eventually be built.

S. R. Sen, discussing the implications of planning for a 'self-generating' economy* recognises the problems inherent in postponing to the Fourth or Fifth Plan period the development of consumer-goods industries, and so delaying the expansion of labour-intensive manufacturing. The heavy industries – steel, fuel, and power, and machine building – are all expensive in foreign exchange and require large amounts of capital investment to be locked up, with small returns in the short term. Such industries tend to be located in a limited number of areas

* In Sen, S. R., *The Strategy for Agricultural Development* (London, Asia Publishing House, 1966), pp. 138–55.

determined by the existence of particular resources, and so their immediate benefits to the community in wages to employees affects directly only a small part of the country.

Consumer-goods industries, on the other hand, are as a rule most economically located close to their markets, the populous areas which are also sources of job-seeking labour.

With the Second Five Year Plan the Government established the politico-economic pattern for the industrial development of a 'mixed economy' in which the public and private sectors have defined fields for enterprise. The Government reserves exclusively to itself the responsibility for certain basic industries (Schedule A industries) while sharing others with private enterprise (Schedule B industries) and leaving the remainder for private investment to develop within the general scheme of Government control.

Schedule A industries include the mining of coal, iron, petroleum, and the main non-ferrous metalliferous minerals; the basic iron and steel and non-ferrous metal industries; heavy engineering, machine tools, air and rail transport, atomic energy, and electric power. Schedule B include aluminium, chemicals, fertilisers, road and sea transport. It will be noted that neither schedule includes the textile or food processing industries.

India is fortunate among developing countries in possessing a reasonable range of industrial resources in the way of raw materials. Among materials essential to industrial development which India has to import, are petroleum and copper. However, being so young as an industrial nation, a great amount of machinery and transport equipment has to be imported, much of it to equip new factories and to maintain the existing physical fabric of the economy. It is in the form of such capital equipment that much foreign aid enters India.

Fuel and Power Resources

India is at a stage when one can see, side by side, industries still persisting at the same craft level as for many centuries before the industrial revolution, and the large scale and technically very advanced industries which are the outcome of that technological and entrepreneurial revolution. One of the hall-marks of the industrial revolution as it occurs in any country is the substitution of inanimate power for muscle. In western Europe, the area first to experience the industrial revolution, steam-power raised from coal was the basis of factory industry which consequently developed mainly on or close to the coalfields. Later the development of electricity as a form of energy which could be readily transmitted over a grid system, and the invention of the internal-combustion engine using petroleum products which are conveniently transported and stored in bulk, freed many industries from the necessity to be located close to a source of power. India thus sets out upon the road to industrialisation from a starting-point very different from that of eighteenth- or nineteenth-century Britain or Germany.

Coal (Fig. 3.4.1)

Most of India's production comes from West Bengal and Bihar, from the Gondwana deposits of the Damodar Valley – the Raniganj, Jharia, and Bokaro fields – and the near-by Giridih field. Most of the deposits are of only moderate quality and coking coal is relatively scarce. However the seams are thick and little disturbed. Apart from these fields there is some production along the northwest-southeast trough extending from the Lower Godavari towards Nagpur, in the Pench and Wainganga valleys (near Chhindwara), at Tandur (northern Andhra Pradesh) and at Singareni (about 100 miles due east of Hyderabad). Small fields at Umaria (northwest of Jabalpur) and near Talcher on the Lower Mahanadi also work Gondwana coal. The total output of coal probably now exceeds 70 million metric tons per annum.

Coals of Tertiary age are mined in Assam, mainly for use in the tea factories. Lignite is being exploited at Neyveli (South Arcot) near Madras, to produce electricity, urea (for fertiliser), and briquettes. An ultimate output of 6·3 million tons per year is expected. A lignite field in Bikaner (Rajasthan) produces briquettes for railway use.

Petroleum (Fig. 3.4.1)

India's output of upwards of 5·6 million metric tons of petroleum (1967) meets between one quarter and one-third of her needs. Supply and demand are increasing rapidly at present, but there is no immediate prospect of self-sufficiency being achieved on the basis of known resources. India's principal oil-field at the head of the Assam Valley

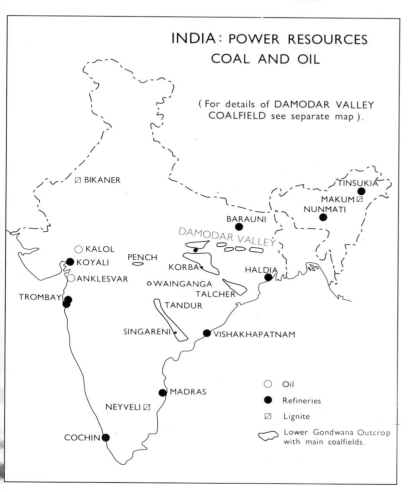

FIG. 3.4.1   India: coal and oil

has been in production for many years, and recently a new field has been opened up in Gujarat, and another in Karikal (Pondicherry) in Tamilnadu has recently been discovered.

Assam oil is refined on the field and at a small refinery at Nunmati, near Gauhati, on the Brahmaputra (capacity 0·75 million rising to 10 million metric tons) and on the pipe-line linking the oil-field via Siliguri, in the corridor of Indian territory north of East Pakistan, to Barauni. Here a larger refinery (capacity 2 million rising to 3 million metric tons) is located about forty miles east of Patna in Bihar and is being connected to Kanpur and to a refinery under construction at Haldia (2·5 million tons), Calcutta's deep-water port being developed on the Lower Hooghly estuary.

The latter is one of several refineries established or under construction to deal with imported petroleum. Others are at Trombay (two) near Bombay and Vishakhapatnam, with a combined capacity of about 7·7 million tons, and at Cochin (2·5 million tons). Gujarat oil is refined at Koyali (near Baroda) where the plant will develop a capacity of 3 million tons. Another refinery planned for production in 1968 is being built in Madras to process imported crude oil (2·5 million tons per year).

Electric Power (Fig. 3.4.2)

Since independence, India's capacity to generate electricity has increased about sixfold and new power-stations are coming into production every year. In total, however, India's output of power (37,900 million kW. hours) is very modest in relation to its population. Countries such as Australia

FIG. 3.4.2   India: electricity

The following large projects are not shown on the map: Matatila (H.E.P.) and Singrauli (Thermal) in Uttar Pradesh; Koradi in Maharashtra.

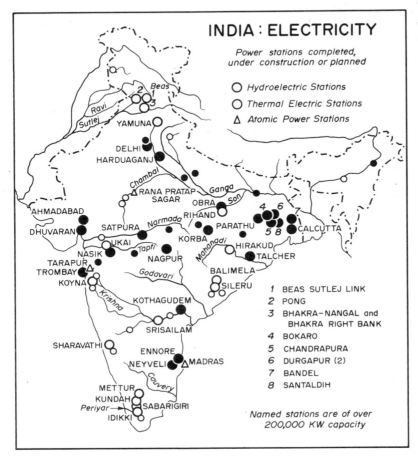

INDIA : ELECTRICITY

Power stations completed, under construction or planned

○ Hydroelectric Stations
○ Thermal Electric Stations
△ Atomic Power Stations

1 BEAS SUTLEJ LINK
2 PONG
3 BHAKRA–NANGAL and
    BHAKRA RIGHT BANK
4 BOKARO
5 CHANDRAPURA
6 DURGAPUR (2)
7 BANDEL
8 SANTALDIH

Named stations are of over 200,000 KW. capacity

(38,900 million kWh.), Norway (52,800 million kWh.), and Italy (96,800 million kWh.) have a greater output and many fewer people; Spain, with one-thirteenth of India's population generates a little more power, 41,200 million kWh.

At present thermal and hydroelectric stations share fairly equally in installed capacity (Table 3.4.3). In the foreseeable future India's economically exploitable water-power resources are likely to be harnessed, and the share of thermal stations will inevitably increase if the rising demand for power is to be met. Plans are being made to establish some nuclear power-stations to supplement the output of the conventional steam, diesel, and hydroelectric stations.

Fig. 3.4.2 shows the location of major hydroelectric stations and places (or districts) having a large capacity for thermal power production.

TABLE 3.4.3

Electricity Generation

	1951	1960/61	1963/64	1965/66
	(Million kW.)			
Installed capacity:				
total	1·83	4·6	6·2	9·0
Steam	1·1	2·4	2·7	4·5
Diesel	0·1	0·3	0·36	0·4
Hydro	0·6	1·9	3·2	4·1

The hydroelectric potential of India's rivers is estimated at 41 million kW. of which approaching one-tenth has been harnessed. The seasonal irregularity of flow of rivers in a monsoon climate will make difficult and expensive the exploitation of this presumed potential. Where water storage for irrigation is an urgent need, multipurpose river developments are politically and economically attractive. The development of the vast potential of the Brahmaputra as it enters northeastern India could hardly be justified in the immediate future since this well-watered region has petroleum as a source of power, and the nearest large market for electricity is at Calcutta, 750 miles away and much closer to cheaper sources of fuel in the Damodar Valley coalfields. The distribution of water-power potential is estimated as follows* (in million kilowatts):

West-flowing rivers of Western Ghats	4·3
East-flowing rivers of Southern India	8·6
Central India	4·3
Ganga Basin	4·8
Brahmaputra	12·5
Indus	6·6
Total	41·1

Recent developments in the techniques of transmitting electricity over long distances give some prospect of the ultimate unification in a single super-grid of India's power generation system. Up to the present local grids have been established in a few more highly industrialised areas such as Bombay, Damodar Valley–Hooghlyside, and linking the major centres of the states of Tamilnadu and Kerala. The Damodar Valley grid is an example of integration of hydro and thermal generation. The rising demand for power here and on Hooghlyside has led to the multiplication of thermal stations on the coalfield, and the Fourth Plan may see the establishment of a huge 1000 megawatt station at Santaldih.

Atomic nuclear power-stations may soon be established to serve the growing industrial areas remote from coalfields. Ahmadabad–Baroda, Bombay, and Madras have been considered as suitable markets for nuclear power. However, the very high capital cost of nuclear power-stations compared with conventional thermal stations will no doubt be a deterrent to their establishment while India is so desperately short of funds. A plant to produce 400 megawatts is under development at Tarapore, Bombay. Planning of another by the waterbody at Rana Pratap Sagar (Rajasthan) is well advanced, and a third is seriously considered for Kalpakkam (Madras).

Other localised resources

Coal, apart from its influence on industrial location through its use in electric power generation, exerts some attraction on the metallurgical industries such as iron-smelting which require it as a reducing agent, usually in the form of coke made from a

* Source: *India Reference Annual,* 1968.

blend of coking coal with non-coking types. The presence of **iron ore** of high grade and in massive quantities has also been a strong factor in locating this industry in the northeast of the Peninsula and in Mysore.

The availability of **raw jute** which could be cheaply transported from the Ganga Delta to Hooghlyside (particularly in pre-partition times) accounts for the concentration of that industry in the Calcutta conurbation. **Cotton** growing in the Deccan may have influenced less directly the location of the cotton industry in Bombay, the chief port through which the fibre was shipped abroad. Ahmadabad and Sholapur within the cotton belt probably owe their strong interest in cotton spinning and weaving to the availability of local raw fibre. However, much of India's industry is located for reasons other than those connected with the proximity of materials. The great ports of Calcutta and Bombay for example attracted commerce, capital, labour and population generally, and inevitably became industrial leaders.

Before considering the distribution of industry it is useful to summarise the principal raw materials India is able to provide from her own territory.

Iron ores of high quality are worked in several parts of the Peninsula both for export and for India's considerable iron and steel industry. The most productive region extends from Singhbhum in southern Bihar across northern Orissa into Madhya Pradesh. Ore from this field is exported from Orissa through Visakhapatnam and a new port which has been constructed for the purpose at Pardeep, at the mouth of the Mahanadi, near Cuttack (see Fig. 3.4.4). Mysore State, the adjacent territory of Goa, and the Ratnagiri District of the south Maharashtra coast have less rich iron ores, some being exported through Marmagao.

Among other metalliferous ores **manganese** is exported from much the same mineral belt in Madhya Pradesh–Bihar as produces the iron ore. India ranks high among world producers. Her exports of **chromite** are less important. This ore also comes mainly from southern Bihar and Orissa. **Zinc,** found in Rajasthan, is of increasing importance.

Copper is mined in the extreme southeast of Bihar but cannot supply all India's needs. Deposits are known in Rajasthan and may soon be developed. **Bauxite** occurs extensively as laterite in the Peninsula, being worked in Madhya Pradesh and Bihar. Some is exported, but more effective use of deposits in these and other states (Maharashtra, Madras, and Orissa) await improved communications and power development. A small output of **gold** comes from the Kolar field in Mysore.

Several important non-metallic minerals are found in India. **Mica,** greatly in demand for the world's electrical industries, is obtained from primitive shaft mines in central Bihar. **Monazite** (a source of the 'atomic' element thorium) and **ilmenite** (a source of titanium oxide) are worked in the beach sands of Kerala. Most of India's **common salt** is obtained by evaporating sea-water along the Gujarat–Maharashtra coast, and in Madras–Andhra Pradesh. Some natural concentrations are worked in Rajasthan (Sambhar Salt Lake).

Distribution of Manufacturing Industry

The map (Fig. 3.4.3) showing India's 'industrial regions' is based on Karan. At the present stage of India's industrial development one has to beware of thinking of these industrial regions as comparable in scale or concentration of manufacturing to the industrial regions of Britain or western Europe. Hooghlyside (see below, p. 81) is indeed a vast conurbation containing much industry within its continuous built-up area. It is strongly integrated with Calcutta's hinterland which includes the Chota Nagpur region and the Ganga Valley at least as far as Kanpur–Lahknau (= Cawnpore–Lucknow) (Fig. 3.4.4), but the other major regions are more loosely structured. Bombay is a good eighty miles from Poona; Madurai is about 230 miles from Bangalore in a straight line, much more by road or rail, yet they are included in their respective regions.

Karan lists five 'major industrial regions':

	('000 factory workers)
1. Calcutta–Hooghlyside	591
2. Bombay–Poona	563
3. Ahmadabad–Baroda	276
4. Madurai–Coimbatore–Bangalore	197
5. Chota Nagpur	159

Table 3.4.4 below shows the breakdown of the industrial labour force in these regions by major industrial groups as in 1960.

TABLE 3.4.4

Percentage of Workers in Each Region by Major Industries.

Region (total workers)	Food	Cotton	Chemicals	Engineering	Mining and Metals	Jute	Miscellaneous
Calcutta–Hooghlyside (591,111)	3·8	8·2	4·0	27·0	1·3	40·0	15·4
Bombay– (563,649)	7·3	41·4	5·4	19·4	1·9	—	24·5
Ahmadabad–Baroda (275,700)	3·0	76·0	3·4	4·8	0·4	—	12·3
Madurai–Coimbatore–Bangalore (197,465)	10·4	56·5	5·1	15·7	1·2	—	11·0
Chota Nagpur (158,867)	10·1	1·5	6·9	19·1	46·9	—	15·4

Except in Chota Nagpur, textiles whether jute or cotton tend to dominate, most markedly so in Ahmadabad–Baroda. Chota Nagpur is seen to be a region of heavy manufacturing where metal, engineering, and chemical industries, based on the coalfields and mineral deposits, account for more than two-thirds of the total employment. One characteristic of these major industrial regions is the minor importance of food processing, which although second only to cotton textiles in the size of its labour force (see Table 3.4.2 above) understandably tends to dominate in the smaller 'country towns'.

The *Calcutta–Hooghlyside* conurbation, home of the Indian jute industry, and the Chota Nagpur region are discussed in more detail below, p. 77.

Bombay–Poona is similarly dominated by textiles, here cotton, but is also an important region for forward-looking engineering industries such as motor vehicle manufacturing and electrical and light engineering. Bombay maintains its advantages as the port nearest to Europe and the Middle East, and is thus in a good position to import and refine petroleum. Fuel and power have always presented a problem, the long railway haul from the Damodar Valley or nearer but lesser coalfields in eastern Maharashtra making for high costs. The abrupt scarp of the Western Ghats made hydroelectric power generation worth while, but it is no accident that India's first nuclear power-station at Trombay is to serve this region. Other signs of modernity are the film industry, and various chemical plants including soap works. The Parsee family of Tata are a major entrepreneurial factor in Bombay (as also in the iron and steel industry at Jamshedpur in Bihar). Poona's industrial contribution to the region is in textiles, rubber, paper, and light engineering.

Fig. 3.4.3 India: industrial areas

As the table shows, *Ahmadabad–Baroda*, some fifty miles apart, are almost mono-industrial in textile manufacturing. Location in the cotton-growing area is an obvious advantage. Baroda is well known for its pottery, and may be expected to expand its chemical industries with the development of the petroleum refinery nearby at Koyali.

It could be argued that the well-separated cities of *Madurai–Coimbatore–Bangalore* hardly constitute an industrial region, or that if they do, then *Madras* with a very similar range of activities (and no further from Bangalore than Madurai) could also be included. Cotton textile manufacturing is the strong common element in their industrial make-up. Bangalore stands apart as the centre of the Indian aircraft industry, important also for its light engineering, machine-tool industry, motor vehicles, and telecommunication factories, and for its higher technical and research institutes. It is greatly favoured by its relatively mild and equable climate at 3000 ft. above sea-level. Despite an early start in industry, Madras had advanced less rapidly than the other cities, partly because of a less productive immediate hinterland. Its future is more promising now that oil refining and exploitation of the near-by Neyveli lignite deposits will guarantee it raw materials and power.

To these five major industrial regions listed in Table 3.4.4, might well be added a sixth comprising the towns of the *Kerala coast*, where, by contrast, food industries processing the products of farms, plantations, and fisheries dominate. Some 140,700 workers are found here mainly in the towns of Kozhikode (Calicut), Cochin–Ernakulam, and Quilon. Cochin is developing as an important deep-sea port with a new petroleum refinery, but the

22.   Ahmadabad, India's mono-industrial *cotton-textile city* in Gujarat. A medium-sized textile mill in the foreground, and many mill chimneys on the skyline.

major industries of the Kerala coast are concerned with rice-milling, coconut-oil extraction, soap-making, fish products (e.g. packing shrimps for the American market), etc.

It would be tedious to enumerate the industrial characteristics of all the towns in the country. A glance at the map, Fig. 3.5.2, shows a great number of urban centres of upwards of 100,000 people, each of which could probably justify a mention. Towns of this scale, whatever the primary reason for their existence, tend to generate some industrial activity of their own accord. They also, especially if well placed in relation to communications, attract industries to them for this reason and the prospect of a labour force. Since the main reason for the genesis of a town is to be a centre to serve the population of the surrounding area, it is to be expected that among the industries most commonly found in the medium-sized towns are those concerned with processing foodstuffs and manufacturing cotton textiles, to feed and clothe the local people.

This is indeed the basic pattern over India. Rice-milling, flour-milling, extracting vegetable oil from ground-nuts, coconuts, cotton-seed, linseed, etc., the extraction and refining of sugar-cane, cotton ginning, and so on, are characteristic of the towns in the agricultural areas which grow the appropriate crops. Light engineering, pottery making, and other

often small-scale workshop industries only a stage removed from the traditional crafts of the village, are wellnigh ubiquitous. Specific mention will therefore be made only of those towns or groups of towns where industry is of considerable importance in differentiating them from the 'average town'.

Several cities of the Punjab–Ganga Plain have large-scale textile industries serving national and overseas markets: Amritsar (woollen textiles and carpets), Delhi–Meerut (cotton), Kanpur (cottons and wool), Agra (cotton). These cities should not be thought of as mono-industrial. Light engineering, chemicals, and food processing are carried on in all of them. Also based on local material but serving a wider market are a group of towns in north Bihar – Uttar Pradesh specialising in sugar-cane processing. Lakhnau, with engineering stemming from its early function as a railway workshop centre, is characteristic of a number of Indian towns which owe their modern importance to the railways. Nagpur, Ajmer, Jabalpur, and Hubli are in the same category: Nagpur has developed a wide industrial base, including textiles, pottery, and glass; Jabalpur is an ordnance factory town of long standing. Ludhiana (Punjab) with a large refugee population is a growing centre for light engineering, particularly sewing-machines and vehicles. A number of other specialised industrial towns in the Chota Nagpur–

Calcutta region and its adjacent areas will be discussed below. Fig. 3.4.3 shows all the industrial towns and districts of note.

A fundamental problem facing industry in India is that of distance. Transport cost are high, and industries far from coalfields, oil, or assured supplies of hydroelectric power may face heavy charges for fuel and power. Distance also affects marketing, and industries located at nodal centres in the communications network enjoy obvious advantages. The Indian railway system operates under considerable strain to handle the increasing demands placed upon it, and in recent years much has been spent on increasing the capacity of the main lines, by double-track construction and in parts electrification, on converting to the broad gauge some important sections of the former metre gauge system, and on constructing new lines to meet new needs, such as the export of iron ore from Madhya Pradesh. Through the manipulation of rating systems particularly for coal and iron traffic, the Government is able to provide some protection for industries which depend heavily on such raw materials and are located far from them.

Important among the many other factors affecting the development of industry in India are the quality of labour and of the market. Modern industry requires many highly skilled technicians and India has had greatly to expand the facilities for training such manpower. With modernisation of the outlook of the younger generation, traditional and caste prejudices against manual work, whether unskilled, semi-skilled, or highly skilled, are being broken down. The mass market, however, remains a poor one, with an exceedingly low purchasing power and a list of 'necessities of life' which would exclude many of the most rudimentary of manufactured items which would be found in the possession of every Western household. It is to the raising of the living standards of the mass of the people that industry looks to create the expanding markets it needs in order to become 'self-generating' and to enable it to provide jobs for the available labour.

Chota Nagpur, Calcutta, and Adjacent Areas

A study of the industrial geography of the area shown in Fig. 3.4.4 which includes the Damodar Valley (see also Fig. 3.4.5) and Calcutta–Hooghly-side (Figs. 3.4.7 and 3.4.8) and such important industrial outliers as Kanpur–Lakhnau, the steel towns of Bhilai, Rourkela, and Jamshedpur and the shipbuilding port of Vishakhapatnam, all within a frame of 700 miles from north to south, 500 from west to east, illustrates the 'open pattern' of much of India's industry.

In dealing first with the scatter of industrial towns outside the more concentrated industrial regions of the Damodar Valley and Calcutta, the towns of the Ganga Plain, with their industrial base in agriculture and the dense agricultural population, may clearly be distinguished from those of the Peninsular Plateau with their base in mineral resources.

Reference has already been made to Kanpur and Lakhnau. Gorakhpur, an important railway town lies in the sugar-growing belt of north Bihar–Uttar Pradesh and has sugar refining and fertiliser works. Both Allahabad and Varanasi (Benares), particularly the latter, on the Ganga owe much to their religious traditions, but as manufacturing cities contain the characteristic 'mix' of cotton textile and light engineering industries appropriate to their size. Industry is less important in the river town of Patna, but may receive stimulus from the completion of the Barauni oil-refinery centre to the east.

On the plateau outside the Damodar Valley manufacturing as distinct from extractive industry based on minerals, focuses on the big steelworks towns. *Jamshedpur* was established in 1907–11 by Jamshedji Tata of Bombay. By the end of the Third Plan period Jamshedpur's steel production was about two million metric tons per year. High-grade iron ore is mined in the hills to the south and west but although manganese and chromite for alloy steels are available in the same Singbhum District, better quality materials are brought in from Madya Pradesh and Orissa. Coking coal is railed from the Damodar coalfield about seventy-five miles away. *Rourkela* some hundred miles to the west of Jamshedpur and also on the main line, Calcutta–Nagpur–Bombay, has been built with West German help in the Second Plan period. Steel ingot production should reach 1·8 million tons by 1967–68. Fertilisers are produced as a by-product. *Bhilai*, established with Russian help lies still further west in the pocket of irrigated rice farming in the Chhatisgarh Plain. Its iron ore comes from the hills to the south. Steel production was stepped up to 2·5 million tons in 1966, making Bhilai the principal producer, and further expansion to 3·5 million tons is under way.

FIG. 3.4.4   India: the industrial northeast

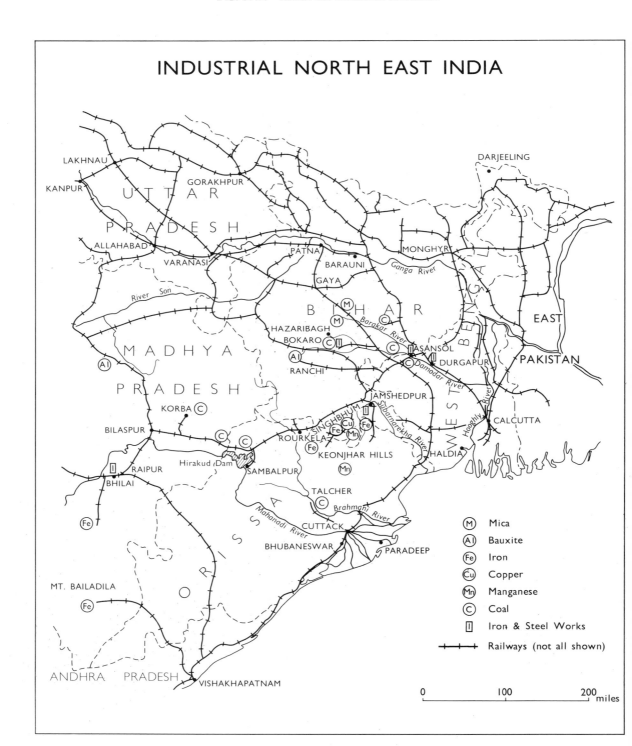

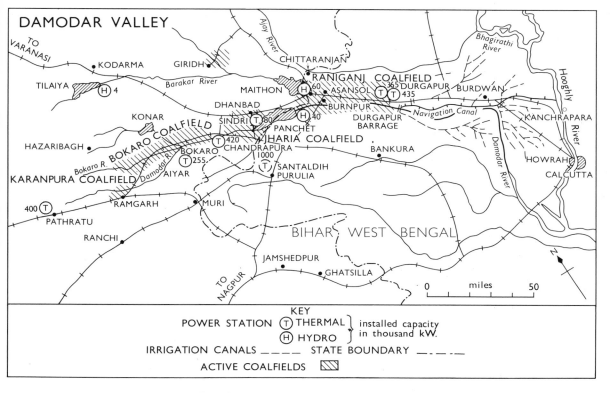

FIG. 3.4.5   India: the Damodar Valley

The Damodar Valley (Fig. 3.4.5) as India's major coalfieldbased industrial region merits more detailed discussion.

The Damodar River and its principal tributaries the Bokaro, Konar, and Barakar drain an elongated basin with its furthest water parting about 240 miles northeast of Calcutta. The river has a long record of disastrous floods and is notorious for the speed at which floodwaters rise after rains in its upper reaches. Its flow ranges from *nil* to 650,000 cusecs. During bad floods vital communications between the Damodar coalfields and Calcutta used to be disrupted, much damage was done to crops in the plains between the lower reaches of the Damodar and the Hooghly, and the stagnating floodwaters became the breeding area for malarial mosquitoes. Several minor measures had been undertaken before independence to alleviate the troubles caused by Damodar floods, and after the disasters of 1943 plans for a comprehensive scheme of multipurpose river development began to take shape. These plans crystallised in the Damodar Valley Corporation Act of 1948.

Under the aegis of the D.V.C. very considerable progress has been made to control the river by dams and barrages to develop hydroelectric power, to provide an assured water-supply for industry, to make water available for irrigation, and to establish a canal link between the coalfield and Calcutta. These developments have enhanced the attraction the coalfield exerted on heavy industry which has expanded greatly over the past twenty years.

Fig. 3.4.5 shows the salient features of the Damodar Valley and its adjacent regions as far as Jamshedpur to the south and Calcutta to the southeast. The several coalfields of the valley have long been India's main source of coal, which still leaves the region in large quantities to supply the fuel deficient areas of the Ganga Plain. The section in Fig. 3.4.6 shows the attitude and distribution of seams in a typical mine in the Raniganj field. In many areas the coal seams, several of them in excess of 20 ft. thick, can be worked very cheaply by open-cast methods.

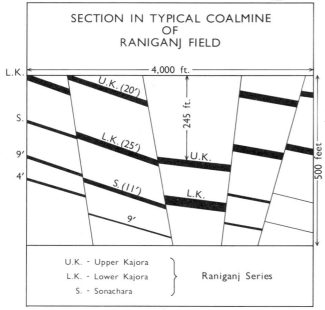

SECTION IN TYPICAL COALMINE
OF
RANIGANJ FIELD

U.K. - Upper Kajora
L.K. - Lower Kajora   } Raniganj Series
S. - Sonachara

FIG. 3.4.6   India: coal-mine section

In underground pits the seams are worked by 'pillar and stall' methods where the dip is moderate, or by 'long wall' methods especially where the dip is steep. In either case sand is generally stowed to support the friable roof.

The visual aspect of the coalfields is to the Westerner at once familiar yet bizarre. Pithead gear is much as in Britain, but rises from paddy-fields; aerial ropeways sweep across country, bringing buckets of sand from the bed of the Damodar for stowing purposes; sari-clad women are seen at work around the pithead, pushing trolleys of pit-props; in the open-cast areas grass-thatched bamboo huts are used for offices and workmen's shelter, only explosives being housed in brick in such a transient landscape; at pithead and in the open cuts loading is as often as not by lines of coolies carrying baskets of dusty coal on their heads to tip into lorry or railway van (closed for fear of pilfering *en route*); more modern pits supplying local coke ovens or power-stations load mechanically into open trucks; by each modern mine stand neat rows of miners' cottages, some flat roofed and maybe topped with a stack of rice straw, fodder for the family cow, and evidence that the miner still clings to remnants of a rural way of life; casual labourers and open-cast miners fare less well as squatter settlers in simple shacks of

matting, mud, wood, bamboo, and straw, grouped on some patch of waste ground.

Power development has been a major feature of the Damodar Valley project. In its earlier days stress was placed on the hydroelectric power which would be made available from the several dams which would regulate the flow of the rivers and correct their tendency to flood the lower valley. Three relatively 'high' dams at present have power-stations: Tilaiya (4000 kW.) in the head-waters of the Barakar, Maithon (60,000 kW.) near this river's confluence with the Damodar, and Panchet (40,000 kW.) on the Damodar close by. Another high dam completed is at Konar on the tributary of that name, and the next major work is to be a low-earth dam on the Damodar at Aiyar. These two latter dams are regulators and for water storage for industry in the first instance. The demand for power has grown more rapidly than the early planners had anticipated, and it has been necessary to establish several thermal power plants to supply a grid that serves not only the valley's own industry, but feeds places as far afield as Jamshedpur, Calcutta, Gaya, and Patna. The completion of several more dams and their associated hydroelectric power-stations has been postponed since thermal power can be more economically produced in the short run, and the dams already established have solved the immediate flood and water-supply problems. The chief thermal power generating stations are at Bokaro (255,000 kW.), two at Durgapur associated with coke-oven plants (365,000 and 435,000 kW.) and the most recent at Chandrapura (420,000 kW.) to supply power for electrification of the railway, and Pathratu (400,000 kW.) near Ramgarh. An important new station is planned to be started in the Fourth Plan at Santaldih, Purulia (1,000,000 kW.). These thermal stations provide power for base load, while the hydroelectric stations are used generally for peak load four hours daily, except during the summer high-water period when they provide base load to capacity.

In addition to their contribution to thermal electric power output the Durgapur coke-oven plants are being linked by a pipe-line to Calcutta so that gas can be fed into that city's supply.

Power and industrial water supplies take precedence over irrigation for the use of Damodar water. Thermal power-stations, the several iron and steel works and other industries are considerable users of water for cooling and other processes. The full potentialities of the basin for irrigation are not likely to be realised for a long time. Quite apart from the high cost of providing storage for the large quantities of water that would be needed to guarantee irrigation throughout the dry season (after all other non-agricultural needs have been met) there seems to have been little urgency on the part of West Bengal to seek more water than is at present available. About 40,000–50,000 acres are irrigated during the rabi crop season by the left-bank canal taking off from the Durgapur Barrage. The canal is designed to water 750,000 acres. A right-bank canal will have a design command of 250,000 acres. It is doubtful if these areas will be fully supplied, since the need to maintain navigation on the canal will presumably have priority over irrigation.

The navigation canal, eighty-five miles in length, carries coal to the Hooghly at Kanchrapara, at the northern end of the Hooghlyside conurbation. It is designed to carry two million tons of coal a year in 200-ton barges. Twenty-three locks, each capable of carrying a tug with two barges are needed to control the descent from Durgapur to the Hooghly, but it is claimed that the journey will take only forty hours.

The scope and scale of industrialisation in the Damodar Valley has reached impressive proportions. The accent is on heavy industry. To the older pig-iron furnaces at Kulti and steelworks nearby at Burnpur (about 1 million tons output) have been added the modern integrated plant at Durgapur (1·6 million tons ingot steel by 1967–68). Development of a steelworks at Bokaro with Russian help has begun. The Bokaro project is for a steel plant with initial capacity of 1·7 million tons, rising to 4 million. Some economists argue that India would do wiser to bring existing steel plants to maximum efficiency and to expand them before undertaking new investment of this scale.

Firebricks for the steel and other industries are made on the Jharia coalfield. Sindri on the same field produces ammonium sulphate and superphosphate fertiliser. Purulia and Muri, south of Bokaro, process bauxite from Lohardaga west of Ranchi, sending alumina to Sambalpur at the Hirakud Dam on the Mahanadi, and to Alwaye in Kerala for electrolytic reduction using hydroelectric power. Dhanbad has refineries of lead and zinc, and is a

23. *Durgapur Steel works:* four blast furnaces at the modern integrated iron and steel works in the Damodar Valley.

centre for toolmaking and radio industries. Heavy engineering is strongly represented in the Chattaranjan railway locomotive works, the Durgapur constructional steel and mining machinery plants, and heavy cable works at Rupnaraianpur.

Calcutta and the Hooghlyside Conurbation are separated from the coalmines of the Damodar Valley by barely seventy miles of paddy-fields.

The sprawling concentration of perhaps $6\frac{1}{2}$ million people that is strung out along the Hooghly for some forty-five miles is not India's fairest nor her most prosperous city. It does, however, epitomise several significant characteristics of the present-day city in India. Calcutta is not an ancient settlement by Indian standards. Until the end of the seventeenth century its site was occupied by a few agricultural villages, lining the levee belt of the Hooghly, then an important distributary of the Ganga. English and French merchants found the Hooghly a convenient point of access to the great cities of the Ganga Plain, with its centres of Mogul administration such as Delhi, Agra, and Allababad, and many other substantial towns.

The Ganga gave access by water, and a route for exporting goods to the transhipping points where ocean shipping could anchor in the Hooghly. The French at Chandernagore, the English at Calcutta, established their factories, and the foundations of India's mercantile capital were laid. Opium and indigo, and fine cotton textiles gave place in the nineteenth century to jute and tea as major exports. With the establishment of the British Indian Empire, Calcutta became its capital, attracting commerce and gradually industry, though even today it is predominantly a commercial rather than an industrial centre. Though it lost to Delhi its function as India's capital in 1912 it continued as capital of the populous province of Bengal. From the middle of the nineteenth century, railways began to displace river and road transport in the trade up the Ganga Valley, though within the Ganga Delta and northeastwards into Assam, inland-water navigation persisted. Railways, and the opening of the Suez Canal in 1869 gave Calcutta's chief rival, Bombay, great advantages of proximity to Britain, and reduced Calcutta's hinterland. Today this includes all of Assam, West Bengal, Orissa, Bihar, and the neighbouring independent state of Nepal, and extends west to include more than half of the states of Uttar Pradesh and Madhya Pradesh.

Railways did much to assist Calcutta's industrial development, linking it to the Damodar Valley coalfields, and to the growing mineral and metallurgical industries of the Chota Nagpur Plateau. The advantages of proximity to these resources has been somewhat neutralised since independence by a Central Government policy which equalises coal and iron traffic rates over India.

Partition dealt Calcutta a serious blow, since up to that time it had held the monopoly of the jute manufacturing industry in British India and the bulk of the raw jute export trade, drawing its raw material mainly from that part of the delta now in East Pakistan. Partition also created human problems for Calcutta, many East Pakistan Hindus seeking refuge there and swelling the flow of workless rural labourers hoping to find work in the conurbation.

The immigration of rural people into cities is a characteristic of India in its present condition: a surplus of people on the land creates pressures which encourage the landless and unemployed to drift to the towns where expanding industry may offer work. As in other Indian cities, and indeed in most great cities receiving migrants, the newcomers tend to congregate in the districts where they have relatives or friends of the same religion, caste, language, or dialect. Half the population of the conurbation has come from outside. The ratio of males: females of 60 : 40 and the predominance in the population of people of working age are clear indications of a population which has yet to achieve demographic normality.

In respect of its demography as in much else, Calcutta has been described as an immature city. People have poured in, but the necessities of urban life have not yet been created to serve them. The city region is cosmopolitan, polygot of Bengali, Hindi, Punjabi, Oriya, Bihari, and English speakers. The over-rapid expansion of Calcutta's population and the failure of urban amenities of even the most rudimentary nature – water-supply, sanitation, shelter – to keep pace are paralleled in other Indian cities, but Calcutta's physiographic site, 'the city in the swamp', aggravates the problems of social hygiene and economics.

Land in a delta is naturally subject to inundation, and although the Hooghly no longer discharges much Ganga floodwater, heavy local rainfall is enough to create serious problems of storm-water and sewage disposal. From the restricted strip of levees close to the Hooghly, the land slopes away into backswamp areas, some of which are perennially water-logged, like the Salt Water Lake four miles from the heart of the city. With proper sanitation available for less than 40 per cent of the people, and rubbish disposal erratic, the effect of storm-water flooding can be imagined. It is little wonder that dysentery is endemic and Calcutta is the main world centre engendering cholera epidemics. Taps supplying safe fresh drinking-water may have to be shared by thirty persons, and it may be easier to use unprocessed water from hydrants intended for sanitary purposes and street cleaning only, or even water from ponds.

A factor in the problem of water-supply is the diminishing flow of the Hooghly, and the resultant increase in the salinity of the river by tidal incursion. The Hooghly is silting up rapidly through the lack of freshets to keep channels clear; over the period

24. *Calcutta:* Garden Reach on the Hooghly where cargo ships load and unload overside into barges.

1955–61 the available draft was reduced by two feet. For India's major port, handling 40 per cent of the exports – tea, jute, and jute products, the main earners of foreign exchange – and 25 per cent of the imports, continued silting would spell strangulation.

It is proposed to rejuvenate the Hooghly as a distributary of Ganga water, by constructing a diversion barrage across the Ganga at Farakkar to increase and control the flow of water into the Hooghly. This it is hoped, will clear silt from the Hooghly, improve the draught for shipping and incidentally help solve the water-supply problem for Calcutta. As in many of the world's great ports, there are problems arising from the increased draft of the largest cargo-carrying vessels, particularly petroleum tankers. To cater for such ships a deep-water outport is being constructed at Haldia, near the entrance to the Hooghly estuary. Haldia will have a petroleum refinery to process imported oil and will handle bulk cargoes of grain, ore, and coal, as well as the 'topping off' of ships sailing out of Calcutta with holds part-empty on account of

shallow drafts. To alleviate the silting problem in Calcutta itself an ingenious scheme is being operated to pump silt from the river-bed to fill in and reclaim for settlement the Salt Water Lake area of backswamp depression (see Fig. 3.4.8).

The urban area of the Hooghlyside conurbation is shown in Fig. 3.4.7. Calcutta and its twin city Howrah, on the opposite bank of the Hooghly, are the largest municipalities and have densities exceeding 50,000 per square mile. The overall density of the Metropolitan district averages 17,000, but quite extensive semi-rural areas are included with densities of 3500–5000. Some of the highest densities are achieved in the slums or 'bustees' where the people are crowded together in crude shacks of matting and tin or sun-dried mud bricks, each individual often having a living space of less than 30 square ft.

The map shows the occupational structure of the labour force in the major towns of the conurbation. Looked at overall, in a work force of 2 million (covered by a recent economic study), 1·27 million were engaged in transport and service (tertiary)

FIG. 3.4.7   India: Calcutta and Hooghlyside: population

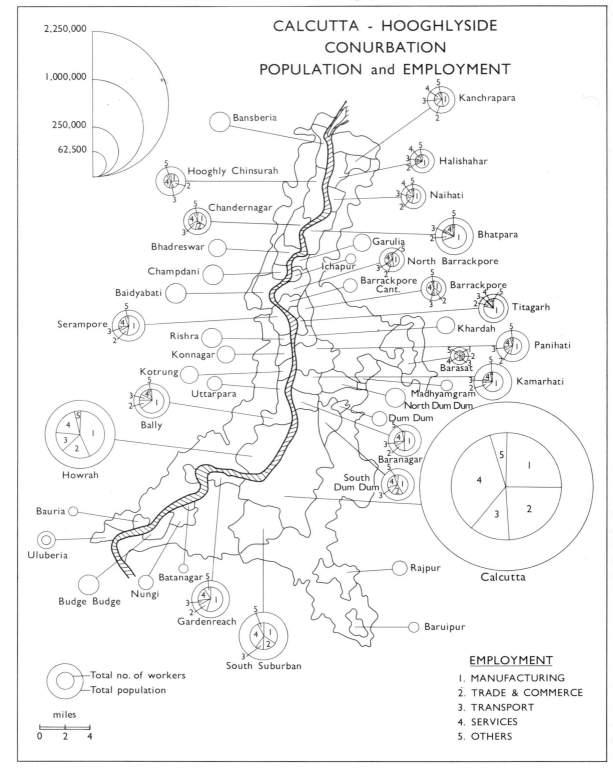

CALCUTTA - HOOGHLYSIDE
CONURBATION
POPULATION and EMPLOYMENT

2,250,000
1,000,000
250,000
62,500

Kanchrapara
Bansberia
Halishahar
Hooghly Chinsurah
Naihati
Chandernagar
Bhatpara
Bhadreswar
Garulia
North Barrackpore
Champdani
Ichapur
Barrackpore Cant.
Barrackpore
Baidyabati
Titagarh
Serampore
Khardah
Rishra
Panihati
Konnagar
Barasat
Kotrung
Kamarhati
Uttarpara
Madhyamgram
North Dum Dum
Bally
Dum Dum
Howrah
Baranagar
South Dum Dum
Bauria
Uluberia
Rajpur
Batanagar
Budge Budge   Nungi
Gardenreach
Baruipur
South Suburban
Calcutta

Total no. of workers
Total population

EMPLOYMENT
1. MANUFACTURING
2. TRADE & COMMERCE
3. TRANSPORT
4. SERVICES
5. OTHERS

miles
0   2   4

industry; 0·24 million in the jute industry; 0·22 million in other types of manufacturing. In terms of value of output, the jute industry is seen more nearly to dominate the economy as the largest single secondary industry (Table 3.4.5).

TABLE 3.4.5

Calcutta–Hooghlyside: Value of Industrial Output*

Jute manufacturing	Rs	1323 m.
Transport and tertiary industry		1327
Manufacturing		950
Chemicals		542
Iron and steel		444
Non-jute textiles		255
Food products		168

There are important differences in occupational structure among the administrative units which constitute the conurbation. For the smaller units no data is available, but for the larger it is convenient to group employment in five categories thus (in order clockwise on the diagram, starting at 12 o'clock): 1. Manufacturing; 2. Trade and commerce 3. Transport; 4. Service industries; 5. Other employment.

In Calcutta the predominance of service industries (employing more than one-third of the labour force) is very marked, as is to be expected in a metropolitan city. Manufacturing employs about a quarter, a smaller percentage than in almost all the other municipalities but in absolute terms nearly four times more than in Howrah the next largest manufacturing centre. Trade and commerce together employ 24 per cent.

The other centres show a proportionately higher importance of manufacturing, five exceeding 60 per cent of their labour force so employed; Bhatpara and Titigarh exceed 70 per cent. Transport nowhere employs more than 15 per cent of the work force, and the largest concentration of labour engaged in this is in Calcutta – Howrah, where docks and railway termini are concentrated.

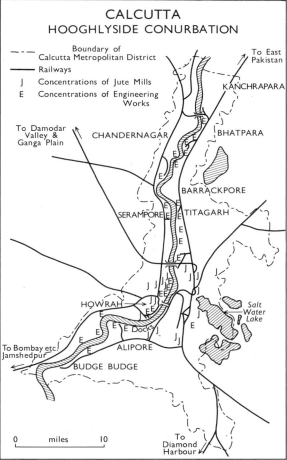

(After Spate and Calcutta Metropolitan Planning Board)

FIG. 3.4.8   India: Calcutta and Hooghlyside

Fig. 3.4.8 shows the railway system of the conurbation, its main dock areas, and the location of jute mills and engineering works. Many vessels anchor in the Hooghly to be loaded and unloaded overside from 'flats' and smaller lighters which collect and distribute cargoes from railway yards, godowns, and mills scattered the length of the conurbation's waterfront.

5. INDIA

POPULATION DENSITY AND CITIES

The overall density of population by districts is shown in Fig. 3.5.1 based upon the census of India

---

* Data from Bose, N. K., 'Calcutta: A Premature Metropolis', *Scientific American*, September 1965.

1961. The average density stood at 370 per square mile for India as a whole, but such a statement has limited meaning. It is more helpful to an understanding of India's geography to recognise the dis-

tribution of density values which seem characteristic
of the main types of man–land relationship.

There is a primary correlation of above-average
densities with mainly alluvial lowland: the Ganga
Plain, Brahmaputra Valley, the deltas and coastal
plains of the Peninsula and their extension inland in
Tamilnadu. The upland areas have few districts of
above-average density and some of these are linked
to important urban centres such as Hyderabad,
Nagpur, Indore, and Bangalore.

A population density map by districts has to
accept the pattern of district boundaries which in
many cases extend across both densely settled alluvium and sparsely peopled hill country. It is danger-
ous, therefore, to generalise too much from Fig.
3.5.1 alone. Rice-growing lowlands have the highest
density – the Ganga Plain in West Bengal, Bihar,
and eastern Uttar Pradesh, and the Kerala coast
have densities of over 750 per square mile, extensively more than 1000. Largely on account of the
way in which district boundaries run, the rice-growing east coast deltas of the Mahanadi, Godavari,
and Krishna do not exceed densities of 500 per
square mile. The west coast in Maharashtra and
Mysore has only moderate densities for the most
part, since the proportion of areas available for rice
cultivation is restricted by the spurs of hilly country
that project to the coast from the Western Ghats.
Almost all these areas where rice cultivation on lowlands is a main support of population, with densities
ranging from average to very high, have a mean
annual rainfall of more than 40 inches. Much of
Tamilnadu is an exception to this general rule;
here tank irrigation is widespread and industrial
urbanisation quite a significant factor.

Up the Ganga Plain in the areas of lower rainfall
westwards from central Uttar Pradesh rice gradually gives way to wheat as the major food crop. A
given area of even the best land under wheat can
support fewer people than the same area under rice.
There is therefore in a general way a progressive
falling off of population density through western
Uttar Pradesh into the Punjab. Urbanisation and
canal irrigation account for the maintenance of
some high density areas. Thus Lakhnau–Kanpur,
Delhi–Meerut, the irrigated Yamuna–Ganga interfluve, and the irrigated areas of the northern Punjab
stand out with densities of over 750. More extensively however, the population density of western

Uttar Pradesh is in the range of 500–750, and that
from Delhi west to the Pakistan border, an area of
still lower rainfall, 350–500.

One further area of above-average density demands attention. North of Bombay, through Surat
and at the head of the Gulf of Cambay around
Baroda and Ahmadabad, despite unreliable rainfall
in the average range 25–40 inches and a general lack
of irrigation facilities, population densities rise to
over 500 per square mile in several districts. Urbanisation, partly as a result of the complex of princely
states in this region in the past, partly in response to
more modern industrial development, provides a
partial explanation. Such political and industrial
urbanisation must also stimulate the economy and
so the population density of surrounding agricultural areas.

Low densities of population in India are associated with arid lowlands beyond the present reach
of irrigation schemes or with mountainous country.
There is a progressive fall in density with reduction
of rainfall towards the Thar Desert where Jaisalmer
District has a density of only 9·5 per square mile.
In Kashmir and the most northerly districts of the
Punjab, the areas beyond the main Himalayan
ranges are extremely remote and for the most part
very dry. Ladakh, on the borders of Tibet, has barely
two persons per square mile. The more humid
areas south of the Great Himalaya in Jammu-
Kashmir, Himachal Pradesh, and Uttar Pradesh
have densities of 25–100 in the more rugged parts,
and upwards of 100 per square mile in the Outer
Himalayan foothills. Higher densities are found
where intermontane basins are extensive enough to
counterbalance the mountain sections in an administrative district. The Vale of Kashmir, the
Kangra Valley, and Dehra Dun stand out with
densities of over 250.

It could be said of these westerly areas that the
harsh physical environment is the strongest factor
accounting for low densities of population. By and
large the cultural level of the people is similar to that
of their rural neighbours in the plains. In the case of
the areas of low density of population in the eastern
half of India, there is a more marked cultural
differentiation from the adjacent lowlands. The
Bastar Plateau on the borders of Orissa and Madhya
Pradesh, and the hill country of Assam are occupied
by peoples who retain a tribal organisation and who

Fig. 3.5.1   India: population distribution

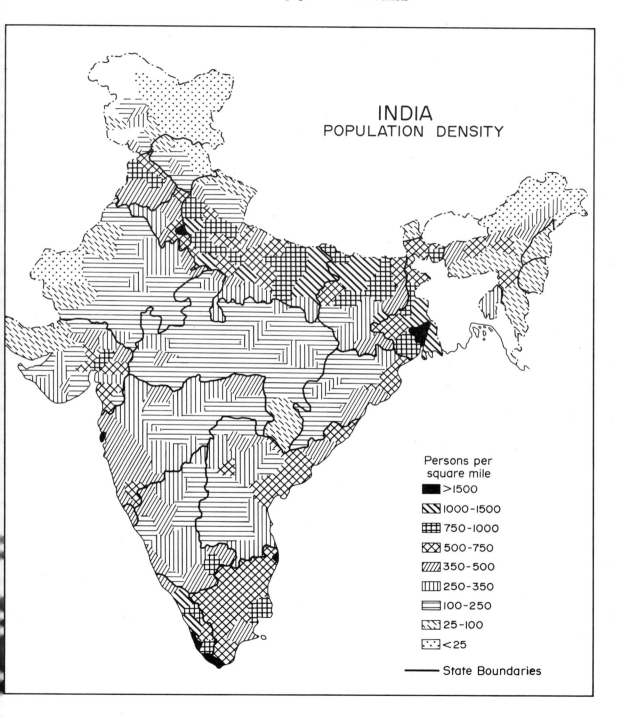

INDIA
POPULATION DENSITY

Persons per
square mile

>1500

1000–1500

750–1000

500–750

350–500

250–350

100–250

25–100

<25

State Boundaries

practise shifting cultivation. Those lower parts of the Assam Hills where extensive tea plantations have been established have above-average densities. The factor of culture, particularly through its different agricultural techniques, must be added to that of a relatively difficult environment in explaining the pattern of population densities in Assam.

The discussion of areas of high and low density of population has left unexamined the larger part of India comprising a wellnigh solid block covering the interior of the Peninsula. Extensively population densities lie between 100–250 per square mile; thus a continuous belt from Rajasthan through Madhya Pradesh into upland Orissa, linking with a belt in central and eastern Maharashtra – northern Andhra Pradesh. Within this mass of fairly low population density the areas able to support higher densities are generally those favoured by better terrain (especially more extensive alluvium) or climate. For example, along the Tapti Valley and east to Nagpur between the Satpura and Ajanta ranges, a line of districts is relatively favoured by terrain and rich lava soils.

Barely separated from the main belt of lower density by the Middle Krishna–Tungabhadra valleys is a block of districts in eastern Mysore – western Andhra Pradesh, a region notorious for its famines, where rainfall averages less than 25 inches.

Cities

Almost 18 per cent of India's population live in towns, defined as places having a municipal administration or at least 5000 inhabitants at a density not less than 1000 per square mile, supporting themselves by mainly non-agricultural activities. Most of the smaller centres are simply rural market towns. The 250 urban centres with over 50,000 population are mapped in Fig. 3.5.2 which shows cities in five size groups.

Among the major factors to be borne in mind in interpreting this map are:

(i) the relationship of urban centres to regional population;

(ii) the importance of the two major ports as foci for the growth of conurbations;

(iii) the political pattern of the past, in particular the urban development associated with the capitals of former princely states.

There is an observable concentration of cities in areas of dense population and conversely a sparsity of cities in areas of below-average population density. The limits of the Ganga Plain can almost be sketched by reference to the map of cities. Delhi dominates with its 2·4 million. Strategically located in relation to movements by invaders from the northwest into the Ganga Plain and the Peninsula, Delhi has long played an important role as capital city of successive ruling powers. From 1773 to 1911 British rule was administered from Calcutta, but the claims of Delhi were reasserted when New Delhi was established as the seat of the Government of India. Thirteen Indian cities have a population of upwards of half a million, and of these six lie in the Ganga Plain (including the delta in West Bengal). Kanpur (971,062), Lakhnau (655,673), and Agra (508,680) all in Uttar Pradesh are among them, and are closely rivalled by Varanasi (489,864), and Allahabad (430,730) in the same state. Patna (364,594) capital of Bihar is a little behind. Outside West Bengal the only other cities of the Ganga Plain to exceed the quarter million mark are Amritsar (398,047) and Jullundur (265,030) in the Punjab, Meerut (283,997), and Bareilly (272,828) in western Uttar Pradesh. The cities of West Bengal are discussed below.

After the Ganga Plain, the most extensive areas of high population density are the lowlands of Kerala, Tamilnadu, and the east coast deltas. With the exception of Madras (discussed separately below) no city exceeds half a million; four cities Madurai (424,810), Cochin (313,030), Trivandrum (302,214), Coimbatore (286,305) exceed a quarter of a million, and three others are very close to this figure: Tiruchirapalli (249,862), Salem (249,145), and Calicut (248,548). All these are towns of some importance industrially and all lie either on the Kerala coast or inland in Tamilnadu. No town in the east coast deltas of Andhra Pradesh or Orissa exceeds a quarter of a million, the largest being Vijayawada (230,397) in the Krishna Delta, a situation that reflects the relative smallness of these deltas as rich agricultural areas, and the lack of industrial development.

It is of interest that seven of the thirteen cities with over half a million inhabitants are 'millionaire' cities. With the exception of Delhi, the largest are ports; Bombay and Calcutta dominate, but it is a matter for debate which may be regarded as the

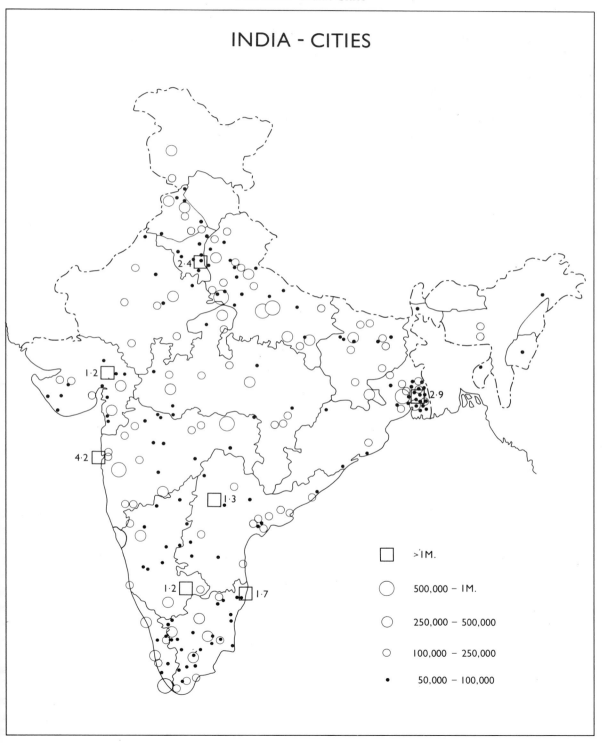

Fig. 3.5.2 India: Cities

25. *Chowpati, Bombay,* probably the most extensive stretch of upper class flats in South Asia. They overlook the muddy shallows of Bombay's Back Bay. Malabar Hill is in the left distance.

larger. Both have become great conurbations, more particularly Calcutta, which with its twin city, Howrah, on the opposite bank of the Hooghly extends for miles along both river-banks (see below). Greater Bombay has an official population of 4·15 million, which might be increased to 4·26 million by the addition of the adjacent town of Thana. Calcutta is officially a city of 2·93 million, but with the adjacent riverside towns could claim at least 5·42 million and more likely 6½ million as urban Hooghlyside dwellers. Both these great industrial cities owe much to the commercial development of India under British rule, for these were the main ports through which India traded with the United Kingdom and other industrial nations. Calcutta was for long the capital of Imperial India and both were capitals of provincial governments before independence, as was Madras (1·73 million) the third 'millionaire' port city.

Ahmadabad (1·2 million) the cotton textile town, now capital of Gujarat, Hyderabad (1·25 million) formerly capital of the Nizam's Dominions, now of Andhra Pradesh, and Bangalore (1·2 million) capital of Mysore State, are the remaining millionaire cities. None is located in particularly rich or populous country; Ahmadabad owes its rise to the cotton industry though as a small city it once had some strategic importance at the head of the Gulf of Cambay. Hyderabad and Bangalore rose to importance as the principal cities of the powerful princely states of Hyderabad and Mysore (despite the location of the Maharaja's court in Mysore City). Bangalore is particularly important as a centre of modern industry.

There remain to mention twelve centres of more than a quarter of a million citizens: half of them were capitals of princely states in pre-independence India, the rest owe their size rather to industrial development and to their importance as regional centres. Poona (737,426) and Sholapur (337,583) are major industrial towns on the Bombay–Madras railway route; Nagpur (690,302) the industrial halfway house on the Bombay–Calcutta line; Jabalpur (367,014) was a centrally located military supply centre on the alternative route from Bombay to Calcutta via Allahabad, and is now the regional centre for the eastern half of Madhya Pradesh. Jamshedpur (328,044) in southern Bihar is India's major steel town, the home of the Tata family's heavy industrial enterprises. These five cities owe much of their importance to modern industrial development resulting partly, in the case of the first four, from their fortunate position on early railway systems. All were in former British India, as was Surat (258,026) the site of the first English 'factory' on a now silted estuary.

The other six cities were capitals of princely states. Jaipur (403,444) has become capital of the new state of Rajasthan which replaced the former Rajputana. Indore (394,941) and Gwalior (300,587) were capitals of princely states now absorbed into Madhya Pradesh. Baroda (298,398), despite loss of capital status on ceasing to be a princely city, seems set on an industrial career, helped by its position on the Bombay–Ahmadabad and Bombay–Delhi railways. Mysore (253,865) no longer capital of the former princely state had even before independence lost the position of leadership to Bangalore. Lastly, Srinagar (295,084) capital of Jammu and Kashmir, retains its status, and may expect to progress as a centre of tourism and fine-craft industries.

In the preceding paragraphs some thirty-eight cities of upwards of a quarter of a million persons have been mentioned. Size is not the only criterion of importance in a city, but the great majority of the cities of present importance in India are among those discussed.

CHAPTER FOUR

PAKISTAN

1. PAKISTAN AS A WHOLE

Pakistan is unique among the countries of the world in having come into being as a national unit composed of two widely separated parts, unified by religion but differing greatly in climate, language, and agriculture. In 1961 Pakistan had a population of almost 94 million, 43 million being in West Pakistan (including the Federal territory of the then capital, Karachi) and 51 million in East Pakistan. West Pakistan is a dry land, very dependent on her rivers for irrigation. With vast areas too arid for settlement, the overall population density in the West wing is 136 per square mile, compared with 932 per square mile in wet deltaic East Pakistan. In effect, Pakistan expresses in her two divisions the extremes of climatic and agricultural conditions and population density to be found in South Asia.

There is little about which one can generalise with reference to the *whole* of Pakistan. None the less the country is a single political unit and the economic fortunes of either part are inevitably tied to those of the other. Separation by 1000 miles of Indian territory overland, or by a week's sea voyage from Karachi to Chittagong, makes for difficult problems of integration of West and East Pakistan. Only a tiny fraction of the population can hope ever to visit the other wing of the country, and the differences in the traditional ways of life in the two wings are such as to pose a considerable problem in creating mutual understanding between their peoples. Even within each wing (the more so in the case of West Pakistan) there is wide regional diversity in living standards and in levels of cultural, economic, and political sophistication.

The unity of Pakistan derives from one positive factor alone – religion. Islam, whose adherents are called Moslems, Muslims, or Mohammedans, was brought to what is now West Pakistan by invading groups who, in the tenth century A.D., attached the Punjab Plains as a province of a principality centred on Ghazni in Afghanistan. From this time on into the seventeenth century, Moslem political power in the Indian subcontinent spread, till Akbar, greatest of the Mogul emperors, ruled over an area stretching from West to East Pakistan and south as far as the latitude of Bombay. Islam was a religion of conversion, and succeeded through the centuries in winning over many of the lower caste Hindus who were attracted from their rigidly stratified society to the Mohammedan creed of equality and brotherhood. It appears that some areas, such as East Bengal (now East Pakistan), were converted *en masse* following their ruler's acceptance of Islam, while in other regions only a minority of the population changed their religion.

Since the time Islam entered the subcontinent, there has existed mutual antagonism between Moslem and Hindu. Their creeds are so different in many respects, that this is only to be expected. Islam is a monotheistic religion demanding strict adherence to the Koran as its holy book. The Moslem, while he will not eat pork, is permitted to kill cattle and other livestock for food. The strictest Moslem insists on the practice of 'purdah' (veiling in public) by his womenfolk. Altogether a Westerner might view Islam as a somewhat uncompromising religion, very traditionalist in outlook. By contrast Hinduism is polytheistic or abstractively agnostic according to approach, deriving ideas from such a variety of sources, some of great antiquity, as to be almost incapable of definition. As a practical way of life it is characterised by its rigid caste system, by which the social system is ordered, and by the sanctity in which the cow is held. While at some levels of its practice, Hinduism contains much that might be styled superstition, the more educationally advanced of its adherents may find it less difficult than do some of their more orthodox Moslem counterparts, to discover a workable religious philosophy for the twentieth century.

It is essential to appreciate the deep-seated nature of the differences between the outlook of Moslem and Hindu in order to understand the political geography of the subcontinent today. During the present century, as the movement for 'self-determination' developed in the undivided British Indian Empire, the problem loomed large of how to devise an independent state in which the rights of the very large Moslem minority would be safeguarded. In due course, the idea of establishing *two* separate nations gained popularity with the Moslems, though it was never favoured by the Hindus or by the more secularly minded Moslems who joined with them in the Congress Party to press for the independence of a united, though possibly federal, India. The outcome of a period of complicated political history was the agreement to the partition of British India by a British arbitrator, Sir Cyril (later Lord) Racliffe. His award set apart the two large areas having clear Moslem majorities, now known as West and East Pakistan. The partition award did not encompass the former Indian 'princely' states, whose rulers were theoretically free to attach their territory to either of the new dominions. Hyderabad in the Deccan, and Junagadh in Kathiawar, both enclaves in the new India, sought unsuccessfully to join Pakistan. The state of Jammu and Kashmir, with a mainly Moslem population under a Hindu ruler, borders on both new states. The ruler chose to join India, and the state has remained a bone of contention ever since. Inconclusive attempts to settle the issue by force leaves India in possession of most of the state, Pakistan administering the western fringe as 'Azad' (Free) Kashmir. At the time of partition, there were about 4 million Hindus in West Pakistan, and 14 million in East Pakistan, while the Moslem population in India totalled about 46 million, distributed unevenly throughout the country. Migration in both directions, particularly across the West Pakistan–India frontier has reduced the proportions of these minority groups, but there still remain some 10 million Hindus in Pakistan, concentrated in East Pakistan where they constitute about one-fifth of the population.

So far we have concentrated on the contrast between Hindu and Moslem ways of life which lay behind the political partition of the subcontinent into Pakistan and India. While it is true to say that there are similarities between West and East Pakistan arising out of their common religious heritage, there are also important differences in the cultural make-up of the peoples of the two wings. The cultural tradition of West Pakistan has for many centuries been predominantly Moslem and looked westwards to Iran for linguistic and literary inspiration. Urdu, written in an Arabic script is the main language. Physically and socially the population owe a heavy debt to invading groups entering over the western and northwestern borders. Whatever cultural traits derive from pre-existing 'Hindu' populations in the area, they are relatively weak. In East Pakistan, however, the case is quite different. Although the mass conversion of its Hindu population to Islam took place in the twelfth century, the new religion was grafted into a society otherwise Hindu in many respects. The number of Moslem migrants from the western nucleus of what became the Mogul Empire was probably quite small. The people preserved their Bengali language and its script, adopting the Arabic script (through the Koran) for religious purposes, and to a small extent Urdu, as the language of the Mogul administration. Even today, in literary matters the East Pakistani is first a Bengali. Thus the new state of Pakistan recognises Urdu and Bengali as official languages in the West and East wings respectively, but uses English as the official state language and as one of the media of instruction in universities. Many townspeople but few country people in East Pakistan can speak and understand Urdu. In West Pakistan the few Bengali speakers, migrants from the East wing, are in the cities, and the language is completely foreign to the vast majority.

The larger and culturally the more advanced part of the population in both wings occupies the lowland plains. There are relatively small populations in the hills and mountains that flank the plains, to the north and west in West Pakistan, and to the east in East Pakistan, and in both cases they may be described as culturally less sophisticated than the lowland peoples adjacent to them. The contrast between hill people and plainsmen is less marked in the West wing, where they share a common cultural heritage in large measure, the inhabitants of the, till recently, semi-feudal states of Swat, Dir, and Chitral, for example, being merely the social and economic victims of long isolation and a harsher environment, rather than representing an alien culture. In East Pakistan the contrast is more fundamental. Here one meets in the Chittagong Hill Tracts the fringe of a culture realm that extends throughout Southeast Asia and even into the Pacific. There are a number of semi-tribal groups of religious affinities ranging through Buddhism and Hinduism to animism, linked physically and culturally with the peoples of Burma rather than with the plains Bengali, and practising shifting cultivation of hill-slopes. Their inclusion within Pakistan was due to the fact that the region could only be administered effectively by whichever of the new nations was to hold Chittagong, the port controlling the entry to the Hill Tracts along the Karnaphuli River. The more backward state of the peoples of the Chittagong Hill Tracts (and of certain hill areas of West Pakistan also) is recognised in the retention by the Central Government of close control of their administration.

Despite all these evidences of human diversity in Pakistan, there is no doubting the unity of the nation as a whole, granted strong leadership. National pride is a strong antidote to fissiparous tendencies, though the marked differences in political attitudes between West and East wings calls for astute handling by the Central Government. In West Pakistan, a more feudal pattern of society, the long tradition of military service, and a lower level of literacy militate perhaps against the growth of democratic institutions as we know them in the Western world. East Pakistan on the other hand had a tradition of vigorous local and regional politics, intellectual pursuits, and a less inegalitarian social structure. The present somewhat authoritarian pattern of government in the country, is trying to introduce afresh, a form of democratic rule while maintaining political stability as an essential prerequisite to economic development. It is upon the latter that all progress must be founded, but here too there are problems resulting from the separation of the two wings.

In the case of areally unified states, investment for development in one particular area is likely sooner or later to benefit all parts of the state to some degree, through the arteries of economic life. The scale of geographical separation of West from East Pakistan makes difficult a really satisfactory level of economic integration. With two such widely separated market areas the full benefits of 'economies to scale' that would benefit entrepreneurs supplying the Pakistan population cannot be reaped. In many respects the economies of the two wings operate independently. Their basic agricultural economies, to a great extent still at the level of local self-sufficiency, have little to exchange, while in those parts of the economy where a measure of interdependence is possible, the high costs of inter-wing transfer may render the exchange of goods uneconomic unless heavily protected from external competition. Thus it has sometimes been more economical to import Japanese cement directly into East Pakistan even though there has been at the same time a surplus of locally produced cement up-country in West Pakistan.

The question of distributing development capital derived mainly from foreign exchange earnings from jute grown in East Pakistan has been the cause of internal political friction. With the finances controlled from the West wing, politicians in the East felt that their wing obtained less than its proportional share of the capital available. In recent years the Government has been careful to distribute development schemes more equitably, in proportion to population. Problems of this kind are common enough in states of a federal type, but in Pakistan the situation is aggravated by physical separation and the cultural differences between the wings.

2. WEST PAKISTAN:
WATER THE KEY TO SUBSISTENCE

Rainfall and Irrigation

To a very large extent the human geography of West Pakistan is an expression of man's ingenuity in harnessing exotic rivers and in learning to survive in an arid region. The rainfall map (Fig. 2.2.9) and dispersion diagrams (Fig. 2.2.7) suggest how precarious agriculture must be where the sole source of moisture is the rain falling on the fields. The only

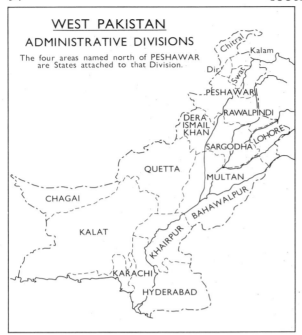

FIG. 4.2.1   West Pakistan: administrative divisions

area of alluvial plain receiving more than 25 inches of rainfall on average is a strip barely 25 miles wide lying parallel to the Siwalik foothills in the north-eastern corner round Sialkot. Parts of the small area of mountain country bordering on Kashmir have over 35 inches though even here the total falls off westwards and as at Chitral (13 inches) is lowest in the sheltered valleys. For the rest of West Pakistan, however, there is no escaping the fact that it is at best a semi-arid region, with a rainfall so low and so unreliable that it may best be looked upon as a gratuitous accident of nature reviving native forage plants and supplementing whatever supplies have been engineered by irrigators. From Dera Ismail Khan on the Indus or Montgomery in the Bari Doab, through both of which passes the 10-inch isohyet, it is a full 500 miles to beyond Hyderabad before that isohyet is crossed again and for half this distance the rainfall fails to average even 5 inches.

Northwards from the 10-inch isohyet in the Punjab Plains, an increasingly large proportion of the rainfall comes in the cool season (see Fig. 2.2.8, dispersion diagrams for Lahore and Peshawar) and is consequently of much greater benefit to agriculture than the same amount received in summer. The importance of the winter rains, whether as the sole or as a supplementary supply of moisture for agriculture is seen in the ratio of rabi (cool season) to kharif (summer) crops. West of the Indus, in the districts running north from Dera Ismail Khan, the ratio of the rabi area to kharif is roughly 2 : 1; in the Punjab Plains 3 : 2; in Khairpur and Hyderabad 3 : 4. Direct rainfall is, however, a secondary and supplementary factor, since about 75 per cent of the total area sown with crops is irrigated. (Administrative divisions may be located on Fig. 4.2.1.)

The main source of irrigation water is the great rivers issuing from the Himalaya, the Jhelum and Chenab principally, but with the Indus playing an increasing part. The political problems of apportioning water resources between Pakistan and India are discussed further below; in brief, it has been agreed by Pakistan and India that although the courses of the Ravi and Sutlej pass through the plains of West Pakistan, their waters are progressively to be diverted to Indian use. All these rivers rise deep in the Himalaya, where the summer melting of snows combined with summer monsoon rains causes their discharge between April and September to be on average five or more times larger than that of winter. The engineering works are designed primarily to divert water into distribution systems commanding the interfluve areas downstream, though the height of barrages may be determined by the need to raise the level of water at that point so it can be channelled at the highest possible level on the interfluve, thus maximising the efficiency of the system. Midsummer, when the rivers are in full spate and the highest channels can be filled, is the main season for irrigation. In winter it may be difficult to maintain the flow of even the lowest channels. Modern engineering techniques offer the possibility of building storage dams on the rivers before they enter the plains (e.g. Mangla Dam). Such dams should permit more reliable irrigation in winter and also, if storage is adequate, protect the farmer against a dry year when the river flow is reduced below its normal high level.

Diversionary barrage systems are not the only source of irrigation water. In a belt close to the major rivers, and along the Punjab submontane belt (where they supplement the moderately good rainfall of 25 inches) wells are commonly sunk to the water-table, here reasonably close to the surface. The water is raised still by traditional methods, the most common being the Persian wheel driven by bullocks or other farm animals. Water from wells costs the farmer more in personal initiative, capital investment, and labour than does canal water, and for this reason it tends to be more carefully used. The few acres which it is economical to water from a well are usually intensively farmed, the fields nearest the well often having the aspect of a well-tended garden. Where the water-table is beyond the reach of hand-excavated wells (or where adequate capital is available) mechanically drilled, metal-lined tube wells are sometimes sunk. Driven by diesel engines or electric motors, tube wells can command a larger irrigated area. Another more general use of tube wells is to drain areas which have become water-logged through years of canal irrigation.

There are other methods of bringing water to cultivated lands, though none is responsible for any appreciable proportion of West Pakistan's sown area. In the Himalayan valleys, streams and small rivers are diverted to water terraced slopes or the valley-floor alluvium. The broad active floodplains of the Indus and the Punjab rivers are similarly watered to some extent by diversion of braided channels. Along the Piedmont Plain that skirts the Sulaiman and Kirthar ranges an unreliable and variable proportion of the infrequent but normally violent discharge of hill-fed torrents is held up behind crude barrages in the steep-sided river-beds and is led to bunded fields to soak into the soil so that a crop can be taken. Lastly, the *karez* system of Baluchistan epitomises the basic problem of agriculture in an arid region, that of concentrating upon a restricted but cultivable patch of land the sparse precipitation that occurs over a wider area. In essence a karez system consists of a near horizontal tunnel driven from the level of the cultivable land near the centre of an intermontane basin to intersect the water-table in the gravelly detritus which constitutes the fans along the mountain foot where intermittent streams from high catchments soak away into the coarse material. At the lower end of the tunnel emerges a small stream of water which is led to the fields. An important advantage of the karez is that the water travels most of its way underground, and so with the minimum risk of loss by evaporation.

Altogether these minor irrigation methods supply perhaps a sixth of the total area irrigated.

Regional Pattern of Land Use

Water availability, rainfall, and landform are the principal variables to be taken into account in explaining the agricultural patterns of West Pakistan. The crops concerned are grouped as in India as *rabi* (winter) and *kharif* (summer) crops. Table 4.2.1 below shows the areas and percentages of the total made up by each of the main crops in the major administrative divisions of the Indus Plains as estimated by a Colombo Plan survey. These figures exclude the highlands of Baluchistan and the northwestern hill country.

Of the **rabi crops** the cereals, **wheat** and to a lesser degree **barley,** are most important. **Gram** and other pulses provide a significant proportion of the protein in the Pakistani diet, in which meat plays a smaller part than in the Western diet. Vegetable oils are supplied by **rape-seed, colza,** and **rocket,** crops which are sometimes useful also as green fodder. **Clover** is the main rabi fodder crop. In some areas, notably the Peshawar Vale, **tobacco** is cultivated as a cash crop for the Pakistani market.

The **kharif crops** are rather more varied. Food grains are represented by millets, rice, and maize. **Millets,** particularly **bajra,** are drought resistant and are therefore widely grown on lands where irrigation water is absent or unreliable. Bajra and the Great Millet, **jowar,** are however more extensively cultivated as irrigated crops. Their stalks are important as cattle feed and much jowar is grown specifically as fodder, often being intersown with vetch. **Rice** the principal food grain of Hyderabad Division tends to be concentrated on the most suitable areas of fine textured soils and reliable irrigation. A valuable characteristic of rice for West Pakistan is its tolerance of saline and water-logged conditions in which most other crops would fail. If rice is the kharif crop *par excellence* of the south, **maize** is the northern crop, used both as food and fodder. In the Peshawar and Bannu vales it is irrigated, while in the Himalayan valleys it is grown on terraced fields dependent mainly on summer rainfall. Dominant as the province's cash crop is **cotton,** now mostly of the American long-stapled variety. Cotton is generally an irrigated crop. Its value is not limited to the fibre which is a valuable export and the basis of a developing textile industry, but extends to the seed which is a useful fodder and ferti-

TABLE 4.2.1

Percentage of seasonally cropped area under main crops. Note the relative importance of rabi and kharif cropping in each region as indicated by the total area of crops at each season.

(Source: Colombo Plan data)

Divisions	Rabi Crops									Kharif Crops										
	Cereals	Pulses	Cereals–pulses mixed	Oil-seeds	Tobacco	Vegetables	Fruits	Fodder	Area (million acres)	Rice	Millets	Maize	Pulses	Oil-seeds	Cotton	Sugar-cane	Vegetables	Fruits	Fodder	Area (million acres)
Peshawar, Dera Ismail Khan	67	16	—	4·5	1·5	2	0·5	7·5	1·2	2	19·5	44·5	2·5	0·5	2	23·5	1·5	1	3	0·5
Rawalpindi, Lahore, Sargodha, Multan	61	15·5	3	4	0·5	1·5	0·5	13·5	11·19	12·5	26·5	6·5	5·0	0·5	22	7	2	0·5	15·5	7·25
Bahawalpur	55	19·5	6	9	—	2·5	—	7	1·32	5	31·5	2·5	14·5	6	20·5	7	1	0·5	10	1·17
Khairpur (1)	54·5	10	—	31	—	0·5	—	—	0·24	10	32·5	—	1	—	30	4·5	0·5	4·5	17	0·18
Sind (2)	50	32·5	—	12	—	—	1·0	3·5	2·46	45·5	24·5	—	0·5	0·5	23	0·5	0·5	1	2	3·25
Baluchistan (3)	57	12·5	—	28	—	—	—	—	0·15	41·5	50·5	—	—	—	—	0·5	—	8	—	0·17
Indus Plains	60	19	2·5	6·5	0·5	1	0·5	10·5	16·56 (100 per cent)	20	27	6	4·5	1	21	6	1·5	0·5	11	12·55 (100 per cent)

Notes: (1) The former Punjab state of Khairpur now incorporated in a larger division of the same name.
(2) Comprising Hyderabad Division and Sukkur District, the latter now part of Khairpur Division.
(3) Only a part of the lowland area round Sibi is accounted for here.

FIG. 4.2.2   West Pakistan: agricultural regions

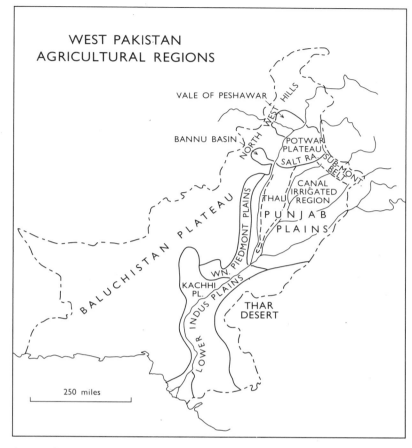

WEST PAKISTAN
AGRICULTURAL REGIONS

250 miles

liser. Another cash crop, for the internal market only, is **sugar-cane**, heavily irrigated in the Vale of Peshawar and areas commanded by wells in the submontane belt in Gujrat and Sialkot districts. Although normally regarded as a kharif crop, sugar-cane requires a long growing season which may extend into the rabi season.

Broad regions of agricultural differentiation in West Pakistan are shown in Fig. 4.2.2 and, for the Indus Plains only, the significant elements of land-form and irrigated land use are shown in Figs. 4.2.3 and 4.2.4. respectively.*

The economically less important regions of the uplands to the west and north of the Indus Plains

comprise areas with a wide range of conditions as far as agriculture is concerned. The **Baluchistan Plateau** with less than 10 inches of rainfall on aver-age except in the higher mountain areas around Quetta, is essentially semi-arid. Throughout, agri-culture depends on water derived from the moun-tains used either haphazardly as in the case of torrent-irrigation, or in a more reliable fashion by use of karez. Rabi crops of wheat and barley are raised; millets as the kharif crop. Karez-irrigated orchards of apricots, peaches, apples, and grapes are generally situated within a few miles of the rail-way by which both fresh and sun-dried fruit is dis-patched to the cities in the plains. Such relatively intensive farming occupies only a fraction of the generally rocky and treeless countryside, concen-trating oasis-like in the more accessible basins. Elsewhere semi-nomadic pastoralism of goats and sheep provides a meagre livelihood. On the Makran coast, dates are grown for consumption

---

* Fig. 4.2.3 'Landforms' and Fig. 4.2.4 'Types of Irrigation in the Indus Plains' are based on maps in Ahmad, Kazi, S., *A Geography of Pakistan*, and Whittington, G., 'The Irrigated Lands on the Indus Plains in West Pakistan', *Tijdschrift Voor Econ. en Soc. Geografie*, 55 (1964), pp. 13–18, by kind per-mission of the authors.

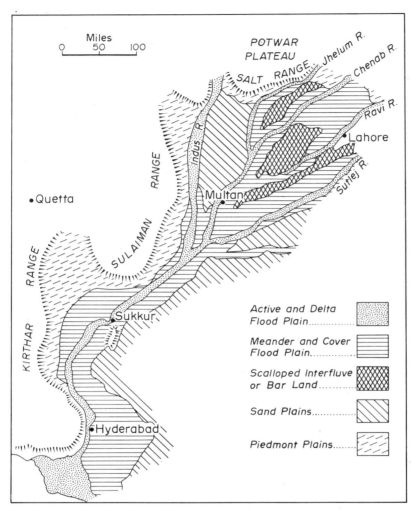

FIG. 4.2.3 West Pakistan: land-forms of Indus Plains

locally and for the Karachi market.

Northwards from Quetta the **Northwestern Hills and Himalaya** enjoy a better rainfall. In the western part although the total rainfall is only 15 to 20 inches its incidence is mainly in winter, and rabi crops of wheat and barley can be grown without irrigation. Maize is the summer crop where moisture is sufficient. In the Himalayan valleys rainfall increases to about 40 inches, and is reasonably well distributed. The steep valley sides are terraced as much as 3000 ft. above the river, and support rabi wheat and oil-seeds, and kharif maize. In spring the valleys present a colourful spectacle, with splashes of brilliant yellow of mustard amid the fresh green of young wheat with the late snows throwing into relief the pine forests on the hill-tops. In some sheltered areas small-scale diversion channels in the valley-floor alluvium irrigate rice fields, e.g. in Swat and Hazara. Small livestock are of some minor importance, sheep's wool being used locally to weave clothing and blankets.

Held within spurs of the Northwestern Hills, the **Basins of Peshawar and Bannu** are areas of intensive cultivation supported by perennial irrigation, and are in effect extensions of the Indus Plains. Rabi wheat and kharif maize are the principal food grains everywhere; sugar-cane and tobacco are important cash crops, supporting industry, particularly in the Vale of Peshawar. Both basins are fringed with a zone of dry cropping in which dry farming techniques are practised, such as repeated ploughing of the soil, bunding to hold rainfall on the land, and

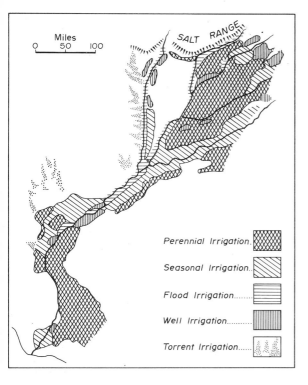

FIG. 4.2.4 West Pakistan: types of irrigation

Perennial Irrigation.

Seasonal Irrigation.

Flood Irrigation.......

Well Irrigation..........

Torrent Irrigation......

sion by contouring the fields and by damming the gullies, but the social problems involved in reallocating land in a land-hungry district so that contour bunds can be constructed, are formidable. An expensive experiment to reclaim the land for cultivation after gullying has carved it into a 'badland' is being carried out by dynamiting upstanding knolls of loess and bulldozing the material into the gullies.

In an area with such an uneven surface, irrigation is only practicable in the narrow valley bottoms. Dry cropping is the rule, and the moderately reliable rainfall of from 15 to 25 inches some of it in winter, supports the usual rabi crops of wheat, barley, oil-seeds and pulses, and kharif millets and maize. The kharif crops become more important towards the east as the proportion of summer rainfall increases.

The Indus Plains. About a quarter of the area of the Indus Plains is commanded by *perennial irrigation* systems. The largest block of such irrigated land lies in the Punjab between the Jhelum and Sutlej rivers, where it occupies for the most part the highest physiographic element, the *scalloped interfluves*, and to a lesser extent the next lower features, the meander and cover plains. Another extensive block

channelling to allow rainfall on several fields to be concentrated on one.

Similarly, dry farming is widespread in the **Western Piedmont Plains.** Here, and along the foot of the Salt Range scarp there is a good deal of torrent-irrigation, but understandably the supply of water is most unreliable and there is a fair chance that a sudden flood will carry away the crude barrage erected to divert it. In the north of the Piedmont Plains, winter rains give some measure of security to the farmer, and rabi cropping of wheat, barley, gram, and oil-seeds predominates. Southwards, the cultivation of kharif millets and some cotton depends on the chance of summer storms.

The **Salt Range** between the Indus and the Jhelum marks the southern edge to the **Potwar Plateau** which extends to the Himalayan foothills. The surface of the plateau is uneven and often rocky, but there are agriculturally valuable areas where loess masks the bedrock. Between Rawalpindi and the Jhelum in particular, however, the loess has been deeply gullied as a result of accelerated erosion brought about by over-grazing and careless cultivation. Efforts are being made to control this soil ero-

26. *Ploughing* with a pair of bullocks drawing a light wooden plough. Kagan Valley (in the same area as Plate 1). The steep slopes are laboriously terraced into narrow fields supported by retaining walls. The unterraced slopes are used for grazing sheep.

27. *Potwar Plateau:* Gullied loess with small wheat fields near Rawalpindi. This type of accelerated erosion has resulted from the destruction of the natural grass and scrub vegetation through over-grazing by sheep and goats.

occupies similar floodplain land in Hyderabad mainly on the left bank below the Sukkur Barrage. Smaller blocks of perennially irrigated land are located in the vales of Peshawar and Bannu (above), in the Thal region in a strip parallel to the Salt Range and in patches along the Indus bank. Rabi crops predominate on lands watered from perennial systems. Since the objective of the engineers of such systems is to guarantee a perennial supply, the canals are designed to carry the guaranteed *minimum* supply, which is determined by the low winter flow. Rabi season water, volume for volume, is twice as effective as that supplied in summer, since in the hot season so much more is lost through evaporation and transpiration.

The 'designed' cropping intensities under perennial irrigation in the Punjab range between 66 and 75 per cent; Hyderabad 81 per cent. Cropping intensity is calculated here in relation to the two crop groups, rabi and kharif. If all fields carried both rabi and kharif crops, the intensity would be 200 per cent. While the designed intensities appear rather low, there is no prohibition of farmers cultivating more land – using, presumably, less water per unit area – and actual cropping intensities in the Punjab are frequently greater than these figures, rising often to over 100 per cent. Intensities of up to 150 per cent are found in Peshawar Vale.

The rabi crops characteristic of most perennially irrigated land are wheat, gram, and fodder. Kharif crops show more areal differentiation; cotton, for example, is not important in Peshawar Division and here millets tend to be replaced by maize.

Where irrigation is strictly *seasonal* the canals deriving from barrages or head-regulators in riverbanks are more generously designed than perennial canals, and farmers can give more water to their fields even though the supply may be less secure. In good years there is water to spare for advance soaking of rabi fields as well as the current irrigation of kharif crops. It is mainly the *cover* and *meander floodplains* that are seasonally irrigated. (Compare Figs. 4.2.3 and 4.2.4.)

Well irrigation for rabi crops often supplements the moisture left after seasonal irrigation. With or without well irrigation, the area commanded by seasonal irrigation works is a little over half that under perennial schemes. Without wells, cropping intensities, though high for kharif alone, are lower for the full year than under perennial irrigation. Wells compensate for the seasonality of irrigation, however, and allow cropping intensities comparable to those supported by perennial canals.

The main kharif crops under seasonal irrigation are millets, cotton, and rice, followed by rabi wheat with fodder crops (where well-water is available) or oil-seeds and pulses (where reliance must be placed on advance watering of fields and on winter rainfall).

The lowest element in the sequence of landforms in the Indus Plains is the *active floodplain*. During the winter and early summer large expanses of floodplain are exposed which during the summer rains are submerged by often swift-flowing floodwaters. Although the risks of losing late spring crops is high, the floodplains are extensively farmed. These lands are shown on Fig. 4.2.4 as areas of flood irrigation. The lowest parts of such lands carry only rabi crops, since summer floods would destroy the plants. At higher levels where the floods if any would be shallow, it may be worth risking a kharif crop as well. Wheat is the rabi crop in the Jhelum, Chenab, and Ravi riverbeds; wheat and pulses are grown beside the Sutlej and Indus. Kharif cropping of millets, pulses, and oilseeds is less widespread. Fig. 4.2.5 is a transect diagram illustrating the relationship of landform and land use in a section of the Jhelum–Chenab interfluve (the Chaj Doab).

The *irrigation schemes* of the **Punjab Plains** are undergoing considerable modification as a consequence of the redistribution of waters under the Indus Waters Agreement. The political partition of the former province of the Punjab between India and Pakistan in 1947 cut right across the irrigation schemes established under British rule. Some canals in Pakistan were separated from their barrage headworks in India. Even before independence, the irrigated areas in the interfluve between the Ravi and Beas–Sutlej (the Bari Doab) had to rely in part on waters brought from further west. The 'triple project' carried Chenab water across the Ravi into the Bari Doab. The problems posed by partition are being tackled along similar lines. Under the Indus Waters Treaty of 1960, India was given control of the waters of the Ravi, Beas, and Sutlej, Pakistan obtaining those of the Indus, Jhelum, and Chenab, together with some financial compensation for the loss of the eastern rivers. The areas in Pakistan formerly irrigated from the Ravi, Beas, and Sutlej will be brought under the command of canal schemes deriving from the rivers further west. The necessary works are being financed with the help of the World Bank and are planned over a ten-year period. They include the following major works (see Figs. 4.2.6 and 4.2.7):

(i) Tarbela Dam on the Indus north of Rawalpindi, to regulate flow by storing about 5 million acre–feet of water.

(ii) Two link canals to carry water from the Indus to the Jhelum from a new Chasma Barrage downstream from Kalabagh and to the Lower Chenab (from the Taunsa Barrage) to maintain irrigation formerly dependent on the Jhelum particularly.

(iii) A new Mangla Dam on the Jhelum upstream of the old Mangla regulator, to hold 5 million acre–feet and feed a hydroelectric power-station.

(iv) A link canal, the Rasul–Qadirabad link, from the Rasul Barrage on the Jhelum across the Chenab where it adds Chenab waters to its load in the Qadirabad–Balloki link. At the latter place the link is to be carried across the Ravi to parallel an existing link across the Bari Doab to Suleimanke on the Sutlej.

28. *A canal distributary* reaches the farmer's fields. Water is led to each field through the side of the channel which is afterwards replugged with earth (left foreground). The nearer fields are under the pulse gram, a bunch of which the man is holding. Beyond is a crop of wheat. View in Jhelum district, West Pakistan, taken at the end of the cool season.

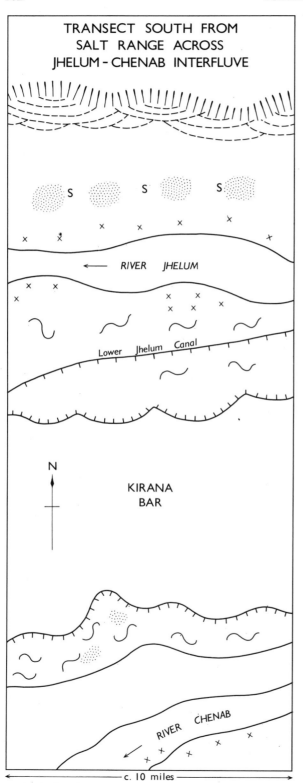

TRANSECT SOUTH FROM
SALT RANGE ACROSS
JHELUM - CHENAB INTERFLUVE

RIVER JHELUM

Lower Jhelum Canal

N

KIRANA
BAR

RIVER CHENAB

c. 10 miles

Fig. 4.2.5   West Pakistan: transect Chaj Doab

Scarp Face of Salt Range. Rugged, steep, and rocky. At best some poor scrub grazing for sheep and goats.

Alluvial Fans coalesce at scarp foot. Intermittent streams sink into the coarse gravels which are too gullied for cultivation.

Piedmont Plain slopes gently towards River Jhelum. Where ground-water seeps to the surface patches of saline soils (s) occur. Dry cropping of winter wheat and some summer millets is practised except near the Jhelum where wells (x) reach fresh ground-water to support intensive cultivation of wheat millets, tobacco, vegetables, sugar-cane, cotton.

Active Floodplain of River Jhelum. Deep flooded in summer, some winter cropping of wheat on channel bed islands.

Meander Floodplain. Immediately south of Jhelum well irrigation supports winter wheat and fodder. (Well irrigation is of little importance in summer due to high evaporation rate reducing its efficiency.) In old meander depressions (~) rice can tolerate the water-logged soils. A little inundation canal irrigation is practised in summer. Some old levee lands are dry cropped in winter only for wheat and gram. South of the Lower Jhelum Canal perennial irrigation allows winter cropping of wheat, gram, oil-seeds, fodder, and summer millets, and cotton.

Scalloped Interfluve. Kirana Bar, formerly a barren waste is now intensively cultivated using water from the Upper Jhelum Canal system which commands this high interfluve area. Rather more than half the fields carry winter wheat, gram, fodder, or oil-seeds. About half grow summer crops of millets and cotton, with maize and sugar-cane of less importance. Orange groves produce a minor cash crop.

Channel Remnant. Below the scalloped edge of the interfluve lies a belt of abandoned channels of the Chenab. Much of this belt is water-logged and there are saline patches. Cultivation is restricted to the higher belts of old levees, where winter crops of wheat and gram are grown without irrigation.

The Meander Floodplain either side of the Chenab's active floodplain has a variety of land uses. Levee remnants above the reach of canal irrigation carry dry winter crops of wheat and gram, or are used for rough grazing. Land commanded by canals grows summer millets, cotton, and rice (the latter on the lowest ground). Well irrigation is used for winter wheat and gram. Salinity and water-logging are locally serious.

Active Floodplain of River Chenab carries much waste grass and scrub on sandy islands. River inundated croplands grow wheat and pulses in low-water winter season. There is a little hazardous well irrigation but the risk of damaging summer floods is a deterrent.
(Based on data in a Colombo Plan project.)

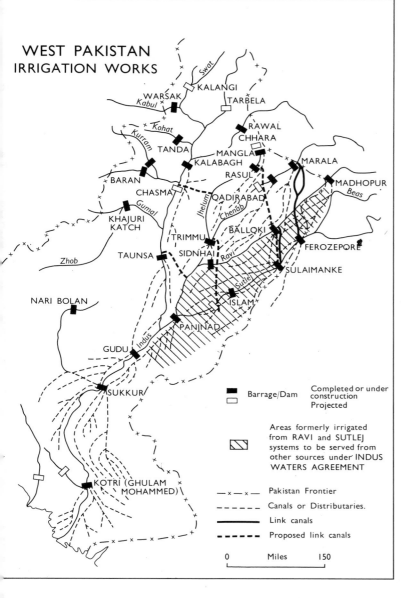

WEST PAKISTAN
IRRIGATION WORKS

■	Barrage/Dam
□	Completed or under construction Projected

Areas formerly irrigated from RAVI and SUTLEJ systems to be served from other sources under INDUS WATERS AGREEMENT

— x — x — Pakistan Frontier

- - - - - Canals or Distributaries.

———— Link canals

▪▪▪▪▪ Proposed link canals

0   Miles   150

FIG. 4.2.6 West Pakistan: irrigation schemes

v) From the existing barrage at Trimmu below the confluence of the Jhelum and Chenab a link canal will carry water across the Ravi at Sidhnai to join the Sutlej at Mailsi.

The **Thal** region forming the Indus–Jhelum interfluve or Sind Sagar Doab is the last extensive area of plain in West Pakistan where irrigation may be able to convert the semi-desert into farmland as was done in the remainder of the Punjab Plain over the past seventy years. It is planned to bring a million

acres under irrigation, but progress cannot be as rapid as was usual in the earlier canal colonisation further east. The Thal contains large areas of hummocky dune country which has to be levelled before farming can begin, and some of which is too sandy for cultivation. A start has been made in the north where Indus water from the Jinnah Barrage at Kalabagh is led eastwards almost to the Jhelum at Khushab. Parts of the western Thal are irrigated as far as 150 miles from the same barrage. These areas

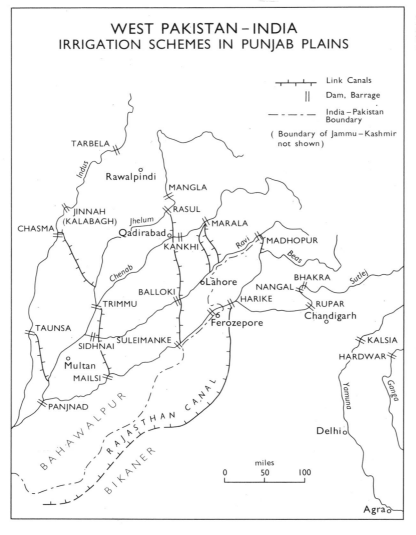

FIG. 4.2.7　West Pakistan–India: irrigation schemes in Punjab Plains

are perennially irrigated but south from Leiah, on the Indus, to the Panjnad confluence there is well and seasonal irrigation in a narrow strip. For the most part however the Thal remains a forbidding region, semi-desert scrub providing poor pasture for sheep and goats, but much of it empty. There is some *barani* or dry cropping of gram, wheat, and oilseeds in the winter and a lesser crop of millets in the summer.

Bahawalpur lying southeast of the Sutlej and Indus, and the adjacent narrow neck of alluvial land in the Indus 'corridor' as far as Sukkur have much in common with Thal. A strip of seasonal irrigation close to the Indus is backed by a zone of perennial irrigation at a higher level, beyond which is the **Thar Desert**, a region of dunes, fixed by sparse scrub which provides forage for camels, sheep, and goats.

The Sukkur (formerly called the Lloyd) Barrage is probably still the largest irrigation scheme in South Asia. With the new Kotri Barrage near Hyderabad, it has brought great areas of the **Lower Indus Plains** in Khairpur and Hyderabad divisions under the command of perennial irrigation. The northern part of the Lower Indus Plain merges, on the right bank, with the **Kachhi Plain** in the Piedmont zone, a rough, often saline area, seasonally irrigated from diversion channels above Sukkur, and by the Sukkur scheme. This is the principal area for rice culti-

29. *Taunsa Barrage*, diverting the waters of the Indus into a link canal transferring water into the lower Chenab system. By raising or lowering the many gates in the barrage the flow of water can be controlled. A barrage of this kind has, however, a very limited capacity to store water.

vation in West Pakistan. In winter pulses and wheat are grown on residual moisture from summer irrigation or by rabi irrigation. The agriculture of the central section of the plains is the chief gift of the Sukkur Barrage. The level terrain facilitates irrigation which is mainly perennial, supporting rabi wheat and kharif cotton and millets. Further south, the plains were formerly inefficiently irrigated from inundation canals but are now largely under the much improved command of the Kotri Barrage. The proportion under perennial irrigation has risen. The cropping pattern is one of kharif rice, millets and cotton, followed by rabi wheat and oil-seeds.

Water-logging and Salinity

The completion of the works proposed under the Indus Waters Treaty will not remove from West Pakistan every problem connected with irrigation.

The design of early irrigation schemes did not usually provide for the long-term changes in hydrology that massive irrigation produces. Water-logging and the increase in salinity of the soil, the consequences of inadequate drainage, are resulting in many acres of once productive land being lost to cultivation. It is estimated that 100,000 acres are going out of production each year quite apart from areas which are becoming less productive through progressive salinification and water-logging.

The basic factor in the problem is the rise of saline ground-water to within reach of plant roots, and its cause is the application, over time, of river-water to plants at the surface. What water sinks into the ground after evaporation and transpiration by plants have taken their share in the form of pure-water vapour, is more saline than the irrigation water that was applied to the land in the first place.

The problem is best illustrated by reference to the experience of an actual irrigation area, but it is a widespread phenomenon in the Indus Plains.

The Khairpur District, close to Sukkur, has been the subject of recent investigations into the problem of water-logging and salinity, undertaken with a view to finding *economic* solutions. From the Sukkur Barrage the large Rohri Canal passes through Khairpur on its way south. No feeder-canals branch from it, but it has some slight effect on the hydrology of the district through the seepage of water from the unlined channel. Smaller canals bring irrigation water to Khairpur's fields.

It was realised from the start of perennial irrigation, in 1933, that a close watch would have to be kept on ground-water movements so that steps could be taken in adequate time to prevent the level of saline ground-water invading the soil and rendering it toxic to plants. The 'water balance sheet' drawn up for the Khairpur area by Hunting Technical Services illustrates the process of water-logging and salinification.

Income of water into the Khairpur Command (the area supplied by the two Khairpur canal feeders) is made up of:

```
2,000,000  acre-feet from the canal feeders;
  310,000  acre-feet from rainfall;
   90,000  acre-feet by seepage from the Rohri
           Canal;
 _____
2,400,000  acre-feet.
```

The *debit* side of the account is less certainly known but is estimated thus:

```
1,000,000  acre-feet transpired by 520,000 acres
           of crops and cultivated soil;
   22,000  acre-feet evaporated from water sur-
           faces;
   20,000  acre-feet draining away from the
           region below the surface;
   30,000  acre-feet being added each year to the
           ground-water held in the area;
1,328,000  acre-feet presumed transpired and
           evaporated from wild vegetation and
           uncropped land.
 _____
2,400,000  acre-feet.
 _____
```

From the 2·4 million acre-feet of water coming into the area, most of it Indus river-water, only 20,000 acre-feet of water drains away; while 30,000 acre-feet stays in the subsurface. Since the water vapour evaporated and transpired by plants is pure water containing no salts, it follows that most of the salt content of the incoming water is being held in the local soil and ground-water, the salinity of which is inevitably increasing. The level of the water-table is rising through the annual addition of 30,000 acre-feet, and it is in this subsurface water that salinity is highest.

Between 1933 and 1959 the mean depth of ground-water was measured in a number of wells and was found to have risen: as much as 16·4 ft, in some cases, and at least 4·8 ft. Over 339,000 acres the ground-water had risen to within about 6 ft of the surface and in almost a quarter of this area it lay less than 3 ft. below ground-level. Where the ground-water has become saline, water-logging at such shallow depths can adversely affect plants or even kill them. About 170,000 acres of the Khairpur Command are regarded as sufficiently saline to affect all field crops. Even without excessive salinity, water-logging alone can create conditions inimical to cultivated plants sensitive to excessive moisture around their roots.

The line of attack upon the dual problems of salinity and rising ground-water levels combines efforts to reduce the ground-water level by pumping from tube-wells with the construction of drainage canals to carry saline water from the region, to the Indus or to irrigation canals, where by dilution the degree of salinity can be kept below danger level. Land already affected by salinity may be reclaimed for farming by leaching out the salts under heavy irrigation.

The problems introduced by irrigation in a semiarid land are clearly exemplified on a small scale in the Khairpur Command. In the Indus Basin water used by Punjabi farmers in Sargodha or Multan may be used again in Khairpur and, if drainage schemes are made effective, again in Hyderabad. If in the long run, productivity of the lands now irrigated is to be maintained, careful controls of salinity levels of water and of the whole irrigated farming system of the basin will have to be worked out.

Population Density in West Pakistan

The map of population densities (Fig. 4.2.8) although it includes the urban population which comprises 22·5 per cent of the total, and is drawn at the district level, gives a reasonable indication of the wide disparity in the capacity of land to support man. Were it possible to draw a map of rural population density per square mile of cropland (like that for East Pakistan in Fig. 4.3.13 below) the contrast between the closely occupied irrigated lands and the rest would be even more marked. Apart from the district of Karachi where high density is the direct result of urban development based upon that port–city's commercial, industrial, and political functions in relation to Pakistan as a whole and to West Pakistan in particular as its only maritime outlet, district densities reflect fairly faithfully the intensity of agricultural settlement.

Thus an outstanding block of districts with high densities of over 500 per square mile extends from the sub-Himalayan districts of Gujrat and Sialkot (where well irrigation supplements a relatively good rainfall) into the canal-fed plains of the Punjab, as far as Lyallpur and Montgomery. A zone of moderately high density (251–500) flanks this block completing the apex of the Punjab irrigated districts in Multan.

Off the Punjab Plains proper, to the north, there are three districts of moderate to high density. Rawalpindi, since 1959, has contained the Pakistan capital (now being transferred to the new city of Islamabad near by) and the district's urban population is responsible for its reaching a density of over 500 per square mile. The two districts of Peshawar and Mardan which occupy the Vale of Peshawar have high densities more closely tied to their agricultural productivity. They are flanked on the west by two districts of moderately high density, rather remarkable in view of the harshness of their mountain environment in which the partly tribal populations are concentrated in the few patches of productive land in the valleys and intermontane basins (namely Khyber and Mohmand).

Densities around the mean for the wing (average 138 per square mile) are found in a continuous belt extending south from the Himalayan foothill districts (Dir, Kalam, Swat, and Hazara) through the Potwar Plateau (Campbellpore), and Kohat–Bannu districts either side of the Indus, and so into the

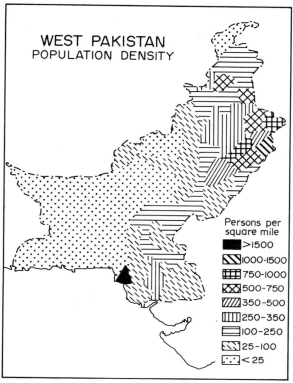

FIG. 4.2.8 West Pakistan: population distribution

Indus Plains proper in Dera Ismail Khan and Mianwali. In the more arid country to the south the moderate densities are limited to the districts which can be watered from the Indus, particularly downstream of the Sukkur Barrage where in Hyderabad the density exceeds 250.

Away from the irrigated tracts, densities fall sharply. Districts in the Indus Plains adjoining those with a substantial amount of irrigated land have densities between 26 and 100 per square mile. Only three upland districts fall into this density category: the districts of North and South Waziribad (in the hills of Dera Ismail Khan Division) and Quetta in the most accessible part of the Baluchistan Plateau. For the rest, the Plateau and the Sulaiman Ranges have very low densities, as little as 2 per square mile over extensive areas, e.g. Chagai and Kharan.

Rural Settlement

The pattern of rural settlement in West Pakistan is generally nucleated. The need to seek, defend, and control water-supplies in a semi-arid land has no doubt contributed to this tendency, but even in the

30. *An Afridi village* in the Khyber Pass, West Pakistan. Stone and mudbrick walls are dominated by the watch-tower from which a look-out can be kept for enemies. Blood feuds have been a tradition in this still partly tribal region. Note the sparse vegetation in this rocky area. Grazing of sheep and goats is important and may partly be blamed for the thin scrub cover.

canal colonies established in the Punjab Plains following the construction of irrigation works, nucleation is the rule, though the canal villages are readily distinguishable from the traditional settlements by their more regular plan, and in the post office guide or on the topographical map, by their codified addresses, each village having a number rather than a name, linking it to the canal system which nurtures it.

In the Himalayan valleys of Hazara the ruggedness of the terrain is perhaps protection in itself, and scattered farms are found clinging to the terraced mountain slopes. West of the Indus mountain settlement becomes more definitely nucleated; witness the fortified walled Afridi villages of the Khyber, with their watch-towers, reminders of the turbulent recent past of the Northwest Frontier, and the persistence of blood feuding in some areas.

3. EAST PAKISTAN:

AN AMPHIBIOUS ENVIRONMENT

The geography of East Pakistan like that of West Pakistan is in large measure a function of its rivers. East Pakistan is, however, well watered by rain, by South Asian standards, and its problems are more often a result of super-abundance of water than of rainfall deficiency. More than 90 per cent of the country is lowland. With the exception of the hill country of Chittagong and Sylhet, on the borders of Burma and India, East Pakistan is the alluvial gift of two major rivers, the Ganges and the Brahmaputra, and of a number of lesser rivers, notably the Surma and Kusiyara which unite in the Meghna, and the Tista (Fig. 4.3.1, Administrative Districts and Rivers). Unlike the rivers of West Pakistan which can be controlled by head-works constructed in solid rock foundations the courses of the great rivers within East Pakistan lie in deep alluvium and carry such enormous quantities of water when in

spate as to defy economic control to protect the delta against floods. Examined in detail many aspects of life in East Pakistan – agriculture, settlement, communications – reflect man's adaptation to the delta's amphibious environment, and his acceptance of the inevitability of flooding and fluvial change. Granted minimal prospects of controlling water within his environment, man has had to make the most of what nature has had to offer. That nature has offered much is testified by the extremely high densities of population the country supports.

Physiographic Evolution

A first step to an understanding of East Pakistan's geography is an appreciation of the variety of its relief and soils. A deltaic river flows on an alluvial ridge of its own making, the highest parts of which are the *levees* immediately adjacent to the river's

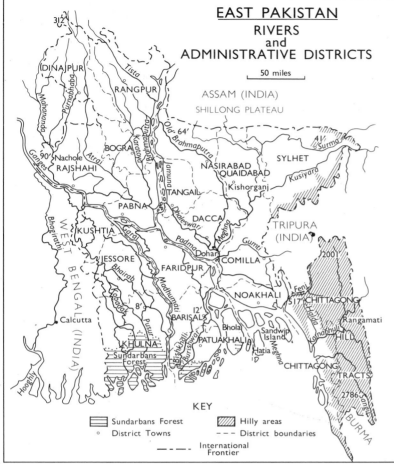

FIG. 4.3.1 East Pakistan: administrative districts, rivers

channel. From the levee crest the land slopes away gently into the lowest areas, the *backswamp depressions*. When in full flood the river overtops its levee. The rate of flow of water away from the main channel diminishes rapidly, and with it, its capacity to carry its load of suspended sand, silt, and mud. Consequently the coarsest part of the load is deposited first, hence the building of a levee which is invariably coarser material than will be found in the backswamp area. The load carried by one river may well differ from that of another, and so the range of textures of the alluvial material making up its levee–backswamp varies. The general principle holds however, for every river at every scale within the delta plain. Backswamp depressions are generally areas of clays and fine silt; levees of sand and coarse silt. The slope between levee and backswamp may be termed the *floodland slope*.

The whole delta plain is made up of these recurring elements: backswamp depressions and the levees forming their rims. But not all such features in the present landscape are in a state of active evolution. Deltaic rivers flowing as they do on an alluvial ridge alter their courses from time to time, so gradually constructing their delta, and the surface details in any area may be in part the product of a past phase of river action. *Meander floodplains* on which the meander belts of former channels can be picked out in old levees and whose courses and backswamps may fill with water in the rainy season, are found particularly in the western part of the delta, in a region referred to as the Moribund Delta. The channels which traverse the Moribund Delta no longer carry much floodwater from the Ganges, which now discharges its main flow further east.

Longer term geomorphological changes have also

had a significant effect on the landscape. The Barind lying between the Ganges and Jamuna (Brahmaputra), and the Madhupur Tract between Jamuna and Old Brahmaputra–Meghna are usually referred to as areas of *old alluvium* and may be regarded as Pleistocene terraces of the present river systems. Smaller patches of similar age and material – lateritic, red, leached, silty clay-loams – occur in the Lalmai Hills close to Comilla and as a benchland formation fringing the hill country to the east of the plains.

If the old alluvial terraces may be regarded as corresponding to the *scalloped interfluves* of the plains of West Pakistan, the *cover floodplain* has its equivalent in the Tippera Surface, intermediate in age between Pleistocene and present. Lying east of the Meghna, the Tippera Surface largely lacks the riverine morphological features such as abandoned meanders and levees that are clearly distinguishable in the younger parts of the delta plain.

Physiographic regions of East Pakistan are shown on Fig. 4.3.2.

1. The **hill country** and its **associated alluvial plains** of Chittagong and the Chittagong Hill Tracts districts has its counterpart in Sylhet where the northern ends of hill ridges extending from the Indian area of Tripura project into the alluvial plain. In Sylhet the hills reach 1102 ft. but ridges generally run at 200–300 ft. above sea-level, and only 10–30 ft. above the plains. South and east the ranges are higher, culminating within Pakistan, in a peak of 3141 ft. in the upper Sangu. The trend of the parallel ridges is roughly north–south and is picked out clearly in the pattern of subsequent drainage. A few major rivers traverse the ridges. Chief among them is the Karnaphuli which has head-waters in Assam and flows southwest across the grain of the country to enter the Bay of Bengal at Chittagong. The Feni River, Sangu, and Matamuhari have shorter transverse courses. All have important subsequent sections which make up a large proportion of their total length. Although the hill country is deeply dissected, and often ridge tops stand a thousand feet above the valley bottoms, the gradient of the rivers is generally slight, and a meandering course is characteristic of their north–south sections.

The benchland features so important as sites for the tea plantations of Sylhet and Chittagong districts are found extensively in some of the longitudinal tributary valleys, standing as better drained but reasonably level (and so accessible) land above the floodplain alluvium. Some of the benchlands are under plantations of teak.

Generally speaking, however, the hill-country slopes are clothed in bamboo jungle extensively used for *jhum* cultivation (shifting agriculture) while the narrow alluvial strips of the longitudinal valley floodplains support permanent fields. These aspects of the region, and its growing importance as East Pakistan's only source of hydroelectric power are discussed further below.

In Chittagong the **alluvial plains** are best developed in the lower tributaries of the transverse rivers, the most extensive being in the Halda Valley.

2. The **old alluvial terraces**. The Pleistocene terrace lands of the Barind and the Madhupur Tract have been slightly deformed by faulting and tilting which have had an influence on their drainage patterns, and may also have been responsible for setting these areas a score or so feet above the adjacent younger floodplains. Perhaps it is this relative elevation which has prevented them being covered by more recent alluvium and so allows their leached soils, lacking exotic sources of plant nutrient in the form of floodwater, to play a part in the areal differentiation of agriculture.

Rivers rising north of the Barind in the sub-Himalayan Piedmont Plain, have cut channels through the old alluvium. It is probable that the Tista, notorious for its changes of course has flowed in several of the channels now occupied by lesser rivers such as the Atrai and Purnababha.

The Madhupur Tract is visually perhaps the more distinctive area since much of its surface is covered in woodland. Both terraces tilt perceptibly southwards towards low-lying depressions, a reminder that recent tectonic movements have contributed, and probably continue to contribute significantly to the pattern of the country's physiography.

3. The **Tippera Surface**,* dated by geologists as Early Recent, extends southwards along the coastal plain as far as Chittagong. Whether its flatness is the result of soil wash having removed evidence of formation by river action or may be taken to indicate that the region is an elevated marine plain is not clear. What matters geographically is that

---

* Tippera District is now called Comilla.

The physiographic types shown on this map correspond in a general way with features described for the Indus Plains. The old alluvium may be equated geomorphologically with the *scalloped interfluve*, the Tippera Surface with the *cover floodplain*, the Moribund Delta and the Stabilised Delta represent the *meander floodplain* at a later and earlier stage respectively, the braided riverain charlands are the *active floodplains*. The North Bengal Sandy Alluvial Fan combines some features of a *piedmont alluvial fan* with those of the *meander floodplain*.

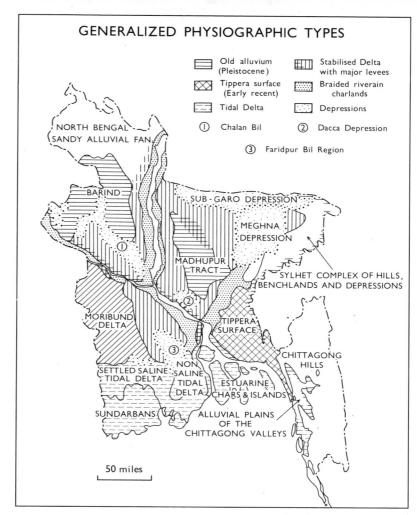

GENERALIZED PHYSIOGRAPHIC TYPES

Old alluvium (Pleistocene)
Tippera surface (Early recent)
Tidal Delta
Stabilised Delta with major levees
Braided riverain charlands
Depressions
① Chalan Bil
② Dacca Depression
③ Faridpur Bil Region

NORTH BENGAL SANDY ALLUVIAL FAN
BARIND
SUB-GARO DEPRESSION
MEGHNA DEPRESSION
MADHUPUR TRACT
SYLHET COMPLEX OF HILLS, BENCHLANDS AND DEPRESSIONS
MORIBUND DELTA
TIPPERA SURFACE
CHITTAGONG HILLS
SETTLED SALINE TIDAL DELTA
NON-SALINE TIDAL DELTA
ESTUARINE CHARS & ISLANDS
SUNDARBANS
ALLUVIAL PLAINS OF THE CHITTAGONG VALLEYS

50 miles

Fig. 4.3.2   East Pakistan: physiography

although it may become flooded along its flanks towards the Meghna, and along the courses of the Gumti and Lower Feni rivers which cross it, its intensive agriculture is generally dependent on direct rainfall.

4. The **North Bengal Sandy Alluvial Fan** is part of the much more extensive submontane belt that stretches the length of the Himalaya foothills from Jhelum in West Pakistan, into the Assam Valley. In that most of its drainage is of local origin it is comparable to the *bhabar* and *terai* tracts (e.g. of Uttar Pradesh) with the swampy terai element dominant. The plain slopes southeastwards with a gradient of 100 ft. in fifty miles, and it is this steeper slope (in comparison to those in the rest of the alluvial lowlands) that sets this corner of East Pakistan aside as a distinct region.

Much of the sandy alluvium that makes up this very low-angled fan has been disgorged into the region by the River Tista. This river rises deep in the Himalaya, draining the Kanchenjunga massif, and

from its point of entry into the plains at 550 ft. above sea-level, and forty-eight miles north of the Pakistan border has varied its course from time to time to build up the fan. In the past the Tista has crossed the Barind to join the Ganges opposite the latter's distributary the Mathabanga. Its removal to the east of the Barind could have contributed to the decay of the Ganges's western distributaries. As recently as 1897 it used a channel more than fifteen miles south of its present course as a main distributary. An earthquake in 1897 appears to have reaffirmed the Tista's present channel, and contributed to the development of the Jamuna as the main course for Brahmaputra water. The Old Brahmaputra which flows east of the Madhupur Tract, is now a much smaller river, carrying Jamuna water only at periods of high flood. Currently a scheme is in preparation to establish a barrage on the Tista by which water can be diverted southwards for irrigation.

The remaining regions may all be regarded as

31. *River Meghna* near its confluence with the Padma (Ganges), East Pakistan. This view, taken in August with the river in flood, shows waterlogged fields of paddy and jute. The dark linear features are settlements, built on river levees, their houses hidden beneath trees. The numerous village sites of this kind are an indication of the changeable course of the river.

representative of the most recent phases in the evolution of the delta.

5. Representing the least active part of the meander floodplain, the **Moribund Delta** lies south of the Ganges and west of the Garai–Madhumati distributaries. Many of its channels are choked with weeds or completely silted up, and its surface is no longer overrun by floodwaters from the Ganges. The Ganges–Kobadak scheme is designed to bring Ganges water back into the region's soils through irrigation, thus rejuvenating them.

6. The **Stabilised Delta** is not so much a region as a widely distributed physiographic element. With the Moribund Delta it corresponds to the meander floodplain element in West Pakistan, but is distinguished from the Moribund Delta on the grounds that it is still flooded periodically. Agriculturally it is the most important feature in the delta. The main channels are reasonably stable, and along the left bank of the Ganges and the Padma (formed by the Ganges–Jamuna confluence) a broad levee has developed. The stabilised delta is an extensive feature in the centre of East Pakistan, around the Ganges–Padma and surrounding the Madhupur Tract.

7. Major **depressions** may be regarded as backswamp depressions to the main rivers, though tectonic subsidence is probably in some degree responsible for their persistence. Chalan Bil* and the Dacca Depression are alike in being at once Ganges backswamps and apparently areas of subsidence related to the tilting of the Pleistocene terraces of Barind and the Madhupur Tract. The bil region of Faridpur District, 700 square miles of marsh, may be seen as a right bank backswamp of the Padma.

* *Bil* is a local term for a lake.

All these bils fluctuate greatly in area between a dry season minimum and a maximum late in the wet season. In the northeast, the sub-Garo and Meghna depressions are almost certainly regions of subsidence, but are also in a sense backswamps to the Old Brahmaputra. Compared with the Brahmaputra–Jamuna and the Ganges, the rivers flowing into the Meghna Depression from the Shillong Plateau and the Assam Hills carry only a small load of sediment, and have been unable to build up their floodplains to keep pace with the subsidence. Some bils in the depression are less than 10 ft. above sea-level, yet almost 200 miles from the sea. It is not surprising therefore, that the Meghna Depression becomes a vast shallow lake for upwards of half the year, unable to discharge its waters southwards through the Meghna because of the higher level of the floodwaters in the Old Brahmaputra, flowing on its 'alluvial ridge'.

8. The **braided riverain charlands** are the active floodplains within which the major rivers are liable frequently to change their channels. The *chars* are the areas of fresh silt exposed at low water. In the case of the Jamuna the river bed is as much as eighteen miles wide and its charlands are very extensive. Those of the Lower Meghna are almost as wide at low water. The firmer levee banks of the Ganges–Padma seem to restrict the width of the charland belt somewhat.

9. In the **tidal delta**, tidal flow in the distributaries has a marked influence on the pattern of channels and the distribution of sediment. Where alternating tidal and river flow is pronounced the distributaries make an elongated hexagonal pattern with their long axis normal to the sea coast. The tides act also to spread the fine sediment more evenly, so that the

TABLE 4.3.1

Monthly Rainfall Medians (in inches)

	Nov.	Dec.	Jan.	Feb.	Mar.	Apr.	May	June	July	Aug.	Sept.	Oct.	Nov.	Dec.
Dinajpur	0	0	0·1	0·2	0·1	2	6·5	11	13	11	11	3	0	0
Jessore	0	0	0	0·5	0·9	4	6	11	11	9·5	8	3	0	0
Sylhet	0·3	0	0	0·8	2·5	10	11·5	30	24	25	20	9	0·3	0
Cox's Bazar	2	0	0	0·2	0·1	4	9·5	28	35	30	15	7	2	0

TABLE 4.3.2

Monthly Variability

	Nov.	Dec.	Jan.	Feb.	Mar.	Apr.	May	June	July	Aug.	Sept.	Oct.	Nov.	Dec.
Dinajpur	∞	∞	200	275	275	60	45	38	34	29	40	113	∞	∞
Jessore	∞	∞	∞	150	122	45	51	23	29	13	38	50	∞	∞
Sylhet	333	∞	100	94	100	41	32	29	25	21	33	72	333	∞
Cox's Bazar	175	∞	∞	150	430	55	39	28	16	31	32	150	175	∞

difference in height between levee and backswamp tends to be less than where river action alone is operative.

The extent to which salt-water penetrates the deltaic distributary channels varies seasonally and depends largely on the vigour of fresh-water flow from the landward side. The **saline delta** extends further inland in the west of the delta where the distributaries are more or less defunct as far as Ganges floodwater is concerned. Only in the wet season does fresh-water gain the ascendancy in the tidal delta west of the Madhumati. East of this the Bishkhali and Burishwar distributaries remain fresh all the year, and salinity affects a much narrower zone at the sea face. The seaward fringes of the estuarine islands – Bhola, Hatia, and Sandwip – and the coasts south of Chittagong may be grouped with the saline tidal delta.

Understandably the whole tidal delta, but particularly the estuarine islands is very vulnerable to cyclones when wind force, low air pressure, high tides, and river floods may combine to devastate wide areas with great loss to human life and property.

Climate

Rainfall is by far the most important climatic element in East Pakistan. The mean annual rainfall ranges from less than 60 inches in the west to over 200 inches in Sylhet, but annual amount is of much less importance than seasonal distribution (Fig. 4.3.3). A distinguished Bengali wrote '. . . rainfall in the months from March to May and again for Sep-

tember and October, rather than the total . . . determines the fortunes of the agriculturalist.'* In other words, he discounted entirely the sparse and unreliable rains of the dry season (November to February), and accepted as adequately reliable the rains of the wettest monsoon months, June, July, and August. He underlined the decisive importance to the farmer of the pre-monsoon (*chota barsat* or 'little rains') and late monsoon rains.

The rainfall dispersion diagrams for Calcutta (lying close enough to the western part of East Pakistan to be characteristic), and Cox's Bazar in Fig. 2.2.7 show clearly the relative reliability of rainfall for the three mid-monsoon months. Sylhet in the northeast corner of the country can rely on an extra month of heavy rain in September. Another way of analysing the seasonality of rainfall is to examine the median value for monthly rainfall at stations representative of the four corners of East Pakistan (Table 4.3.1 above).

Three seasons are clearly seen: dry, little rains and monsoon rains, though their duration is not everywhere identical. The eastern stations have shorter dry seasons, Sylhet having an earlier opening to the 'little rains' in late February–March, Cox's Bazar a later conclusion to the monsoon rains which trail on with decreasing reliability into November.

The relative unreliability of rainfall outside the monsoon rainy season is seen in Table 4.3.2. in which monthly variability for the same four stations is calculated as the proportion expressed as a per-

* Mukerjee, Radhakamal, *Changing Face of Bengal* (Calcutta, 1938), p. 51.

FIG. 4.3.3   East Pakistan: seasonal rainfall (four maps)

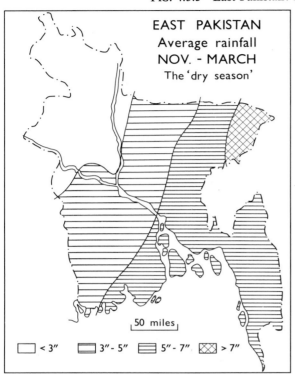

EAST PAKISTAN
Average rainfall
NOV. - MARCH
The 'dry season'

50 miles

☐ < 3"   ▤ 3" - 5"   ▦ 5" - 7"   ▨ > 7"

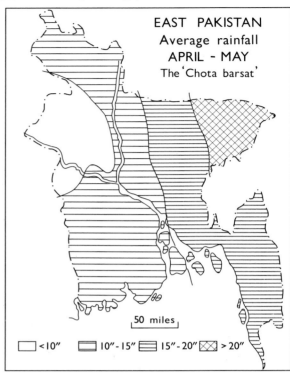

EAST PAKISTAN
Average rainfall
APRIL - MAY
The 'Chota barsat'

50 miles

☐ <10"   ▤ 10" - 15"   ▦ 15" - 20"   ▨ > 20"

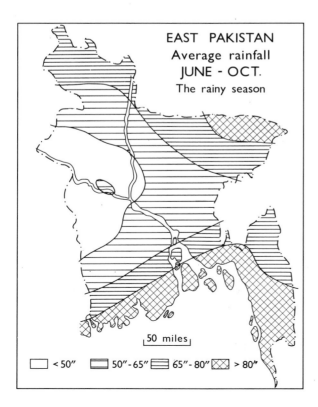

EAST PAKISTAN
Average rainfall
JUNE - OCT.
The rainy season

50 miles

☐ < 50"   ▤ 50" - 65"   ▦ 65" - 80"   ▨ > 80"

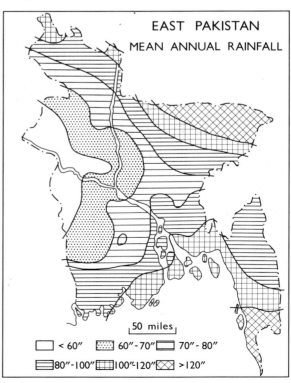

EAST PAKISTAN
MEAN ANNUAL RAINFALL

50 miles

☐ < 60"   ▦ 60" - 70"   ▤ 70" - 80"
▤ 80" - 100"   ▦ 100"-120"   ▨ >120"

Fig. 4.3.4   East Pakistan: October rainfall (two maps)

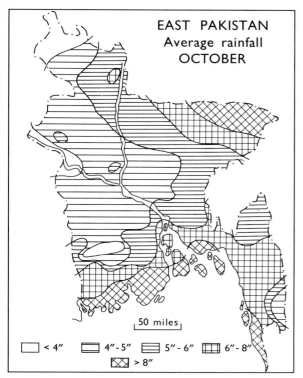
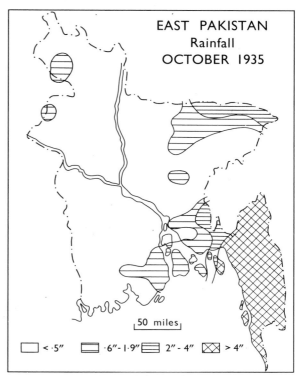

centage, of half the interquartile range to the median value.

Tables 4.3.1 and 4.3.2 taken together indicate the negligible value of dry season rainfall, and the high degree of unreliability of rains everywhere from November to March inclusive. Although more reliable, the range of variation within the low values of April rainfall (in all stations but Sylhet) is high enough to embarrass farmers. Similarly towards the end of the rainy season in October, reliability decreases sharply.

Deficiency of rain in September–October can be very damaging to late rice crops. That fluctuations in late monsoonal rain may affect a large part of East Pakistan simultaneously is seen in the maps (Fig. 4.3.4) showing alongside average rainfall in October, that of a particular month, October 1935. The maps of seasonal and annual rainfall (Fig. 4.3.3) show a longitudinal pattern of rainfall distribution strongly developed in the dry season and little rains. This division into a drier west and moister east in the seven months outside the rainy season proper is important to an understanding of the pattern of

agriculture, especially the distribution of double cropping of rice.

Agriculture

Human ingenuity spurred on no doubt by the pressure of population on the land has brought almost all the surface of East Pakistan into productive use. The mainly self-sufficient Bengali farmer has evolved methods of cropping well adapted to the diverse physiographic conditions of the deltaic lowlands. In the Chittagong Hill Tracts people akin to the hill tribesmen of Burma and Assam combine the practice of sedentary agriculture, in the Bengali style, along the valley bottoms, with jhum cultivation, a form of shifting agriculture or 'swidden' farming, on hill slopes. On the benchlands between, fringing the hill country in Chittagong but more particularly in Sylhet, highly efficient tea plantations represent a third distinct type of agricultural development.

Farming in the Lowlands

Before looking at the regional pattern of agriculture

FIG. 4.3.5   East Pakistan: cropping calendar

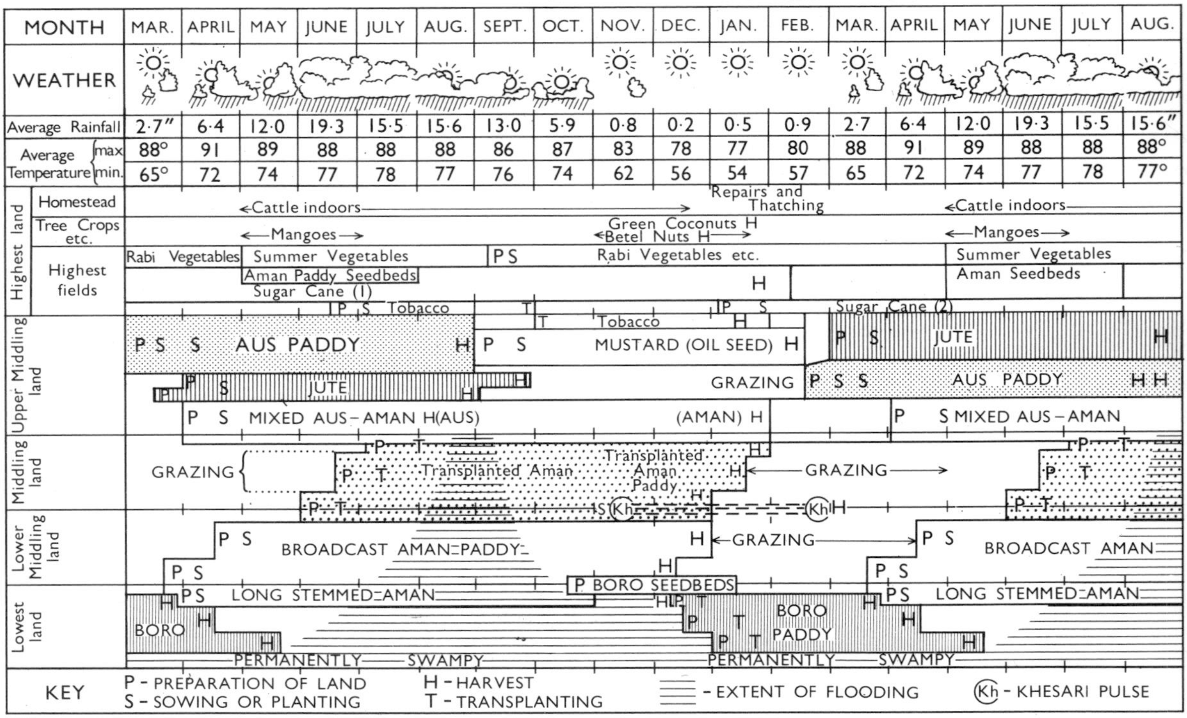

MONTH	MAR.	APRIL	MAY	JUNE	JULY	AUG.	SEPT.	OCT.	NOV.	DEC.	JAN.	FEB.	MAR.	APRIL	MAY	JUNE	JULY	AUG.
Average Rainfall	2.7"	6.4	12.0	19.3	15.5	15.6	13.0	5.9	0.8	0.2	0.5	0.9	2.7	6.4	12.0	19.3	15.5	15.6"
Average Temperature max	88°	91	89	88	88	88	86	87	83	78	77	80	88	91	89	88	88	88°
min	65°	72	74	77	78	77	76	74	62	56	54	57	65	72	74	77	78	77°

Highest land

- Homestead: Repairs and Thatching H — ←Cattle indoors— ... ←Cattle indoors—
- Tree Crops etc.: ←Mangoes→ ; Green Coconuts H ; ←Betel Nuts H→ ; ←Mangoes→
- Highest fields: Rabi Vegetables | Summer Vegetables | P S | Rabi Vegetables etc. | Summer Vegetables
  - Aman Paddy Seedbeds ; Aman Seedbeds
  - Sugar Cane (1) ; H

Upper Middling land

- TP S Tobacco T T Tobacco IP S H Sugar Cane (2)
- P S S   AUS PADDY   H P S   MUSTARD (OIL SEED) H P S | JUTE | H
- P S | JUTE | H   GRAZING   P S S   AUS PADDY   H H
- P S   MIXED AUS–AMAN H(AUS)   (AMAN) H   P   S MIXED AUS–AMAN

Middling land

- GRAZING {   P T   Transplanted Aman   Transplanted Aman Paddy H ←GRAZING→   P T
- P T (Kh) H   S (Kh) H

Lower Middling land

- P S   BROADCAST AMAN=PADDY   H ←GRAZING→ P S   BROADCAST AMAN
- P S   H

Lowest land

- H P S   LONG STEMMED=AMAN   P BORO SEEDBEDS   H P S   LONG STEMMED=AMAN
- BORO H   P T   BORO PADDY   H
- ——PERMANENTLY——SWAMPY—— ——PERMANENTLY——SWAMPY——

KEY	P – PREPARATION OF LAND	H – HARVEST	= – EXTENT OF FLOODING	(Kh) – KHESARI PULSE
	S – SOWING OR PLANTING	T – TRANSPLANTING		

Fig. 4.3.5.   The seasonal use of the different levels of land in the old Brahmaputra flood plain in Quaidabad District (part of the former Mymensingh District). The chart covers more than a year to show more clearly how all the different farming activies overlap. (Chart from the author's "East Pakistan", courtesy Ward, Lock and Co.,)

the basic factors influencing the Bengali farmer in his choice of crop from season to season and from one type of land to another may be gauged from a study of the chart of farming activities (Fig. 4.3.5)* Corresponding to the three rainfall seasons discussed above, there are three cropping seasons in East Pakistan:

(i) the *rabi* or dry season, from October to March or April during which, although only 20 per cent of the cultivated land is cropped, a great variety of crops is grown both 'dry' and by irrigation, e.g. vegetables, wheat, mustard (for oil), pulses, tobacco, and *boro* paddy.

(ii) the *bhadoi* (=kharif) or rainy season, from March or April to August, which starts with the 'little rains' and lasts throughout the months of the heaviest monsoon rains. *Aus* rice and jute are the main crops.

(iii) the *Aghani* or *Hemantic* season, when the main rice crop, *aman*, is grown, occupying land from June to November or December and so overlapping with both bhadoi and rabi seasons. Since little else other than aman paddy is grown this cropping season may conveniently be termed the *aman season*.

In any part of the delta (with the exception of the old alluvial terraces) soils differ in texture as between the levee crests (the 'highest land' in the chart) and the backswamp depressions ('lowest land'), often ranging from light sandy loams to heavy clay loams in the space of a few hundred yards and an altitudinal range of a score or so feet. The lighter higher soils are easier to work than those of the heavier lower land, and can often be tilled dry or with the minimum of moistening from early rains in March. Close to the homesteads for which sites are selected on the highest parts of the levee in order to avoid most floods, vegetables and spices may be grown in kitchen fields all the year round, and a small area of sugar-cane cultivated under fairly close supervision. Seed-beds of tobacco and aman paddy may also be planted. These lands receive

* This chart is based on the farming practices characteristic of the centre of the Old Brahmaputra floodplain in Quaidabad District, part of the former Mymensingh District.

most of what little there is to spare in the way of animal manure after domestic needs for fuel have been satisfied, and their crops are usually fenced to protect them from stray cattle and goats looking for forage. Fruit trees, mangoes, jack fruit, betel nut, and coconut-palms, shade the homesteads and provide a supplement to the farmer's diet and to his income. Apart from the fields immediately around the homestead, most of the agricultural land is unfenced, and the farmer has little choice but to cultivate his scattered fields in the same way as do his neighbours. So although the village lands may be farmed by a number of individuals, there is little apparent variety to distinguish one plot from another.

The highest 'open fields' carry aus paddy and jute in the bhadoi season, both crops which rely on direct rainfall for moisture and which prefer not to grow in standing water. Aus paddy is an 'upland' variety, sown broadcast in non-flooded land. It is harvested in August, when the weather is wet, hot, and very humid. Because of its poor keeping qualities, partly related to these conditions, aus rarely enters into trade. Jute is more tolerant of floods, but deteriorates in quality if left long to grow in water. However, the farmer may have to harvest it in water waist-deep if the monsoon rains are exceptionally heavy. After cutting the jute is retted by soaking in water until the fibres can be stripped from the

33. Loose skeins of *jute fibre* being unloaded from a country boat at a jute mill at Narayanganj, East Pakistan. In the background is a large 'flat' or cargo barge.

stem, washed and bundled in skeins for baling in hydraulic presses at collecting centres.

Some of the land that has carried one of the two bhadoi crops may be ploughed during September and sown with mustard to produce seed for cooking-oil before being cultivated in readiness for the next bhadoi season. Tobacco can also be fitted into this period, the seedlings being planted out from the plots nearer the homestead.

On some of the land sown to aus, aman paddy may be broadcast with the aus seed, to mature after the aus has been harvested. This practice is regarded as an insurance against either crop failing, but does not get the best yields of either. Aman may also occasionally be intersown with jute.

In any village, the greater part of the land will probably be 'middling' land or lower. Here aman is the main crop. These lands are generally too heavy for early ploughing, and have first to be thoroughly soaked by the little rains. The best yields come from aman which is transplanted from seed-beds into rain-flooded fields early in the monsoon. Heavy rains and sometimes river floods, keep the paddy-fields thoroughly wet, and the latter introduce soluble plant nutrients as well as essential moisture Later transplanted crops may need rain in October for best results, after which the fields dry out and

32. *Cutting jute* near Dacca, East Pakistan. The harvest takes place during the wet season, and it is not uncommon for the farmer to have to work waist-deep in flood water.

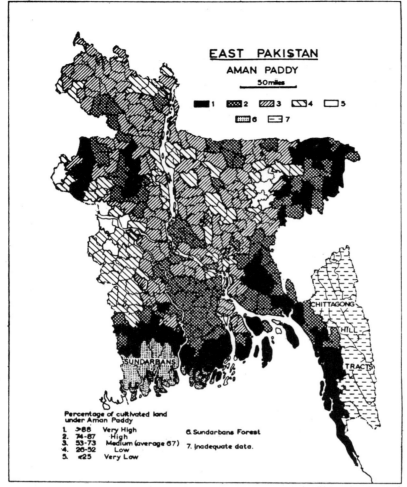

FIG. 4.3.6   East Pakistan: Aman paddy

the crop ripens to be harvested in the clear sunny days of November–December. A common practice is to sow a pulse, *khesari,* among the ripening aman so obtaining a useful 'catch' crop for food and fodder early in the dry season.

On lower land the risk of flooding is naturally greater, and consequently broadcast varieties of aman are sown, among them long-stemmed types. Preparation of land for broadcasting aman can be more cursory than for transplanting, and the object is to get the aman plant well established before the onset of floods, so that the plant can grow quickly when the floods come, keeping its head above the rising water. Aman can grow at the rate of at least an inch a day, some varieties as much as 12 inches in twenty-four hours. The long-stemmed aman can produce a stalk 23 ft. long, and often has to float in

water 15 ft. deep. As the floods recede the stalk subsides and puts out rootlets from its 'joints'.

Where the combined 'little' and monsoon rains last long enough, it is sometimes possible to follow aus with aman on the same land, but the presence of both crops in a farming system usually means they are grown separately.

The lowest land of all, in the backswamp depression may flood too soon for aman to be grown, but is in some areas cultivated as soon as the floodwaters (or accumulated local rain-water) have receded enough to allow a plough team to work knee-deep in water and mud. The dry season *boro* paddy is transplanted before the fields dry out, and has to be irrigated throughout the rainless months of January and February. Water scoops operated on the canti-lever principle, water shovels, and baskets swung

FIG. 4.3.7 East Pakistan: Aus
paddy

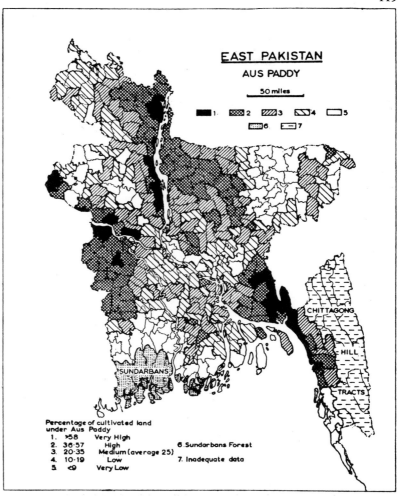

on ropes are used to raise water from the dwindling
backswamp lake, into which the boro fields advance
as the water recedes. Diesel pumps are becoming
widely used to increase the efficiency of boro production, and it may be advantageous to speed the
initial cultivation by tractor ploughing since the
secret of success is to make the most of the water
left over after the end of the rains before it evaporates. Although it is nutritious and yields well, growing in the clear dry season sunshine, boro paddy is
relatively coarse and not popular in trade.

A final element in the chart is grazing. Cattle
and water buffalo are used in ploughing, and to a
small extent as milking animals. During the dry
season the beasts are grazed communally on the
paddy stubble, but while aus or aman crops are in
the open fields they have to be fed near the home-

steads on rice-straw or cut-grass.

Agricultural Regions

While the local diversity of physiographic site in
relation to soil texture and water is reflected generally in diversity of crops and cropping practices
over short distances, the relative importance of the
chief elements in lowland agriculture shows enough
areal differentiation to form the basis of a system of
crop association regions.

The distribution of the main crops or groups of
crops grown is shown in Figs. 4.3.6–4.3.10.* These
maps show in each case the proportion of the cultivated land under the crop. The range of values in

---

* The maps are based on 1944–45 information, later statistics
not being available in such detail.

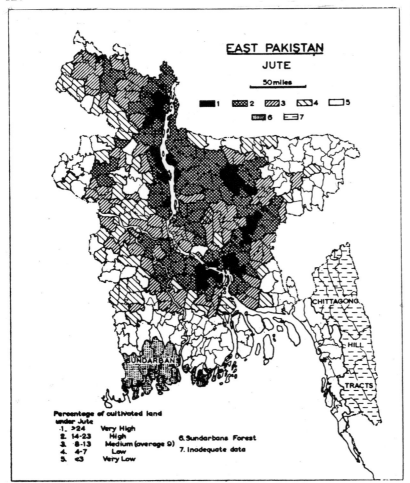

FIG. 4.3.8   East Pakistan: jute

the case of each crop is calculated around a central value representing the percentage of the cultivated land occupied by that crop in East Pakistan as a whole. Thus aman paddy occupies 67 per cent, aus 25 per cent, jute 9 per cent, 'dry' rabi crops 15 per cent, and boro paddy 3½ per cent of the net cultivated area. The maps show in effect how much more or less important a crop is in a particular area than in the country as a whole.

In Fig. 4.3.11 is suggested a scheme of generalised crop association regions which points up the main regional differences in the factors affecting agriculture. The major regions may be distinguished as follows:

1. Areas tending to *aman monoculture.*

   (i) The **Saline Delta** carries little else but aman,

since only after the rains have washed out the sea salt from the soil can a crop be planted. The south coast of Chittagong District has similar conditions.

(ii) The **Barind** with its heavy clay soils developed on old alluvium is in the drier half of the country. The clay soil cannot be ploughed by traditional methods – scratch ploughs drawn by weak oxen – until soaked by the rains, and so, as in the Saline Delta, time allows only a single crop. Southwards the Barind is fringed by depressions (e.g. Chalan Bil) where the land is too water-logged for crops other than aman, or occasionally boro paddy.

(iii) In the **sub-Garo Depression** and **eastern Sylhet** flooding is a major factor giving aman

FIG. 4.3.9 East Pakistan: 'dry'
rabi crops

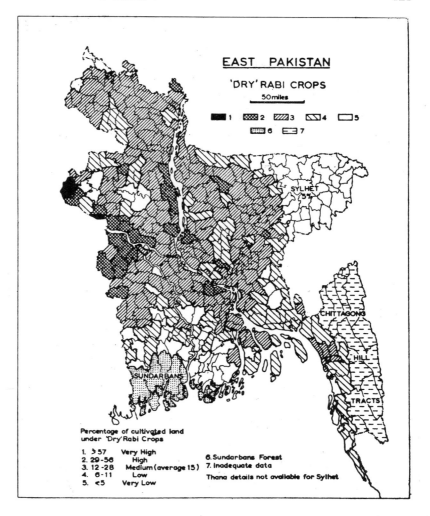

EAST PAKISTAN

'DRY' RABI CROPS

50 miles

1 2 3 4 5
6 7

Percentage of cultivated land
under 'Dry' Rabi Crops

1. > 57   Very High
2. 29-56   High
3. 12-28   Medium (average 15)   6. Sundarbans Forest
4. 6-11   Low   7. Inadequate data
5. < 5   Very Low
                                    Thana details not available for Sylhet

FIG. 4.3.9 East Pakistan: 'dry'
rabi crops

preference over aus. In any case, aman because of its higher yields and adaptation to
the sequence of rainy season and dry is the
preferred crop, other things being equal. It
may well be that the relative lack of population pressure in these areas is a factor discouraging cropping diversification.

(iv) In **Dinajpur** this factor appears to dominate.
Agricultural intensity is low. The severity
and length of the dry season may help to
explain the lack of diversification.

(v) In the **Meghna Estuary** flooding is again a
restrictive factor, but except on the seaward
side of Bhola Island and Hatia, both shown
on the map as I (i), salinity is not a serious
problem, and dry rabi crops can be grown
in the cool season.

2. *Aman paddy and jute* form a dominant association in the **Padma Plain** and adjacent areas, the
richest agricultural region of East Pakistan. Every
year extensive flooding brings into the region fresh
silt and enriching floodwater on the basis of which
fertility the cash cropping of jute on the higher lands
depends. Aman alone can tolerate the flood conditions in summer, often being broadcast early in
order to be strongly enough rooted to withstand the
flood currents and keep pace with deepening water.

3. *Double cropping of aman and aus paddy* (not
necessarily on the same land) is found in the southeast on the **Tippera Surface** extending from Comilla
through Noakhali to the coast and valleys of north
and central Chittagong. Aman generally dominates
here, and an important factor giving aus preference
over the alternative bhadoi crop, jute, is the absence

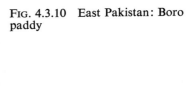

Fig. 4.3.10 East Pakistan: Boro paddy

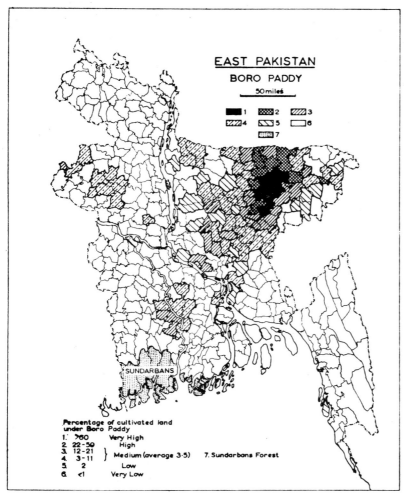

of floodwaters over much of the eastern and southern part of the region. In this eastern part of East Pakistan the dry season is shorter and the little rains more abundant than in the west, so that the effective growing season for paddy is longer.

4. The lighter alluvium of the **Tista and Brahmaputra–Jamuna Plains** is well suited to the bhadoi crops, *aus paddy and jute*. These are relatively very important here, though only in a few areas do they together exceed aman in the proportion of the cultivated land they occupy. The lower ground carries aman paddy, and in the rabi season some areas along the Jamuna banks (and in the charlands in its bed) as much as half the cultivated area is cropped, vegetables and mustard then being important. The region extends along the floodplain of the Old Brahmaputra, enveloping the Madhupur Tract on

either side. Apart from the latter area the region floods extensively each year. Since much of it is forested, the old alluvial Madhupur Tract does not figure largely enough in the agricultural picture to be differentiated in the same way as the Barind.

5. The **Moribund Delta** and the adjacent levee belt north of the Ganges is distinguished by its high concentration of *aus paddy and dry rabi crops*. Aman takes second place to the bhadoi crops, though jute is nowhere very important, since the region's soils lack refreshing floodwaters. The light soils are easy to cultivate even in the dry season, when vegetables are the chief crop, but being relatively unretentive of moisture, aus dependent on direct rainfall is preferred to aman, which needs to be able to stand in water.

6. The heart of the **Meghna Depression** is unique

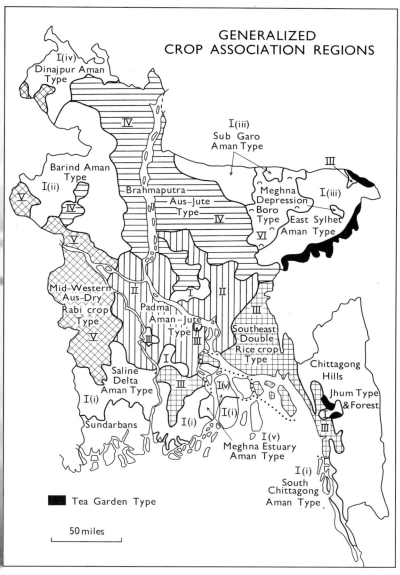

GENERALIZED
CROP ASSOCIATION REGIONS

I(iv)
Dinajpur Aman
Type

IV

I(iii)
Sub Garo
Aman Type

III

Barind Aman
Type

I(ii)

V

IV

Brahmaputra
—Aus–Jute
Type—

IV

Meghna
Depression
Boro
Type

VI

East Sylhet
Aman Type

I(iii)

V

Mid-Western
Aus-Dry
Rabi crop
Type

V

II

I

II

Padma
Aman–Jute
Type

III

III

III

Southeast
Double
Rice crop
Type

Chittagong
Hills

Jhum Type
& Forest

Saline
Delta
Aman Type

I(i)

III

I

III

I(v)

I(i)

III

Sundarbans

I(i)

I(v)
Meghna Estuary
Aman Type

I(i)
South
Chittagong
Aman Type

■ Tea Garden Type

50 miles

FIG. 4.3.11   East Pakistan: crop
association regions

in having most of its land under *boro paddy*. From
May to November vast lakes cover the region,
leaving above water only the artificial mounds on
which the settlements perch along the levee crests.
As the land reappears, hasty ploughing and transplanting of boro paddy begins a dry season busy
with irrigating. There is more cultivable land for the
six months of winter and spring than local farmers
can cope with, and numbers of migrants come from
neighbouring districts by boat to grow boro paddy
and to graze their cattle on the rich pastures. After
boro, the crop next in importance varies from place
to place depending on local conditions.

Shifting Cultivation and Plantation Agriculture
The people of the **Chittagong Hill Tracts** although
possessed of a culture quite different from that of
the plains Bengali, have added permanent field
cultivation in the Bengali style to their traditional
swidden or *jhum* agriculture. Jhum farming involves
clearing slopes covered in a three- or four-year
growth of bamboo, burning the dried rubbish, and
planting mixed crops of *upland rice, maize, millets,
cotton, bananas, and vegetables*. Sowing takes place

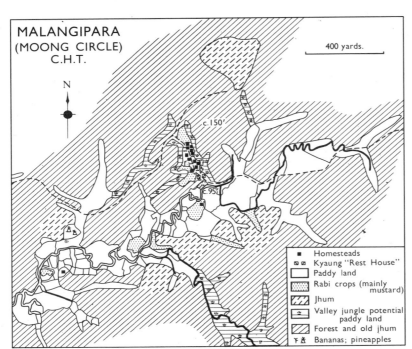

Fig. 4.3.12 Malangipara: a typical village of shifting and permanent cultivators.

Map legend:
- Homesteads
- Kyaung "Rest House"
- Paddy land
- Rabi crops (mainly mustard)
- Jhum
- Valley jungle potential paddy land
- Forest and old jhum
- Bananas; pineapples

Map labels: MALANGIPARA (MOONG CIRCLE) C.H.T. — N — 400 yards. — c.150' — c.95'

during the little rains, and the crops are harvested as they mature. After a single season's cropping the slope reverts to bamboo jungle for three years or more. The jhum land is not owned by the individual cultivator, but is distributed by the village head-man among applicants who pay a capitation fee.

Along the valley bottoms a narrow strip of paddy land is cleared and generally carries *aus paddy* though *transplanted aman* may also be grown. Some light lands have a rabi crop of *mustard, tobacco,* or *vegetables.* Permanent fields such as these are held as individual property. Jhum cultivation is often the occupation of the younger families, who inherit permanent fields later in life. Some tribes in more rugged parts of the region have little land other than jhum. The map in Fig. 4.3.12 shows a typical valley in the Chittagong Hill Tracts.

The tribal population supported by this mixed system in the Hill Tracts numbers about 180,000.

Plantation agriculture occupies large areas in the fringe of the Sylhet Hills and a few blocks in Chittagong. About 76,000 acres of tea are registered, and there are small experimental areas under rubber and coffee. Fig. 4.3.11 shows the distribution of tea estates which lie along the benchlands above the alluvial floodplains but below the steeply sloping hills. The Pakistan tea gardens are among the most efficient in the world in terms of yield per acre of tea. They produce heavily for nine months of the

year, and the labour force (averaging exactly one per acre) spends the three dry months pruning the tea bushes and on general estate maintenance. The tea produced is 'bulk' tea, strong low cost leaf for blending by importers with more flavoured leaf.

Although the plantations are being taken over progressively by Pakistani entrepreneurs and management, the Scottish element is still strong, and the United Kingdom ownership accounts for two-thirds or more of the area. The labour force is composed mainly of third generation descendants of indentured labour brought from Orissa and West Bengal in the 1870s. Female labour is much used in plucking the leaf, but the local Muslim Bengali has as yet shown little liking for the idea of his women-folk working in public, and leaves this task in the hands of a Hindu minority group.

Cropping Intensity

On average about a third of the cultivated area carries more than one crop in a full year. The map of cropping intensity (Fig. 4.3.13) highlights the importance of physical factors in East Pakistan's agriculture. The key is based on the octile distribution of values (i.e. one-eighth of the calculated values is covered by each octile).

The highest intensities of cropping are found generally where readily workable soils, a long rainy season or assured floodwaters to supplement rain-

34. *Chittagong Hill Tracts* near Rangamati. Dissected Tertiary sandstones and shales. The near slopes carry mixed crops of upland rice, millets, beans, cotton, etc., planted by shifting (*jhum*) cultivators. A patch of bananas can be seen near the bamboo hut. The hillsides are cleared of bamboo and scrub in rotation every three or four years. The valley floors are under permanent cultivation for paddy: a farmer is seen pulling seedling rice for transplantation.

fall occur together. Thus the lands along the Ganges, the Jamuna, the Old Brahmaputra, the lower parts of the Padma and Meghna stand out with relatively high cropping intensities. These areas mainly in active or meander floodplains have lighter alluvial soils, annually enriched by floodwaters. The aman–aus 'double cropping' region of the Tippera Surface has the advantage of a longer rainy season than areas to the west. However, it would be rash to discount the possibility that man is himself a potent factor encouraging high intensity of cropping. As will be seen below, high rural population densities are found in much the same areas as high cropping intensities. Physical conditions make possible high population densities, they do not dictate them.

Low intensity of cropping, in a country such as this where population pressures are severe, can generally be explained in terms of the difficulties the terrain presents to farmers equipped only with traditional implements and skills. The Barind and Madhupur Tracts, the Saline Delta, the Dinajpur Sand Plain, the sub-Garo and Meghna Depressions and parts of the Moribund Delta all have certain characteristics which make difficult the multiple cropping of the land.

Agricultural Development: Irrigation
It is somewhat paradoxical that in a country ap-

35. *Pruning tea bushes* Sylhet District, East Pakistan. This operation is carried out during the short dry season when growth of young shoots is minimal and so picking has ceased. The wide branching trees are a planted cover to reduce direct sunlight. The women are Oriyas, third generation descendants of migrants into Sylhet from Orissa, brought in to establish the tea industry in an area where the local Moslem women do not generally work in the open away from home.

parently so well watered as East Pakistan, irrigation should rank high among schemes to advance agricultural productivity. Rainfall is, however, highly seasonal, and in much of the drier western third of the country there are no floodwaters from outside the area to compensate for the shortness of the rainy season.

It is here that the country's two major agricultural development projects are located. The *Ganges–Kobadak* scheme is in an advanced stage of development. It is the largest project undertaken anywhere under the direction of the United Nations Food and Agricultural Organisation. Its first objective is to pump water from the Ganges at Bheramara (near the Hardinge Bridge by which the broad guage railway crosses the river) into a canal system which will lead water southwards through the Moribund Delta, an area which will benefit greatly from a perennial supply of water. The soils of the Moribund Delta no longer receive regular inundations from nutrient-bearing water, and it is expected that irrigation with Ganges water rich in plant nutrients will upgrade the quality of the area's soil as well as providing moisture whenever required. A further objective is to bring fresh Ganges water into the settled Saline Delta that lies south between the Moribund Delta, and the Sundarbans Forest. Agriculturally this region has been deteriorating as the Ganges distributaries decayed. With less fresh-water passing through their channels, salt-water has been able to encroach more and more from the sea, affecting the soil and so restricting cultivation to the rainy season. A system of polders to keep out salt-water and canals to provide fresh-water with which to sweeten the soil could reverse the present progressive wasting of the lands of the Saline Delta.

North of the Ganges another major irrigation project is being undertaken to control the waters of the unruly *Tista* by a barrage located near Hatibandha, close to where the river enters East Pakistan. It is proposed to irrigate 800,000 acres in an area south of the river extending towards Bogra.

A project of a very different kind involves the distribution of small diesel engine pumps of a capacity capable of irrigating a hundred acres or so. Such pumps are designed to draw water from rivers, depressions such as backswamps and meander cutoffs which become flooded during the rainy season, and excavated tanks. A pump can operate with

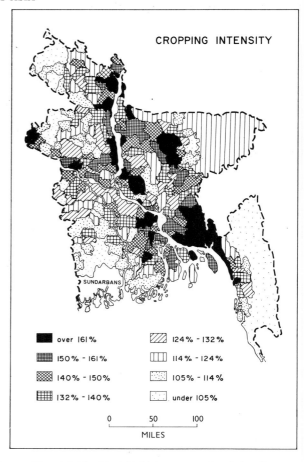

FIG. 4.3.13   East Pakistan: cropping intensity

greater efficiency than the traditional methods used for raising water. In particular water can be raised to a greater height than would be economically practicable using hand-operated methods. Furthermore, a pump being reasonably mobile by road or by river-boat it can be moved to make use of water bodies in several localities at different times of the year.

A major objective of all irrigation schemes is to release the farmer from his dependence on an unreliable rainfall. In East Pakistan temperatures permit cultivation of crops at all times of the year if water is available. At present less than a quarter of the land used for cultivation carries a winter crop, yet good yields of rice, oil-seeds, wheat, pulses, etc. can be obtained at this time of year. But it is not only in the acutely dry season of winter that irrigation can be profitably employed. Cultivation of the

FIG. 4.3.14 East Pakistan: population density per
square mile of crops and of net cultivated area

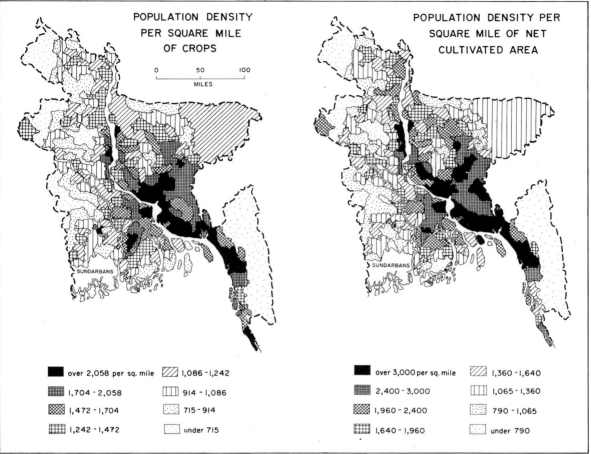

bhadoi crops of aus paddy and jute is frequently
hazardous since ploughing and sowing may be de-
layed while farmers wait for the notoriously unreliable 'little rains' of April and May. Were irrigation water available, farmers would not have to wait
for rain before sowing. Irrigation makes possible a
revolution in cropping practices, allowing the maximum use of the land during the year. Current practices because they have to take account of the risks
of late or inadequate rains too often fail to produce
the best results: the sowing of mixed crops as an
insurance against the failure of one is an example.
In West Pakistan irrigation is so much a matter of
life or death that farmers have come to expect it and
are willing to pay for the water provided. In East
Pakistan, however, where traditional practices do
not depend on irrigation but are adjusted to the
seasonal rainfall, farmers are less ready to pay for

irrigation which is not absolutely necessary for cultivation. As with so many aspects of agricultural
development in South Asia, there is a serious problem of communication to be overcome. The farmer
has to be convinced that additional expenditure on
water will be more than repaid from the additional
productivity of his land.

Rural Population Density
Fig. 4.3.14 shows density of rural population in relation to the total area of crops and of land used for
cultivation, the latter relating rural population to
the area actually used to support it. Naturally the
land which can carry two crops or more annually is
able, other things being equal, to support a greater
number of people than land on which only one crop
can be taken in a year. Cropping intensity (see Fig.
4.3.13 above) is not the whole answer to the prob-

36. *A Bengali homestead* in East Pakistan occupied by a 'joint family' of several related adults and their children. Each separate bamboo matting, grass roofed hut is the home of a man, wife and family. Rice which is being dried on mats in the sun is being swept up by the woman in the foreground. Rice straw is stacked beyond. The dark patch on the ground to the left of the children is cow dung being dried for fuel. The trees provide shade and fruit. The light bamboo fence protects a small spice and vegetable garden from goats.

lem however. In the map showing rural population density in relation to the area of crops, the factor of cropping intensity is taken into account, yet the pattern of densities is still closely similar to that for population per square mile of net cultivated area. In other words, the removal of the factor of multiple cropping, while it reduces the densities of population somewhat at the higher values, does not alter materially the overall differentiation of population density.

The scale of values used in the maps of rural population density represent the distribution of densities by *octiles*, i.e. each step of the eightfold range of values covers one-eighth of the 360 administrative areas concerned. Nine rural areas have densities of over 4000 persons per square mile of cultivated land, the highest value being 6054. At the other end of the scale six areas have below 500 per square mile, the lowest value being 263.

There is a remarkable concentration of areas of high density in the southeastern quarter of the country, notably the districts of Tangail, Quaidabad Dacca, Faridpur, Comilla, Noakhali, Barisal, and Chittagong. Eight of the eleven largest towns lie in this area, and must through their demand for food, and for jute for their industries, exert a strong economic incentive to agricultural productivity upon their tributary areas. Apart from these influences, high population densities may be explained by the same factors which were discussed above in connection with cropping intensity.

Areas of high density in relation to cultivated land or crop areas are an indication of the relative suc-

cess of traditional farming methods in those areas. Areas of relatively low population density may be areas producing a surplus of crops for export to high density rural and urban areas. But as these lands include the most extensive areas of low cropping intensity they must also be considered as areas of possibly unexploited potential. In these areas, while traditional methods may be unable to exact more from the soil, there may remain significant possibilities for increasing crop production and cropping intensity by the application of advanced technology. It is interesting to note that the main irrigation schemes are situated in the areas of low cropping intensity and low population density, e.g. the Ganges–Kobadak and Tista projects and the more diffuse efforts to introduce diesel pumps into the Meghna Depression.

Overall Population Density

In order to allow direct comparison of overall population densities in the countries of South Asia, Fig. 4.3.15 shows the total population in each district in relation to the total area of the district. It is of course a much cruder measure of population density than those employed in Fig. 4.3.14. Since the total area is used, including rivers and lakes, jungle and other non-productive elements in the landscape, the densities tend to be lower. The larger size of administrative unit also tends to obscure the range of geographical conditions within the country. Granted these shortcomings, none the less the high concentration of population in Dacca–Comilla stands out, with the lowest densities being

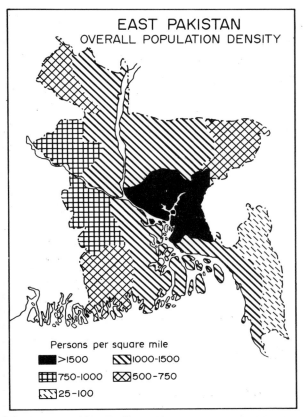

EAST PAKISTAN
OVERALL POPULATION DENSITY

Persons per square mile

>1500   1000-1500

750-1000   500-750

25-100

FIG. 4.3.15   East Pakistan: population: overall density by districts

found in the Chittagong Hill Tracts, and the agriculturally marginal districts in which the Barind, the Moribund Delta, the Saline Delta, and the Meghna Depression dominate the scene.

Rural Settlement Patterns

In a country where even if there may not everywhere be an annual risk of flood there is the certainty of very heavy seasonal rainfall, man has tended to seek out the highest points for settlement sites. In many areas even the levee crests provide an inadequate height to guarantee against regular flooding, and homesteads are raised on earth plinths to gain a few feet of added protection. Not all settlements can find levees convenient to their farm lands and some have had to build artificial mounds on which to concentrate their houses.

The normal unit of Bengali settlement is the joint-family homestead which consists of several bamboo huts grouped within a fence. Such a homestead is occupied by a man, his wife, his unmarried children, and the wives and families of his sons. Villages in the sense of close nucleations of houses are uncommon in the lowland areas except where artificial mounds force a closer settlement for the sake of economy. Normally the homesteads spread, often continuously for miles, along levees. From the air the

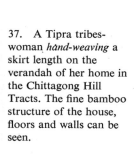

37. A Tipra tribeswoman *hand-weaving* a skirt length on the verandah of her home in the Chittagong Hill Tracts. The fine bamboo structure of the house, floors and walls can be seen.

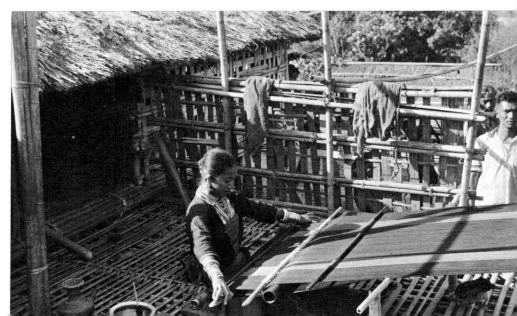

clearest indication of a levee in this so nearly flat land is a line of homesteads nestling beneath the shade of fruit trees and palms. Passing through the most densely populated areas when the paddy is green in the fields an impression might be obtained of wide open grasslands fringed by woods, with hardly a soul in sight. Enter the tree belt and the close packed homesteads teeming with life become clearly evident.

Settlement in the Chittagong Hill Tracts is more clearly nucleated in pattern and water-seeking in site. During the jhum cultivating season a propor-tion of the population may be temporarily dispersed in isolated huts in the lands distant from the village. Building styles are in complete contrast to those found in the plains. Bamboo is still the most im-portant building material, but the houses are erected on stilts, the floor standing 4 ft. or more above ground-level.

The tea garden employees are housed by the plan-tation companies in well-planned nucleated villages close to the centre of the estate where a Hindu temple, a dance house, a market, post office, and clinic will usually be found.

4. PAKISTAN: DEVELOPMENT PROBLEMS

Pakistan faces the problem, common to many of the world's developing countries, of having to feed an ever-increasing population (expanding at the rate of about 2·4 per cent per annum) while simultane-ously striving to raise living standards. The pros-pects of achieving these ends are closely tied to the country's ability to attract development capital as loans or grants from abroad, to accumulate such capital internally, and to earn foreign exchange by the export of goods or services. Where the vast majority of the population are peasant farmers with a very low standard of living the scope for capital accumulation within the country is small, and the need to seek aid or to borrow or earn capital from abroad is correspondingly great. Economists speak of the problems of bringing a backward economy to the stage where it can 'take off' on its own, to become viable and self-regenerating. Before the economies of underdeveloped countries can reach this point, much capital has to be poured in, not only as finance, but as machinery, technicians, and advisors also. Despite the vital part in her economy played by foreign aid, it is worth noting that foreign exchange earnings (Rs. 2950 million) exceeded the total of foreign aid in 1964/65 (Rs. 2750 million). This fact underlines the importance to under-developed countries, as large exporters of raw materials, of stability in the world's commodity markets. A fall in price paid for jute or cotton, while welcome to the industrialists and consumers in Western countries, means a fall in Pakistan's earned income, and forces her to seek to make good the loss of earnings by obtaining increased loans or grants, perhaps from the same countries.

Pakistan's earned income derives mainly from the export of fibres in the raw and manufactured state. Table 4.4.1 shows the composition of her export earnings in 1966. The targets for exports by the end of the Third Five Year Plan (1969/70) are also shown.

TABLE 4.4.1

Export Earnings

(Source: *Pakistan Monthly Statistical Bull.*, Sep. 1968; *Third Five Year Plan (1965–70)*, 1965.)

(Million Rupees and percentage of total)

	1967–68	%	Target 1969–70	%
Raw jute	758·9	24·3	750	18·5
Jute manufactures	619·6	19·8	800	19·8
Raw cotton	441·8	14·1	550	13·6
Cotton manufactures	416·5	13·3	350	8·6
Hides and skins	7·0	0·2	80	1·9
Leather and leather goods	126·8	4·1	80	1·9
Wool	37·0	1·1	90	2·2
Carpets (woollen)	30·9	1·0	?	?
Fish	56·8	1·8	100	2·5
Rice	149·4	4·8	250	6·2
Other primary products	205·9	6·6	230	5·7
Other manufactures	273·9	8·8	770	19·0
TOTAL	3124·6	99·9	4050	99·9

It is clear from the table above, that Pakistan relies heavily on the agricultural sector of the eco-nomy and on industries themselves based on the products of agriculture, to earn foreign exchange. The relative importance of foreign aid (mainly loans) compared with export earnings is expected to de-cline during the current plan period (1965–70) though the absolute value of foreign assistance will increase from Rs. 2750 million (1964–65) to Rs. 3400 million in 1969–70.

The pattern of imports is shown in Table 4.4.2. The fact that food is a significant item in the list of imports, and has over several years been also imported by way of what amounts to a gift (e.g. through the United States Public Law–480 programme) is a matter of concern to Pakistani economic planners. If the country is to balance its external trading account, and indeed if it is to generate capital internally, it must look to develop its main resources which lie in agriculture: land, water, human energy, and skills. Agricultural productivity, whether it is directed towards achieving self-sufficiency in foodstuffs for home consumption or to producing exportable surpluses of fibres for export, raw or in manufactured forms, so that the short fall in food can be purchased abroad, must be of highest priority in Pakistan development planning.

TABLE 4.4.2

Principal Imports 1967–68

(Million Rupees and percentage of total)

Machinery	1065·1	22·9
Iron and Steel manufacturers	428·1	9·2
Transport equipment	407·0	8·7
Electrical goods	302·1	6·5
Food grains	620·2	13·3
Chemicals, dyes, medicines	540·2	11·6
Others	1292·0	27·7
TOTAL	4654·7	99·9

(Source: *Pakistan Monthly Statistical Bull.* Sep. 1968)

Like India, Pakistan has been the recipient of aid by means of grants and loans from a number of countries, both 'Western' and 'Communist'. The distribution of commitments to economic assistance during 1965–66 amounting to loans of $278·7 million and grants of $16·8 million illustrates this point. Most aid came from a group of Western countries operating as the 'Aid-to-Pakistan Consortium', and from international agencies. The U.S.A. ($54 million), Canada ($31 million), and Japan ($30 million) head the list of consortium members; comparable commitments came from the International Bank for Reconstruction and Development either directly ($30 million) as interest-bearing investments or through its special agency the International Development Association ($44 million) as interest free long-term loans. Among the countries offering assistance outside the consortium are Czechoslovakia ($17 million), U.S.S.R. ($14 million), and China ($11 million).

Agricultural development

Regional agricultural development has already been referred to in preceding chapters. The planners of economic development set the following among the targets of the Third Five Year Plan: the achievement of self-sufficiency for food; meeting the de-

8. *A water mill* in the mountains near Abbotabad north of Rawalpindi. Three vertical waterwheels for grinding wheat and maize flour are fed by chutes of water diverted from the dam seen in the right background.

39. *Bidi* making in East Pakistan. Bidis are small cheap cigarettes made by packing dry tobacco 'chaff' into a rolled piece of tobacco leaf. Twenty bidis might cost a few pence/cents. The industry is notorious for its low wage rates.

mand for export commodities; increasing the economic well-being of the cultivators; improving the organisational structure of the agricultural economy to facilitate these developments, e.g. through cooperatives, regional warehouses, credit, etc.

New irrigation projects and reclamation schemes will eventually make more land available for agriculture, and permit more intensive use of some of the present areas under cultivation, but against these gains must be set the continuing losses due to salinity and water-logging. Ultimately the problem of productivity will have to be solved at the farm level by the adoption by the farmer of better methods of cultivation. The Food and Agricultural Commission set up in 1959 recommended an immediate 'crash programme' to set improvements in motion. The programme consisted of 'Five Firsts' which could be implemented with the minimum of disturbance of the existing economic and social conditions of traditional agriculture: better seed, artificial fertilisers, plant protection from pests and disease, better though simple techniques of cultivation, and the provision of easily obtainable short- and medium-term loans to help finance the other improvements. It was estimated by the commission that improved yields per acre of up to 20 per cent could be obtained from better seed, of 40–50 per cent from the use of fertiliser, 15–20 per cent by

plant protection, and 25–30 per cent from better techniques. The greatest difficulty in the way of implementing such improvements in Pakistan (as in India or Ceylon) is that of establishing communication with the cultivator who for generations has followed time-honoured methods.

Important among long-term handicaps to agricultural development has been the landholding system. Much has been done recently to reduce the evils of the old system under which the tenant cultivator was often little better off than the bonded serf of Europe in medieval times. The consolidation of holdings and their rearrangement into economic farm units will require many years of patient work but progress is promising. Legislation has been passed to prevent the subdivision of holdings in West Pakistan below a level of 12½ acres in the Punjab Plains and 16 acres in the Lower Indus Plains.

Industrial Development

At the time of partition, Pakistan entered independent economic life with a very poor basis of industrial and commercial equipment: no jute spinning and weaving mill, sixteen cotton mills, one small hydroelectric station, and a disrupted transport system. The industrial picture has improved remarkably but the best prospects for economic development still lie in the agricultural field. Resources for industry are meagre for such a populous

40. *The village potter* puts a finishing touch to bowls being sun-dried before firing. Photograph taken in a Rajput (Hindu) village at Chhor on the Pakistan side of the border of West Pakistan and India, at the edge of the Thar Desert.

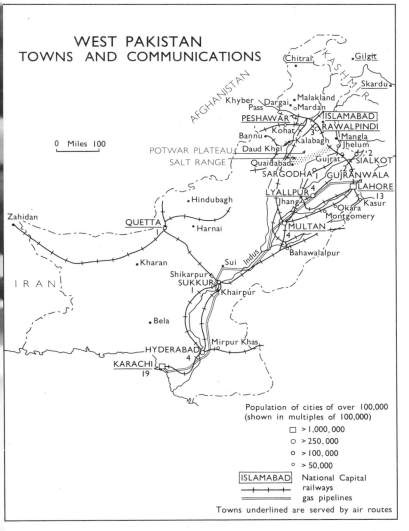

WEST PAKISTAN
TOWNS AND COMMUNICATIONS

FIG. 4.4.1   West Pakistan: econ-
omic development and cities.
Note that Gilgit and Skardu are in
Pakistan-occupied 'Azad Kashmir'.

nation. Pakistan has a much less solid basis for
heavy industry than has India. Furthermore, the
separation of East and West wings, and the widely
dispersed nature of the internal market within each
wing, apply a considerable 'friction of distance' to
the developmental process by raising costs of transfer of power, raw materials, and manufactured
goods.

With so meagre an industrial basis in 1949, Pakistan applied its efforts first to the processing of its
agricultural raw materials. In the current Third
Five Year Plan some greater attention is being
given to the gradual establishment of capital goods
industries so as to make the industrial economy
more self-reliant for its basic equipment.

Resources for Industrial Development (see Figs.
4.4.1 and 4.4.2)

Agriculture provides the main basis for industry
through the fibres **jute** and **cotton**. Efforts have been
made to increase the proportion of these fibres
which is exported as manufactured gunny or
cloth.

East Pakistan, the world's major producer of raw
jute, has 35 mills (258,000 spindles, 17,609 looms)
and a production of 487,087 tons of jute goods in
1967/68, almost 70 per cent of which would be
available for export. The mills are located in
Narayanganj, Khulna, Dacca, and Chittagong.

The small cotton industry of 1947 expanded
rapidly from 177,000 spindles and 4800 looms to

41. *Carting sugar cane* to a crushing mill in Kushtia District, East Pakistan.

1·95 million spindles and 29,000 looms in 1960. By 1967/68 there were 2·7 million spindles and 37,000 looms. Although the industry draws most of its raw cotton from West Pakistan and has its main development there, it is also found in several centres in East Pakistan (notably Dacca, Khulna, and Chittagong) where most of the planned expansion under the Second Plan (1960–65) took place in an endeavour to diversify that wing's economy. In West Pakistan Karachi, Hyderabad, Multan, Khairpur, Sargodha, Lahore, Lyallpur, and Peshawar are important among a great number of cotton manufacturing centres. Production of cotton yarn (254,316 long tons) in 1967/68 placed Pakistan a little ahead of Britain (234,800) in the world table.

The small woollen industry is based on **wool** produced in West Pakistan. Harnai (in Quetta Division) Bannu, and Quaidabad are the chief centres for weaving cloth, the production of which meets most of Pakistan's needs.

In both wings **sugar-cane** is grown for local crushing and extraction, and an increasing proportion of output comes from modern refineries. There are four large refineries in the Vale of Peshawar, two in Thal, and others in Gujranwala and Lyallpur all drawing their cane from irrigated areas. In East Pakistan sugar growing and refining is widespread in the centre and northeastern districts. There seems no prospect of any surplus of sugar for export.

Based partly on agricultural by-product **straw,** but mainly on **forest products**, the manufacture of *paper* has developed since partition. The largest mill is at Chandragona near Chittagong, where bamboo floated down the Karnaphuli is made into good grade paper. Another mill in East Pakistan at Khulna draws its soft woods from the Sundarban forests and a planned mill in Sylhet will use reeds from the swamps of the Meghna Depression. In West Pakistan straw is the basis for paper and cardboard manufacture in Gujranwala and Nowshera. It is expected that newsprint and paper will become increasingly valuable as minor items in the export trade.

Hides and skins provide raw materials for **tanning industries** which are widely distributed on a small scale. Major tanning centres are near Chittagong and Dacca, and in Hyderabad, Khairpur, and Sukkur. Factory scale shoe industries are found in

Lahore, Hyderabad, Karachi, and Narayanganj, but as a cottage industry the manufacture of foot-wear is still widespread.

The *food processing industries* will be of increasing importance as living standards rise and as more people change to urban ways of life. **Wheat** flour-milling, **rice**-milling, and **oil-seed** crushing are found on a small scale in many country towns as well as in the major cities. **Tea** factories on the plantations in Sylhet and Chittagong districts of East Pakistan processed 66 million lb. for local consumption in 1967/68. Increased demand has removed tea from the export list (cf. 7 m. lb. in 1965/66, worth Rs. 11 m.).

In *non-agricultural resources* Pakistan is far less well endowed than India. Only one exportable mineral, **chromite,** is present in abundance. It is worked at Hindubagh northeast of Quetta. Lean **iron ores** are plentiful at Kalabagh where the Indus cuts across the Salt Ranges, but as yet there is no serious prospect of an indigenous iron industry. Smaller reserves of high-grade ore occur in inaccessible Chitral.

Petroleum, natural gas, coal, salt and limestone are of more immediate value.

A small oil-field has long been worked in the Potwar Plateau (Attock and Rawalpindi districts) but supplies only 20 per cent of the country's needs. Production amounts to about half a million metric tons annually.

Natural gas is the subject of Pakistan's major success story since independence. The best known reserves around Sui (east of Jacobabad in West Pakistan) are estimated to contain the energy equivalent of 316 million tons of coal. Sui gas is piped south to Hyderabad and Karachi, and north to Multan, Lyallpur, and Lahore. A branch from Lyallpur to Islamabad is under construction. Gas is also exploited in East Pakistan in Sylhet District from where it is piped to Fenchuganj and Dacca. Sui gas is thought to be among the cheapest in the world even at the end of its 350-mile journey to Karachi. In both wings the gas is used as an industrial fuel and as a chemical raw material, forming the basis of the urea (nitrogenous fertiliser) industry at Fenchuganj and Multan. By 1967 production of natural gas was running at about 2000 million cubic metres per annum.

Pakistan's deposits of **coal** are of indifferent quality and lie mainly in the Salt Range and around Quetta. Production amounts to about three-quarters of a million tons. Good quality coal has to be imported. In East Pakistan peat and lignite deposits are known in several places but are unlikely to attract development in view of the active exploitation of natural gas. The Gondwana coals of the Indian Damodar field are known to extend beneath parts of Bogra District but their economic potential is uncertain.

Salt and **gypsum** are worked from associated deposits in the Salt Range. **Limestone** is of widespread occurrence in the hill country of West Pakistan but restricted to a single source in Sylhet in the East.

42. *Natural gas well,* Sui, West Pakistan. From here the gas is piped to the major cities. Note the sand dunes and semi-arid vegetation of this typical landscape on the edge of the middle Indus Plains north of Sukkur.

43. Looms for weaving gunny (sacking) in a modern *jutemill* East Pakistan.

Cement works in both wings are located close to limestone deposits.

Electric power. The total installed generating capacity was expected to reach 2·89 million kW. by 1970, rather more than two-thirds of it in West Pakistan. Several hydroelectric schemes have been completed since partition, some of them in association with irrigation development. The main schemes are:

(*a*) In West Pakistan:
Warsak (160,000 kW.) on the River Kabul.
Malakand–Dargai (40,000 kW.) on the Swat Canal.
Rasul (22,000 kW.) on the Jhelum Canal.
Mangla (45,000 kW.) on the River Jhelum.

(*b*) In East Pakistan:
Karnaphuli (80,000 kW.).

The Mangla Dam, now inaugurated, will eventually generate 300,000 kW. A smaller scheme under construction is the canal fall project in Gujranwala.

With the development of natural gas the share of thermal power-stations in total output is likely to increase. Thermal stations are concentrated in the industrial cities, the larger units being in Karachi, Hyderabad, Sukkur, Multan, Montgomery, Lahore, and Daud Khel (cement works) in the West, Dacca, Chittagong, Khulna, and Fenchuganj in the East. Many more or less isolated towns maintain small

thermal or diesel plants for domestic and light industrial use.

It follows from the discussion of industrial resources that any metal-working and engineering industries must for the present be established on imported raw materials. A small start in steel-making (from imported pig-iron and scrap) has been made in each wing at Karachi and Chittagong, and there are steel re-rolling mills at Karachi, Lahore, and Multan. Engineering industries are as yet little developed and of a fairly rudimentary type, e.g. vehicle assembly, railway workshops, agricultural (especially irrigation) machinery, but development of a machine tools industry is in hand. There is a small shipbuilding yard at Karachi designed to construct vessels (up to 10,000 tons dead-weight) for coastal and interwing traffic.

Location of Industry

With the exception of industries strongly orientated towards materials (e.g. tea packing, jute pressing, sugar refining, paper making, and cement manufacture) or to ports of entry of materials (steel, petrochemicals) industry appears to be attracted to existing centres of population, where a ready labour supply, a local market and developed communications and public utilities are available. Most such centres are in the areas of better developed agriculture, only Karachi having no firm local agricultural base. As a long established port Karachi has an assured future as an industrial city, and has acquired oil refineries in addition to a wide range of light manufacturing. Chittagong and Khulna combine the advantages of ports and centres of productive agricultural regions. Chittagong has East Pakistan's first oil refinery. Perhaps only Narayanganj (itself fast becoming a suburban satellite of Dacca) could claim to be a predominantly industrial town, almost wholly devoted to processing raw jute and manufacturing jute goods.

Urban Development

West Pakistan is considerably more urbanised than the East wing with 22·5 per cent of its population in urban centres compared with 5·2 per cent in the East. Twenty-three cities in the West have 50,000 inhabitants, nine in the East. In the West, two cities, Lahore (1·3 million) and Karachi (1·9 million) rank in the 'millionaire' class, and five others exceed

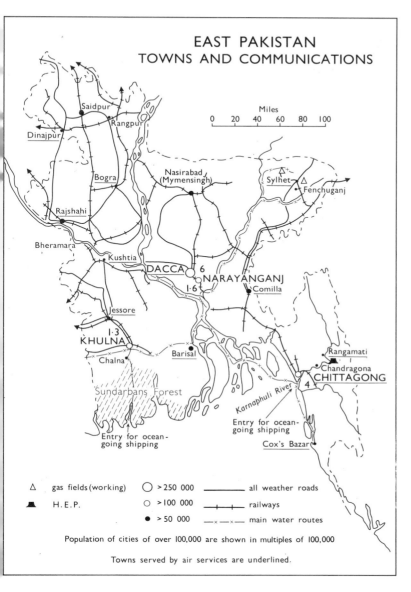

EAST PAKISTAN
TOWNS AND COMMUNICATIONS

Miles
0   20   40   60   80   100

△   gas fields (working)   ◯ > 250 000   ——————— all weather roads
▲   H.E.P.   ○ > 100 000   +—+—+—+ railways
                           ● > 50 000   —x—x—x— main water routes

Population of cities of over 100,000 are shown in multiples of 100,000

Towns served by air services are underlined.

Fig. 4.4.2 East Pakistan: economic development and cities. A good road now joins Dacca–Chittagong–Cox's Bazar.

200,000: Hyderabad (435,000), Lyallpur (425,000), Multan (358,000), Rawalpindi (340,000), and Peshawar (219,000). East Pakistan has no 'millionaire' city, and only two exceed 200,000: Dacca (557,000) and Chittagong (364,000).

The disparity between the wings in this regard cannot be due to their total populations which are not very dissimilar (West Pakistan 42·9 million, East Pakistan 50·8 million) and in any case favour the East wing. Political history provides a partial explanation. Before partition most of East Pakistan was a part of the province of Bengal with its capital at Calcutta and its whole economy orientated towards Calcutta and the Hooghlyside jute industry. Except for a brief period between 1905–12 during an earlier partition of Bengal, Dacca was merely a district headquarters town. As a port Chittagong was overshadowed by Calcutta. West Pakistan on the other hand was constituted from several former provinces and so inherited their administrative capitals: Lahore, a fine and ancient city, was capital of the Punjab, the pride of British India, and became

44. *Rawalpindi* which has served as Pakistan's capital pending completion of Islamabad, a new city lying between Rawalpindi and the Murree Hills seen in the background. Note the numerous horse drawn 'tongas' which serve as the average man's taxicab, and also may turn to load-carrying. Small shops, stalls, and a cinema surround the junction. The twin white minarets of a mosque can be seen in the centre. A sunny afternoon in the cool season.

capital of West Pakistan: Peshawar was capital of the Northwest Frontier Province; Karachi, developed as a port for the regions of canal colonisation in the Punjab and Sind, became capital of the latter province and later of the new Pakistan state. In addition, there were historic cities such as Hyderabad (once capital of Sind) and Multan. Other towns developed in the twentieth century with the canal settlement of the Punjab Plain and Sind – a feature quite absent from East Pakistan. Thus, for example, Lyallpur, Montgomery, Sarghoda, Jhang, Sukkur, and Mirpur Khas owe their present importance to the transformation of their regions by modern irrigation.

All in all, the distribution of urban centres in West Pakistan reflects that of population generally, which in turn is closely linked to agricultural development. Most cities lie in the Punjab Plains (14 out of 23) Rawalpindi in the Potwar Plateau, Peshawar and Mardan in the Vale of Peshawar, and Kohat in its basin, form a second group in the better watered north. Sukkur, Hyderabad, and Mirpur Khas form a southern group based on Lower Indus irrigation. The remaining two are Quetta, a strategic town commanding the Bolan Pass route from the Baluchistan Plateau to the Indus Plains, and Karachi, port, commercial capital, and till recently the national capital.

Of the nine urban centres of East Pakistan, seven have long been district headquarter towns. Saidpur, a railway town in Rangpur District, and Narayanganj the jute handling centre a dozen miles south of Dacca are the only non-administrative towns with over 50,000 persons. The towns which stand apart from the rest by reason of their size are those which have benefited most from the wing's fast growing economic activity: Dacca as capital of East Pakistan has developed as its most important industrial centre; Chittagong and Khulna (the latter with its developing outport of Chalna) are rivals for the export traffic in jute, and are themselves thriving industrial towns. Chittagong handles the tea trade, being the terminus of the metre gauge railway system which links it with the Sylhet tea garden belt as well as with Dacca. Khulna the terminus of the broad gauge railway system which runs through the country west of the Jamuna–Padma is also accessible by river-steamer traffic from Dacca.

Finally, although it has a long way to go to reach the population status of the cities listed above, mention must be made of Islamabad the new capital city designed by Doxiades. Islamabad lies a few miles from Rawalpindi at the foot of the mountains, which rise steeply to nearly 3000 ft. above the site. As Islamabad expands it will probably link up physically with Rawalpindi to form a large specialised administrative quarter in a single city.

CHAPTER FIVE

CEYLON

1. CEYLON: THE HERITAGE OF THE PAST*

The island state of Ceylon has been beset by many problems since obtaining its independence within the British Commonwealth in 1948. It was probably in Ceylon that the demographic impact of the insecticide D.D.T. as a killer of the malaria-bearing *anopholes* mosquito became first apparent. Prior to 1947 the population of Ceylon had been increasing at the relatively moderate rate of 1·6 per cent per annum. Immediately following World War II an extensive scheme of spraying with D.D.T. was undertaken, which, along with other measures to improve health, led to a rapid reduction of the death-rate, and so to an upsurge in the rate of population increase. Over the ten-year period, 1953–63, the population increased by 31·2 per cent, bringing the total to 10,624,507 at the 1963 census. The birth-rate remains high though it has fallen from 38·7 per 1000 in 1953 to 35·5 in 1962. The death-rate has been falling also, from 10·7 per 1000 in 1953 to 8·0 in 1961 and 8·5 in 1962.

This rapidly expanding population is in itself a major problem for Ceylon, aggravated on the one hand by a relative lack of developable physical resources, and on the other by political tensions and instability which militate against effective internal economic advancement. The tensions stem in part

_____

* Principal sources for this and the following chapter are:
Farmer, B. H., 'Ceylon', in Spate, O. H. K. and Learmonth A. T. A., *India and Pakistan*, (London, 1967).
ibid., *Pioneer Peasant Colonization in Ceylon* (London, 1957).
ibid., *Ceylon, a Divided Nation* (London, 1963).
Ludowyk, E. F. C., *The Story of Ceylon* (London, 1962).
Cook, E. K. (revised Kularatnam, K.), *Ceylon: Geography, Resources and People* (London, 1953).
International Bank for Reconstruction and Development, *Economic Development of Ceylon* (Colombo, 1952).
De Silva, S. F., *Regional Geography of Ceylon* (Colombo, 1954).

from the complicated cultural make-up of the population. There are problems too, arising from Ceylon's external relations. Although following an avowedly neutralist line in her foreign policies, Ceylon's internal and external economic affairs have sometimes shown strong leftist tendencies, which have perhaps been at the same time an embarrassment and a spur to the Western nations, particularly the U.S.A., seeking to help her advance economically, and an encouragement to countries of the Communist bloc seeking to align Ceylon more definitely with themselves.

Before one can begin to understand the present-day geography of Ceylon, it is necessary to appreciate the various phases in man's occupation of the island, and how through past ages the physical environment interacted with man's aspirations. As is the case with every nation, there are features of Ceylon's distant past which seem to permeate strongly into its present national consciousness, and perhaps even to bias judgements in favour of following lines of development which might resuscitate memories of past glories long forgotten. This study cannot attempt to examine every facet of the complicated 'human' environment of Ceylon, but will seek to explain the more significant aspects of its modern human geography.

The People

The origins of the people of Ceylon are somewhat obscure. The earliest inhabitants were probably the ancestors of the present Veddahs, a relatively primitive group now numbering about 6000, few of whom are however pure-blooded. The Veddahs are gradually losing their identity by physical and cultural absorption into the Sinhalese population, which latter group constitutes about two-thirds of the population of Ceylon today. Anthropologists find affinities between the Veddahs and some hill tribes of Peninsular India and it is probable that, like the latter, they were in part absorbed and in part driven into the less attractive highlands by invading peoples. As a separate ethnic entity, the Veddahs can be said already to have disappeared.

Apart from the Veddahs, there are two distinctive cultural groups forming the bulk of the population, and which may owe their origins to separate – but if so probably closely related – racial strains, but whose physical identity might well be impossible to establish clearly today. The role of migration in the genesis of the Sinhalese people, the larger of the two groups, is uncertain, but it cannot be discounted that they may have entered Ceylon from India at an early date. Possibly through continued contact with their homeland, they received Buddhist missionaries sent by Asoka, ruler of northern India in the third century B.C. Thus the Sinhalese acquired their Buddhist religion and its associated Aryan language of Pali with its Brahmi script. The Sinhalese language as it has since developed has been much modified by the fusion of Dravidian linguistic elements, derived from the other major group in Ceylon, the Tamils.

The Sinhalese established an advanced civilisation in northern Ceylon during the first millenium of the Christian era. Close proximity to the Tamil country of Southern India ensured some degree of cultural contact and physical mixture, probably from the very earliest days. It was customary for Sinhalese kings to seek brides from Southern India. Ludowyk suggests that for several centuries after the introduction of Buddhism into Ceylon 'over large tracts of the northern plain Tamil and Sinhalese must have been indistinguishable from each other. In these years there were Tamil rulers who had been patrons of Buddhism, then flourishing in South India. (Hindu) Brahmins were officials in the court of Sinhala kings, and the gods of the Hindu pantheon were respected by Hindu and Buddhist alike.'* These idyllic conditions must have been strained and ultimately shattered by the more aggressive turn taken in Tamil relations with Ceylon from about the tenth century A.D. As so often today the threat of political and economic competition

between differing cultural groups led to the exaggeration of their differences and the more fierce 'protection' of their respective cultural badges, of language, religion, and social custom. From this early phase of Ceylon's history derives the continuing mutual antipathy of Sinhalese and Tamil: the Sinhalese, with his Buddhism coloured by fervent nationalism, views the Tamil as the political and economic aggressor from overseas. Prejudices built up over a millenium cannot be expected to disperse overnight.

The early Sinhalese colonists of Ceylon were attracted to the drier parts of the island. The principal focus of settlement was the north-central lowlands, where the Buddhist kingdom of Rajarata was established by the third century B.C., and from which Buddhism probably spread to other 'kingdoms' such as Ruhuna in the southeast and to parts of the lowland west (Fig. 5.1.1). It seems that the 'wet zone' in general, forming the southwest quadrant of the island, and the highlands over 3000 ft. within that zone in particular, was rather neglected by these colonists who perhaps found in the dry zone (as Farmer puts it) 'a region analogous to the part of India from which they came and to which their techniques of agriculture and irrigation were adapted'. Both tank-fed irrigated paddy farming in valley floors and *chena*, a form of shifting cultivation on interfluves, were practised by the Sinhalese. In common with many parts of Asia, agricultural methods have changed surprisingly little in the course of two thousand years.

By the eleventh century A.D. pressures from the Tamil Cholas kingdom on the mainland reached the level of military invasion, and there began a period of progressive 'Tamilisation' of northern Ceylon, as a result of which the Sinhalese were eventually pushed southwards. Thus in A.D. 1017 the south Indian Cholas captured the ancient and glorious Sinhalese capital of Anuradhapura, compelling the Sinhalese to move their capital to Polonnaruwa, fifty miles to the southeast, where there developed a civilisation more strongly influenced by the Dravidian culture of the Tamils. Invasion and migration from India persisted in the twelfth century, resulting in the establishment of a strong Tamil kingdom in northern Ceylon, based on Jaffna. The Tamils were, and are still, mainly Hindu by religion and their language belongs to the Dravidian linguistic family.

---

* Ludowyk, E. F. C., op. cit., p. 58.

FIG. 5.1.1 Ceylon: administrative and historical

These two cultural characteristics have persisted, keeping Tamil and Sinhalese apart throughout the centuries by discouraging intermarriage and minimising close social contact between the groups, whose separateness today remains probably the most potent problem in Ceylonese politics.

By the thirteenth century the old Rajarata kingdom of north-central Ceylon had decayed, and with it many of its splendid feats of irrigation engineering. From this time up to the arrival of the Portuguese early in the sixteenth century, there were three principal political foci in Ceylon: (i) the Tamil kingdom in the far north, centring on the Jaffna Peninsula and separated by a now somewhat desolate and extensive region in the northern third of the island

from (ii) the Kandyan kingdom of Udarata, extending eastwards across the island from the lower hill country in the north of the wet zone, and (iii) the kingdom of Kotte inland and northeast from Colombo on the west coast.

The Country

It is appropriate to pause here to consider what kind of country it was that the Sinhalese and Tamils were striving to colonise, and by what techniques of land exploitation they were able to support themselves. The present-day map of population distribution in Ceylon probably bears very little relationship to the situation that obtained in A.D. 1500 immediately prior to the establishment of European

45. Thuparam Dagaba, Anuradhapura; a typical *Buddhist monument*. In the foreground granite pillars and lintels of an ancient building can be seen.

contacts with the island, and still less to that of A.D. 1000 when the Sinhalese kingdom based on Anuradhapura was at its height. The early Sinhalese colonists, and after them the Tamils, who established their civilisations in the northern half of the island did not occupy the areas which we today would regard as the most favourable to settlement. We can only speculate as to why the better watered southwest quadrant of Ceylon was for so long neglected. In so small an island, measuring very roughly 250 miles by 150, it is unlikely that people in one part remained long in ignorance of conditions in another. A more likely explanation is that the agricultural techniques available to the colonists were found to be adequately effective in supporting within the dry zone the population attained within the first millenium A.D., while the heavy forest cover of the wet zone deterred settlement.

The fundamental limiting factor in Ceylon, as far as agricultural activity is concerned, is rainfall (Fig. 5.1.2). Ceylon lies between 6° and 10° latitude north of the Equator and is exposed to the open ocean on all sides except the northwest, where along for perhaps one-fifth of its circumference its shores may be said to be lapped by the 'enclosed' sea areas of Palk Strait and the Gulf of Manaar. Proximity to the Equator combined with insularity are important influences in the island's climate and make for Ceylon's rather more complex rainfall regimes compared with those of South India.

The southwest monsoon, that most dominant of climatic phenomena throughout western India and the eastern shores of the Bay of Bengal, strikes forcibly against the southwestern coast of Ceylon, bringing heavy rainfall to the coastal lowlands from Negombo through Colombo to beyond Matara, and deluging the western facing hill country in May and June. From July to September the rain-giving force of the monsoon air-stream slackens somewhat as the wind dies down to make way for the doldrum conditions of October to December.* During the months of the southwest monsoon, two-thirds to three-quarters of Ceylon is experiencing its dry season, during which some rainfall occurs, but of an extremely unreliable character.

In common with much of the states of Tamilnadu and Kerala, most of Ceylon enjoys an important rainy season from October to December. This rain has been attributed to what is called the 'retreating monsoon' but, in so far as the word monsoon generally conjures up impressions of strong winds, it may be better to think of this rainfall as coming from unstable air-masses stagnating over Ceylon as it lies temporarily becalmed in the doldrum belt. Crowe's studies of the consistency of the trade wind systems indicate that the northeast monsoon does not firmly establish itself over Ceylon until January, by which time the period of maximum precipitation has passed (see Fig. 2.2.7). In the southwest of the island, most sheltered from the northeast trades, January and February are the months of lowest rainfall, but even so precipitation is far from negligible in quantity and is reasonably reliable (Colombo averages 3½ inches in both of these months).

With the return of doldrum conditions in March and April the relative importance of inter-monsoonal rainfall to many parts of the island is again demonstrated. At several stations in the dry zone

---

* Crowe, P. R., 'The Trade Wind Circulation of the World', *Trans. Inst. Brit. Geographers* (1949), p. 37.
ibid., 'Wind and Weather in the Equatorial Zone', *Trans. Inst. Brit. Geographers* (1951), p. 23.

(e.g. Mannar) there is a secondary maximum in April – the 'little monsoon' – after which monthly totals *decline* as the southwest monsoon sets in in May.

These several factors affecting the rainfall of Ceylon may be seen resolved in Fig. 5.1.2 showing mean annual isohyets. The boundary between wet and dry zones into which Ceylon is conventionally and conveniently divided (Fig. 5.1.1) is seen to enclose in the wet zone all the areas receiving over 75 inches of rain with the exception of the 'bulge' eastwards into the lowland country of Bintenne Division where the rainfall regime contains little of the southwest monsoon element and is therefore more in line with that of the dry zone. The Land Utilisation Map of Ceylon at the scale of four miles to one inch, provides confirmatory evidence for so drawing the wet–dry zone boundary as to include within the wet zone practically all rubber- and tea-growing areas. The wet zone is then a region of generally abundant rainfall, reaching in some highland areas a mean total of over 200 inches per year. Characteristically there are two maxima, the greatest in the southwest monsoon in May–June, and a lesser peak in the doldrum season of October–November. As the run of the annual isohyets suggests, the wet zone gives place rather abruptly northwards and southeastwards to the dry zone. Indeed there is a transitional zone which now and then is invaded by dry zone conditions.

To the traveller from West Pakistan or even from the driest parts of Tamilnadu 'dry' might seem an inappropriate epithet to apply to regions that receive mainly over 50 inches of rain, and only rarely below 40 inches. The driest place in Ceylon – between Puttalam and Mannar on the west coast – receives an average of 34 inches. Only a small area of this northwest coastal strip, together with a fringe of the southeast coast has under 50 inches on average. However, the general tendency for areas of lower rainfall to experience greater variability holds here, and it is the occasionally high annual (or monthly) rainfall that tends to raise the average above the median figure which represents the balance of probability. (Trincomalee, for example, with a mean annual rainfall of 64·8 inches had totals ranging from 95 inches to 34 inches between 1871 and 1920). Flying over or driving through the north-central parts of the dry zone one is struck by the

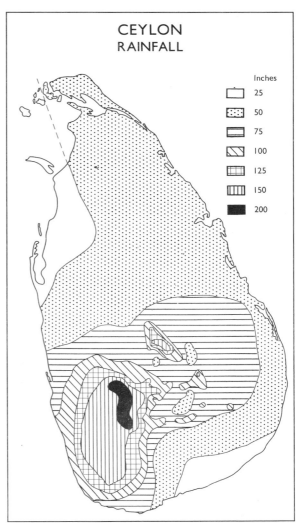

(Isohyets reproduced by permission of Ceylon Meteorological Dept.)

FIG. 5.1.2   Ceylon: rainfall

apparent luxuriance of the woodland vegetation. Trees and shrubs with their deep-root systems are able to withstand periods of drought better than shallower-rooted field crops, and so cannot be taken as an entirely reliable index of the agricultural potentialities of the climate. For agriculture the big problem is the unreliability of a rainfall which from year to year fluctuates about the point which a farmer trying to grow crops (without the added insurance of irrigation) would regard as adequate. This is typical of South Asia's traditional 'famine districts', which lie not where the rainfall is regularly too little for cultivation but where it is usually adequate but may occasionally, or for a run of years be disastrously insufficient.

In the dry belt, rainfall comes mainly from October to December, this wet season being prolonged with January's trade winds particularly on the east coast. The secondary 'little monsoon' rains of April are more marked away from the east coast. June to September, when the southwest monsoon is blowing, are the months of lowest and least reliable rainfall, conditions which are aggravated, as far as crop growth is concerned, by the desiccating effect of the winds.

Rainfall through its influence on the growth of natural vegetation and as a limiting factor in agricultural activity, was the dominant, but not the sole climatic factor affecting man's occupance of the land. Ceylon rises to 8281 ft. in Pidurutalagala and there are twelve peaks exceeding 7000 ft. In the south centre of the island, the highlands rise to over 3000 ft. over a roughly elliptical area measuring fifty miles from east to west by thirty-five miles north to south, and in addition to this continuous upland there are substantial areas northeast of Kandy, east of Badulla, and south of Rakwana, which exceed this altitude. Temperatures in these highlands are, of course, 10° F. and more below those in the surrounding low country, but whether it was the cooler climate, the high rainfall, or the heavy forest cover that discouraged them, the Sinhalese had not settled there, and the region awaited development by British plantation owners in the mid-nineteenth century.

The early colonists of Ceylon were concerned principally with the lowlands, and with the dry zone lowlands at that. Their staple food, rice, was grown in irrigated fields in valley bottoms. In the dry zone tank storage of water was essential to guarantee a paddy crop, while in the wet zone the perennial streams had simply to be diverted to water the fields, and floods rather than drought would have been the problem (as still they are today). Over many centuries the Sinhalese and Tamils built thousands of tanks and some elaborate and finely executed irrigation systems. Tanks, many of them in a state of disrepair, silted up and abandoned, are found throughout the dry zone. The greatest concentration of tanks, and some of the largest, are to be seen in the North Western and North Central Provinces. The Eastern Provinces and the northernmost part of Uva Province have relatively few tanks, but they are concentrated again in the southwest of

Uva in what must have been a most populous district of the ancient Ruhuna kingdom. A few large tanks are in the nature of barrages in the upper and middle reaches of fair-sized rivers, such as the Kala Oya (Kala Wewa Tank), Malwatu Oya (Nachchaduwe Tank); some, like the Giant's Tank and many small storage systems in Mannar District, derive their water from rivers by means of diversion weirs; but the vast majority are small storage reservoirs tapping minor catchment areas in the tributary valleys of the major rivers. In the Jaffna Peninsula the low relief, lacking surface streams, does not lend itself to tank construction. There are ponds but the larger water bodies are saline and the Jaffna Tamils still sink wells for their drinking-water supply, while relying on rain for rice growing. Supplementary to paddy farming (and in a few areas independent of it) the early Ceylonese, like their modern counterparts, utilised interfluve areas for *chena* (shifting) cultivation, growing dry crops such as millets and oilseeds. Round their homesteads they no doubt cultivated – as is the practice today – fruit, spices, and vegetable gardens, but their economy was one of local self-sufficiency. What trade there was had little direct effect on the peasant. The export of gemstones, pearls, and elephants through Arab and Chinese traders helped enrich the king and his officials in the capital, but, to quote Ludowyk, 'the kingdom's prosperity was based on the prosperity of its rice fields'. Ludowyk suggests that the kingdoms stagnated through the progressive imposition on the cultivator, whose techniques did not develop, of too great a burden of supporting the State and the religion.

Irrigation schemes on the scale developed in the north-central lowlands by the twelfth century A.D. depended for their continued success on an efficient and centralised administration. The proper maintenance of tank bunds, weirs, and canals would have been beyond the means of simple villagers. In the wet zone, however, where paddy-fields can be watered by diverting streams and impounding rainfall, there would be no such complex administrative problems. The centuries of political disintegration which followed the relative stability of the Anuradhapura (250 B.C.–A.D. 1029) and Polonnaruwa (A.D. 1111–1215) periods saw the decay of many of the irrigation schemes and the impoverishment and probably the partial depopulation of what is now the North Central Province. From what must have been a quite highly centralised and unified island state, Ceylon (as mentioned above) lapsed into three weaker kingdoms and an unnumbered array of 'warlordships' under local leaders. It is perhaps significant that the three kingdoms were based on areas where subsistence agriculture could be pursued without State initiative or control: Jaffna had its wells and rain-fed paddies, the kingdoms of Kotte and Kandy (Udarata) lay mainly in the wet zone.

For perhaps three centuries there was little change in the situation in Ceylon, but in 1505 a new factor appeared on the scene. Up to this time Ceylon's overseas contacts had been primarily Asian – Arabs, Moslem Indians, Malays probably and Chinese had used the island as an entrepôt, conveniently sited midway between the Red Sea and the Persian Gulf, gateways to European trade, and the Straits of Malacca leading to China's sphere of trading influence. With the sixteenth century Europe ceased to be content to leave this profitable commerce in Asian (especially Arab) hands, and following exploratory voyages in the late fifteenth century, the Portuguese were quick to establish a chain of trading centres around the shores of the Indian Ocean. Their acquisition of Colombo in 1505 must be viewed in the wider context of other bases in Ormuz, Diu, Goa, Cochin, Madras, Hooghly, Chittagong, Bassein, and elsewhere, which formed the foundation of one hundred years of trading monopoly. The arrival of the Portuguese to trade in the high grade wild cinnamon that flourished in the west coastal lowlands, saw the beginnings of that commercial agricultural economy that was to reach its culmination in the nineteenth century. The cinnamon trade which predated the Portuguese in Ceylon probably brought to the fore a sociological phenomenon which is only now beginning to weaken in the face of economic necessity. Cinnamon grew wild on the royal estates, and a labour force had to be found to peel the cinnamon twigs to obtain the commercially valuable bark. The Sinhalese Buddhist of whatever social level, while willing enough to labour on the land for himself and his family, has always regarded toil for another as distasteful. Whether or not this was the major reason, from the fourteenth and fifteenth centuries South Indian labourers had been imported to peel cinnamon, and

these opposite attitudes to paid employment formed yet another element in the Sinhalese–Tamil problem.*

A continuing feature of the political geography of Ceylon from the medieval period up till 1815 was the independence of the Sinhalese kingdom based upon Kandy. The Portuguese failed to establish unified political control over Ceylon, though they set up fortified ports in Jaffna and Galle in addition to Colombo, and effectively dominated trade. By the early seventeenth century European trade rivalry showed itself in Ceylon, when the Dutch treated with the Kandyan king on how to rid the island of Portuguese! By 1640 the Dutch were in Galle, by 1656 in Colombo and in Jaffna by 1658. Furthermore they built forts on the east coast at Trincomalee and Batticaloa in their efforts to monopolise the trade of the Indian Ocean. With the Dutch came (as in the East Indies) the embryonic plantation system. Cinnamon gardens were planted and with areca nuts dominated trade; pepper and coffee trees were introduced; coconut planting increased; and commercially valuable field crops such as sugarcane and tobacco were encouraged. Under the Dutch, the idea of commercial plantation agriculture blossomed with their Sinhalese official class, the Mudaliyars, becoming wealthy land-holders in the process. The problem of feeding a partly non-subsistent agricultural population made itself apparent. Rice had to be imported from India, and slave-labour was introduced from Tanjore (Southern India) in an effort to reclaim some of the land which had been lost to paddy cultivation during the Portuguese period.

By the end of the eighteenth century the effect of many decades of commercial activity and peace could be seen in the prosperity of the west coastal lowlands, though the Kandyan kingdom remained relatively poor and backward with a traditional economy.

The events which led to the Dutch abandoning their possessions in Malaya were paralleled in Ceylon. The English, strongly established in Madras, were at war with France at the end of the eighteenth century and intense rivalry for the naval bases essential to trading nations existed between them in the Indian Ocean. Trincomalee first attracted the

---

* Ludowyk, E. F. C., op. cit., p. 195.

attention of the English, who after losing it to the French regained control and returned it to the Dutch in 1784. With the overrunning of Holland by the French, England (in the form of the Madras Presidency of the East India Company) stepped in as a 'caretaker' of Dutch interests in Ceylon, as in Malaya and the East Indies, and remained in possession thereafter. Ceylon became a crown colony in 1802, and thus began the last volume of the trilogy of domination by a European power.

Ludowyk describes the British accomplishment in Ceylon as a modernisation of the structure laid down by the Dutch. Against the wishes of the home authorities the Governor in Ceylon proceeded to 'tidy up' the political situation by bringing to an end the independent existence of the Kandyan kingdom. By building roads as a means to political control the economic possibilities of the interior of the island could begin to be realised. British colonial rule heralded a new era of plantation development, in which the mixed economy of wild cinnamon collecting and the cultivation of export tree-crops such as coffee, pepper, and coconuts alongside traditional subsistence agriculture gave place to a more specialised and commercial economy for much of the wet zone. Coffee was the prop of the new economy and was grown on Ceylonese smallholdings as well as European-owned estates. Booming in the 1840s it reached a peak of exports in 1875 (856,570 cwt. from 250,000 acres) but was hit by blight which ruined most of the trees in the late 1870's and brought production down to less than 180,000 cwt. by 1886. Botanists had long been active, however, and were ready first with cinchona and then tea to replace coffee and so enable the whole complex structure of the economy, including roads, railways, and ports, to continue in use. Tea planting, begun commercially in 1867, went ahead apace on both lowland plateaus and in the high country, where (from 1840 with the passing of the Crown Lands Encroachment Ordinance) much land was alienated to British private ownership, in some cases certainly depriving the Kandyan villagers of their traditional common woodland – in which they could pasture animals, cultivate *chenas* and, when population pressure compelled, build and cultivate paddy terraces. Rubber joined tea towards the end of the century to compete for the lower hill country and to add to the demand for plantation labour. Unlike

tea and rubber, the coffee harvest is seasonal and temporary labour was generally recruited in South India to work under extremely poor and unhealthy conditions. For tea a more permanent work force was needed and, since the Sinhalese prejudice against wage labouring was still strong, the planters had to create villages of Indian Tamils on their estates. These 'Indian Tamil' immigrants, separated by a thousand years of history from the 'Ceylon Tamils' of Jaffna, are even more distinct than the latter, from their Sinhalese neighbours. For four generations now they have lived on their estates remote from their ancestral homeland yet largely out of contact with Ceylon. Under an Agreement with India, 525,000 Tamils are to be repatriated (with their assets) over a period of 15 years, and 300,000 allowed to apply for Ceylonese citizenship.

In the overseas trade of Ceylon, tea and rubber have held dominant positions since World War I, but in worthy third place has stood another tree crop, coconuts. Of greater seniority than tea or rubber in Ceylon's economic history, coconut growing is mainly the preserve of Sinhalese estate owners and smallholders, and is extensively grown in the sandier coastal lowlands, especially northwards from Colombo to Chilaw and Puttalam. Profits in coconut plantations have never compared with those to be gained in tea or rubber, with the result that European interest therein has been slight.

Soon after the end of World War II came the end of British colonial rule and Ceylon achieved once more the state of unified independence that history suggests may have been hers a millennium ago. Independence has brought little change in the economy which is still tied to the fluctuating fortunes of plantation commodities on a world market. The rapid upsurge in population numbers underlies the urgency of solving problems whose existence has long been realised.

Not least among Ceylon's problems is that of welding into a national unity the several more or less distinct communities. The population strength of the various groups is shown in Table 5.1.1 below.

The Low Country Sinhalese dominate in the districts of the southeast and southwest coastal belts where they everywhere exceed three-quarters of the population. Kandyan Sinhalese make up from half to three-quarters of the population in all the central, non-coastal districts with the exception of Nuwara

Eliya where Indian Tamils are in a majority. The latter group form a substantial proportion of the total in the other important tea-planting districts of Badulla and Kandy. Ceylon Tamils form a relatively small fraction of the population in all districts outside Jaffna (where they are overwhelmingly predominant) and the west coast. The Ceylon Moors are concentrated in the coastal fishing settlement of the west and east coasts of the dry zone.

TABLE 5.1.1

Population by Communities

Community		1963 (thousands)	Per cent
Low Country Sinhalese	4473 42·2% ⎫	7520	71
Kandyan Sinhalese	3047 28·8% ⎭		
Ceylon Tamils		1170	11
Indian Tamils		1121	10·6
Ceylon Moors		622	6·3
Indian Moors		27	0·3
Burghers and Eurasians		46	0·4
Malays		24	0·2
Others (including Veddahs, Europeans, etc.)	20		0·2

(Source: *Statistical Pocket Book of Ceylon*, 1966.)

2: CEYLON: REGIONAL VARIETY

Geologically Ceylon is a fragment of the ancient block of Peninsular India. About nine-tenths of its area is underlaid by Archaean metamorphic and crystalline igneous rocks: the Khondalite series of metamorphosed quartzites, schists, and limestones, granites, and gneisses. The significance of these formations lies rather in the 'grain' their structures impart to the relief and drainage patterns of the country, than in their mineral constitution, though mention should be made of the gemstones found in alluvial deposits derived from the Khondalites, and of graphite which represents Ceylon's only substantial mineral export. Sedimentary rocks are found only along the northwest coast. Two insignificant patches of Gondwana (Jurassic) sandstones east and south of Putallam, are followed along the coast northwards from Kalpitaya (Puttalam Lagoon) by a ten- to twenty-mile-wide strip of Miocene limestones which reach their greatest development in Jaffna. Here the limestone is a valuable aquifer in a riverless region, and enables Jaffna to support an amazingly dense population. It also forms the basis for a small cement industry at Kankesanturai. Pleistocene 'plateau deposits' overlying impermeable Archaean rocks on interfluves in the northwest, and recent sand-dunes on the west coast (north of Colombo), and along the east coast, have some value as local aquifers. Some of the coastal sands north of Trincomalee and south of Batticoloa may have an economic future as a source of ilmenite. The sandy coastal belts are important for their agricultural qualities, often giving rise to a narrowly defined belt of coconut or palmyra farms.

In common with Southern India the most extensive physiographic element is the dissected plateau.

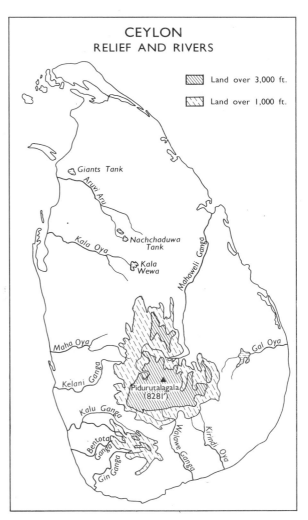

FIG. 5.2.1 Ceylon: relief and rivers

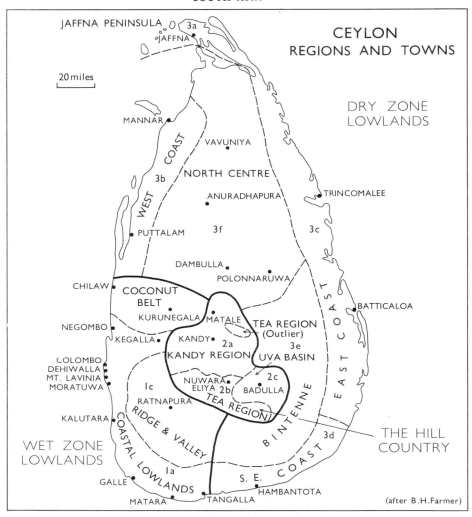

FIG. 5.2.2 Ceylon: regions and towns

Tertiary block movements may have dislocated and differentially raised parts of the highlands, while changes in the relative levels of land and sea have had important effects in the lowlands. As in other coastal areas of South Asia, there is a characteristic association of geomorphological 'sites'. Multiple sandbars enclosing shallow saline lagoons into which the rivers empty through tidal marshes are common round Ceylon and indicate relatively recent but slight submergence of the coast. Rivers are still actively consolidating their floodplains and extending them into the lagoons, but a little way inland the evidence of uplifted eroded surfaces multiplies and one finds, as in Kerala or the Chittagong coast, raised platform or benchlands generally carrying a leached red soil standing a little above the modern floodplain. These platforms represent the lowest series of erosion surfaces which constitute much of the land surface of Ceylon, and into which the drainage is more or less incised. As one would expect in a humid tropical climate, dissection has been generally intense.

The rivers of Ceylon (Fig. 5.2.1) although short, have complex long profiles, steep in their upper reaches but flattening prematurely in their middle and lower reaches to form often marshy floodplains. Despite their shortness, the rivers have a bad reputation for flooding, as might be anticipated from their flattened long profiles. Extremes of variability of flow are characteristic of all the rivers, and many hat rise mainly in the dry zone, may dry up completely for a season. The Mahaweli Ganga is the only major river flowing through the dry zone which has an appreciable watershed within the wet zone; yet at Peradeniya close to Kandy, before it leaves the wet zone, its peak discharge of 180,000 cusec contrasts with an average flow of 2421 cusec. Unfortunately this perennial river has a poor development of floodplain, and is thus of only limited value for irrigation. The contrast in a mainly dry zone river, the Aruvi Aru, in north-central Ceylon, is between a maximum of 150,000 cusecs and an average of only 699 cusecs at Tekkam Anicut, less than twenty miles from the river's mouth. Rivers rising in the wet zone and flowing to the southwest lowlands have a superabundance of water. Here flood protection is needed in several areas to render the floodplains cultivable. The generally radial pattern of drainage combined with its incised nature makes it excessively expensive to attempt any major artificial readjustment in Ceylon's hydrology by transferring surplus flow from wet zone to dry. So far schemes – such as on the Gal Oya – are limited to controlling water within a single catchment. It may be reiterated that the ancient irrigation schemes of the north-central plains were not based on diversion of perennial rivers but on storage tanks holding back floodwaters in dry zone rivers.

The Regions of Ceylon (Fig. 5.2.2)

Man's mode of utilisation of the natural environment in Ceylon has obviously been most strongly influenced by rainfall, and the primary regional division of the island must be into wet and dry zones. Cutting across this otherwise simple division is the complicating factor of altitude with its indirect effect upon present-day land use. Whether deterred by cold or merely lacking inducement the Kandyan Sinhalese did not settle in the hill country over 2500 ft, thus leaving it available for plantation development in the nineteenth century. In some areas, e.g. around Kandy itself, the relief is so varied that high level tea gardens and low level paddy-fields on the sides and floors of the valleys are closely juxtaposed, and whatever regional boundary is drawn will incorporate in any one region quite distinct cultures and modes of land use. These two cultural traits persist into the eastern lobe of high country, the Uva Basin, which strictly speaking lies

outside the wet zone as defined above so that in this sector the human factors must be allowed to predominate over the climatic in determining the regional boundary. Similarly in the 'ridge and valley' subregion of the southwest lowland zone, an area extensively over 1000 ft, and in places over 3000 ft. high, the predominance of *lowland* forms of subsistence combined with the presence of non-Kandyan Sinhalese sways the balance in favour of grouping the area with the lowlands.

Enough has been said to warn the reader that regions cannot be defined with scientific precision, and the attempt to differentiate and describe regions must always be regarded as a means to obtaining a better understanding of the geography of an area rather than as an end in itself. Following Farmer, we have three major regions, each subdivisible into smaller areal units:

(1) The wet zone lowlands
    (a) Southwest coastal lowlands
    (b) Coconut belt
    (c) Ridge and valley country
(2) The hill country
    (a) Kandy region
    (b) Tea region
    (c) Uva Basin
(3) The lowland dry zone
    (a) Jaffna Peninsula
    (b) West coast
    (c) East coast
    (d) Southeast coast: Hambantota
    (e) Bintenne
    (f) North centre

The Wet Zone Lowlands

The wet zone lowlands contain about 60 per cent of Ceylon's population, 75 per cent of the total 'urban' population, and 17 of the 29 municipalities and urban council areas with over 10,000 population (1953). District population densities (in 1963) everywhere exceed the country's average of 419 per square mile, and in the four coastal districts from Colombo south to Matara densities do not fall below 988 per square mile (Fig. 5.2.3). Only in the 'transitional' districts of Kurunegala (464 per square mile) half of which lies outside the wet zone proper, and Ratnapura (438 per square mile) the rugged 'ridge and valley' subregion mentioned above, do overall den-

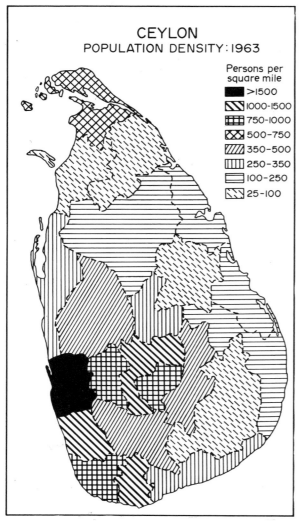

FIG. 5.2.3   Ceylon: population

sities approach the average, and these figures mask some very abrupt contrasts in land use within large districts.

Nowhere in the wet zone lowlands can one find extensive areas of homogeneity. The repeating patterns of physiographic and human geographical features are drawn to a small scale. The main morphological elements of the landscapes have already been touched on: low plateaus closely dissected and interfingered by the floodplains of many short but occasionally vigorous rivers, with the grain of the Archaean substructure frequently apparent in the alignment of ridges from almost east to west in Ratnapura, to north to south in the northern parts

of the region. The subdivision of the wet zone low lands could be based on the 'proportional represen tation' of these elements. Common to the imme diate coastal zone there are, of course, the add tional features of beach ridges and lagoons.

Farmer's threefold regional subdivision of the we zone lowlands is followed here. From the mai stretch of coastal lowlands he separates a norther subregion, the coconut belt, largely on grounds c land use, while inland of these lies the 'ridge an valley' country.

The **Southwest Coastal Lowlands** (1a on Fig. 5.2.2 extend from Tangalla to Negombo, north of Colom bo. Behind Tangalla and Matara the coastal low land is about fifteen miles wide (e.g. near Galle) bu westwards it narrows in places to barely three mile in width. North of the Bentota Ganga the coasta zone widens progressively from an average of fiftee miles to a maximum of almost thirty miles in th latitude of Negombo.

The agricultural economy of the southwes coastal lowlands is characterised by the importanc and variety of the 'cash' crops raised. Paddy i grown as the subsistence crop in all the valley flood plains, but until recently its cultivation did nc receive as much capital or attention as did the mor profitable 'upland' crops. Flooding is a major draw back to paddy cultivation and in some valleys (e.g Kelani Ganga and Gin Ganga) there is great nee of flood protection works. Paddy relies largely o direct rainfall supplemented by water led from th streams in small channels known as *elas*. Althoug the rainfall is everywhere over 70 inches per annun and is normally well distributed throughout th year, occasional dry spells occur, more often in Jan uary–February but sometimes also in August, whic make the maintenance of the *elas* a worth while in surance. By Asian standards, paddy cultivatio techniques are at a mediocre level. The high propo tion of cloudy days militates against the attainmer of really high yields, but part of the blame must b placed on the field practices which are not intensive Transplantation is exceptional, and pre-germinate seed is broadcast on to the puddled land. Bone mea and fish guano are traditional manures. Much i now being done to extend the use of artificial fert lisers, and to encourage better practices generall with the aim of reducing Ceylon's heavy dependenc on imported paddy for more than one-third of he

6. *Coconut plantation* in the lowland wet zone, Ceylon. Such plantations are generally on a relatively small scale compared to those of tea. They are owned by Ceylonese.

equirements. The main paddy crop is the *maha*, own from August on into mid-October (by which ime rainfall is abundant) and harvested in the relatively dry and sunny months of February and March. The *maha* crop is much more reliable than he *yala* crop, which, sown in April, has to grow throughout the increasingly rainy and cloudy months of the early southwest monsoon to be harvested in July and August when conditions are seldom ideal for ripening, cutting, drying, and storing he grain.

With the exception of patches of unreclaimed swamp (often at the junction of tributary and main river floodplains where the high-water level in the main stream ponds back floodwaters in the lower reaches of the tributary) the one inch survey maps how all low-lying ground to be occupied by paddyields. However, although the paddy lands may run continuously for ten miles at a time in the zone parallel to the coast, linking one lagoon with another, along the river courses the width of alluvial floodplain development seldom exceeds one-third of a mile. Fig. 5.2.4 shows the land-use pattern typical of this region of southwest Ceylon.

The coastal beach ridges and the dissected platforms which form the interfluves between the tongues of paddy-filled floodplains carry an entirely different land-use assemblage, in which tree crops predominate. Here the unit of organisation (and landholding) varies from the tiny homestead gardens, with its mixed tree cover of coconut, jack, mango, and breadfruit, undercropped with plaintains and kitchen spices and vegetables, to the smallholdings and commercial plantations of single crops. The sandy beach ridges where deep subsoil water is apt to be brackish beneath the surface layer of fresher water, carry only coconut groves and homestead gardens. On the benchlands a greater variety of land use is encountered, though there is a degree of local specialisation. Coconut growing extends inland across the full width of the coastal lowlands. Because of the heavy rainfall, sun-drying of copra is less important than elsewhere, and the tree is mainly used for the arrack, toddy, and vinegar that can be produced from its sap, and for coir fibre obtained from the coconut husk. Smallholdings and plantations of rubber occupy wide areas, especially in Kulatara District, and the southeast of Kegalle District. Rubber is found not only on the relatively gentle slopes of the low plateaus but also on the steep hill ridges which interfinger with the lowlands. Lowland tea is grown to a small extent. Both rubber and tea crops prefer ample rainfall, and are mostly grown where precipitation exceeds 125 inches per year. In the south in Matara District citronella grass is a speciality, while small, old, scattered cinnamon gardens (now no match for Javanese exporters) continue to produce between Negombo and Galle.

The southwest coastal lowlands contain Ceylon's

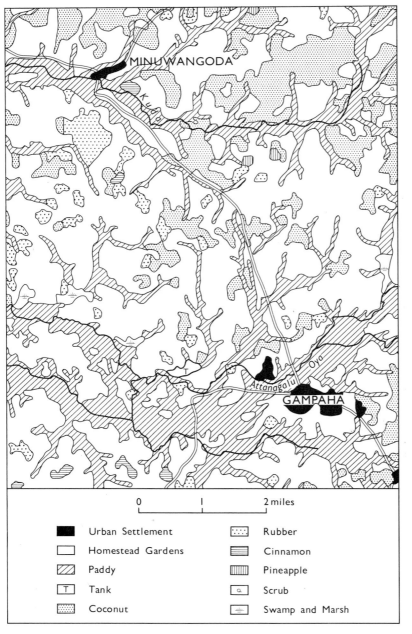

CEYLON
LAND USE : WET ZONE S.W. LOWLANDS

MINUWANGODA

GAMPAHA

Attanagalu Oya

0   1   2 miles

Urban Settlement

Homestead Gardens

Paddy

Tank

Coconut

Rubber

Cinnamon

Pineapple

Scrub

Swamp and Marsh

Fig. 5.2.4
Ceylon: wet zone land-use sample
Based upon a map of the Ceylon
Survey Department with the
sanction of the Surveyor General

Gampaha lies about twenty miles northeast of Colombo. The area shown on the land-use map opposite is a low platform dissected into a rolling landscape by the many flat-floored valleys which may be picked out on the map by their coincidence with wet rice cultivation. The highest parts of the platform reach generally a little over 100 ft. above sea-level, though a rocky hill across the Attanagula Oya from Gampaha reaches 228 ft. The floors of the major rivers lie generally less than 30 ft. above sea-level. Patches of swamp at the junction with the Attanagula Oya of several tributary valleys are due to ponding back of the tributaries by floodwaters in the main river. Settlement is widely dispersed along the many roads which follow spurs. Gampaha, an urban centre, and Minuwangoda in the northwest are the only sizeable concentrations of settlement.

The dominance of two elements in the land-use pattern – paddy in the valley floors and homestead gardens on the interfluves – reflects the high density of settlement. For the rest, land use consists of tree crop cultivation, coconuts, and rubber being widely grown. A few small areas of cinnamon occur, and a similar scatter of pineapple fields.

greatest concentration of towns. Colombo (510, 947), Dehiwela–Mount Lavinia (111,013), and Moratuwa (77,632) are tending to merge into a coastal conurbation stretching south from Colombo while northwards ribbon development links the capital to Negombo (47,026). Other towns of importance are Kalutara (25,286), Galle (64,942), and Matara (32,284).

The **Coconut Belt** (1*b*) lies in the triangular area between Negombo and Chilaw, twenty-five miles apart on the coast, and Kurunegala almost forty miles inland. Quite abruptly, north of the latitude of Chilaw, one enters the dry zone, and it is the liability of the whole area to occasional spells of dry zone conditions that has allowed the coconut to remain unchallenged as a cash crop. The coastal lowland is wider here than to the south, but the alluvial floodplain element, with its paddy-fields, is rather less extensively developed. The low hill country dominates, giving way to more rocky outcrops towards the east. For ten miles inland from the coast, strips of paddy land provide almost the only break in coconut's monopoly, but further inland again one finds a more varied assemblage of coconut groves, paddy-fields, and homestead gardens. This region of transition between wet and dry zones has a less cloudy climate than the more southerly coastlands, and consequently coconut is grown here for its oil, since the copra can be sun-dried before pressing. Most of the production is from smallholdings, practically all of them Ceylonese owned, and the region indeed suffers economically from over-reliance on this single saleable commodity.

On the population map (Fig. 5.2.3) the coastal section of the coconut belt is shown with a lower density than it merits, owing to the regrouping of Chilaw District with the dry zone coastal district of Puttalam. At the 1953 census Chilaw had a population density of 649 per square mile while that of Puttalam was only 65. The 1963 density of the combined district was 258.

The **Ridge-and-Valley Country** (1*c*) is transitional in

another sense. It lacks the coastal morphological features that with the coconut–paddy crop association give some unity to the rest of the wet zone lowlands, but its very characteristic relief and its generally low altitude resulting in rather different development in human and economic terms set it aside from the hill country proper. Only a small part of the subregion rises to over 3000 ft., but what it lacks in absolute altitude it makes up in ruggedness. In a characteristic transect due east of Ratnapura, in a distance of twenty-three miles, eight ridges are crossed at heights ranging between 1500 ft. and 2700 ft., with intervening valleys at 200 ft. to 1200 ft., giving a vertical relief ranging from 600 ft. to 2350

47. Hillsides are *terraced for wet paddy cultivation* in the wet zone in Ceylon, and in several areas of India, notably in the Middle Himalaya. Terrace systems such as this represent an immense investment in labour over generations. View from the Kandy-Colombo railway.

ft. This indicates the difficulties of access into the southern part of the ridge and valley region, much of which remains undeveloped at the present time, though some colonisation is now taking place from the coastal flank. But for a few insignificant areas of smallholders' rubber, tea, and cinnamon, the hill slopes are covered in forest and scrub, while the narrow valley bottoms are beaded with paddy lands.

The relatively high population density of Ratnapura District (438 persons per square mile) is attributable to the easier communications along the valleys of the upper Kalu Ganga system and the southern tributaries of the Kelani Ganga. Although paddy occupies a considerable acreage in the valleys, rubber dominates the economy, with tea becoming more important in the higher (and slightly drier) east, e.g. round Balangoda. Agricultural possibilities were not, however, the only attraction in Ratnapura District. This has for long been the centre of the mining of gemstones which are found in alluvial gravels. Elsewhere this subregion is rather sparsely peopled. Between Ratnapura and the coastal lowlands behind Galle, population densities of under 100 are found over considerable areas, and around Morawaka the density is below 50 persons per square mile.

The Hill Country

Its higher parts for so long neglected, and its lower regions at first places of refuge for Sinhalese and Veddahs retreating from the dry belt, the hill country has become the cornerstone of Ceylon's economy.

After the southwest coastal lowlands and the coconut belt, the hill country contains the most closely settled districts of Ceylon: Kandy with 1150 to the square mile, Nuwara Eliya with 857. The region supports about 20 per cent of the country's population. Most of the Indian Tamils are found here, and they make up more than half the population of Nuwara Eliya District and about one-third of Kandy and Badulla districts.

The hill country may conveniently be divided into three regions: the Kandy region, the Tea region, and the Uva Basin.

The **Kandy Region** (2a) is largely the basin of the Mahaweli Ganga. The country is deeply dissected, the relief often amounting to 2000 ft. or more between valley bottom and ridge top. The grain of the country runs roughly northwest to southeast. The district has been long settled by Sinhalese who terrace the slopes for paddy cultivation and utilise the jungle for grazing and timber supply. Cultivation is fairly intensive and the yield of paddy, 52·9 bushels (*maha*), 44·2 bushels (*yala*) per acre, is well above the average for the country (37·8 bushels maha, 38 bushels yala). Small hilly gardens of tea and rubber interfinger with the paddy lands which are concentrated on the lower slopes and valley bottoms. Northwards towards the dry zone where the hill country enters the Matale District, cocoa growing is of some importance. Larger tea estates are also significant in the region, their population

accounting for almost one-third of the total for Kandy District. It is here that the invasion of Sinhalese lands by foreign tea-planting companies and their Indian Tamil labour force gives most cause for intercommunal resentment, since the two groups often have to co-exist in close proximity, and the tea gardens sometimes occupy lands regarded by the Sinhalese as their own.

In many respects the Kandy region may be looked upon as one of transition between the higher hill country to the south and the lowlands of Kegalla District to the west and southwest. Southwards Kandy District rises and tea gardens begin to dominate. Kandy itself with a population of 67,768 (1963) is the religious centre of the Sinhalese Buddhists and the former capital of the last Sinhalese kingdom. Near by at Peradeniya is the University of Ceylon and the famous Royal Botanic Gardens. A little to the northeast of Kandy is a small area which Farmer isolates as an outlier of the tea region.

The **Tea Region** (2b) is physiographically a continuation of the Kandy region but rises much higher, with extensive areas exceeding 5000 ft. The deeply cut valleys in the heart of the highest parts of the hill country may be as much as 3000 ft. below the ridge levels. The high rainfall of over 100 inches per annum supports rain forest but the latter has been extensively cleared for tea estates. The population is almost wholly non-indigenous with Indian Tamils in the majority; 63 per cent of the population are recorded as estate population. Tea is the backbone of the economy of Ceylon and comes mainly from this country. In recent years two-thirds of the value of Ceylon's export trade was due to tea. The high rainfall and relief suggest some potential hydro-electric power which may eventually be developed, though output will never be spectacular and is likely to be expensive owing to the wide seasonal variation in the flow of all monsoonal rivers. Communications, although difficult on account of the steep slopes, are more highly developed than almost anywhere in Ceylon. A railway penetrates the heart of the hill country reaching a height of about 6250 ft. Nuwara Eliya (population 19,988) stands at over 6000 ft.

The **Uva Basin** (2c) is a truly transitional region. It has some characteristics of the Kandy region being an historic area of Sinhalese cultural development. It contains some high tea gardens and is thus economically associated with the tea region. At the same time it belongs climatically to the dry zone (albeit the wettest part) with rainfall generally close to 75 inches: Badulla receives 72 inches on average. Rice farming, using irrigation water derived from ancient tank systems is important. The population density of Badulla District is 491 per square mile.

The Lowland Dry Zone

The lowland dry zone comprises two-thirds of Ceylon by area but contains perhaps only 20 per cent of the population. Densities are generally low with the outstanding exception of Jaffna District with a density of 614 per square mile, locally over 1000. Otherwise densities are generally less than 50 to the square mile with a few small patches of closer settlement particularly on the fringes of the wet zone and in places on the Batticaloa coast. On the land-use map the dry zone (without Jaffna) stands out as an area mainly lacking in cultivation, in marked contrast with the variegated cultivation of the wet zone. Rice farming is patchy; coconut groves are restricted to the coastal belts for the most part and much of the region stands apparently empty though a good deal of it may be used for chena cultivation where it is not set aside as forest reserve. The widespread relics of old tank systems and the efforts now being made to colonise the dry zone suggest a potential yet to be fully developed. The total scope for settlement is finite however, and the people of Ceylon have to guard against being over-optimistic about the dry zone's capacity to absorb settlers.

The lowland dry zone falls into six subregions of very unequal importance. The Jaffna Peninsula stands apart as a region of highly individual character. A threefold division of the coastal belt into west, east, and southeast is in some degree arbitrary. There remain then the heart of the dry zone – the north centre of Ceylon, and the Bintenne region adjoining the hill country on its southeast.

Jaffna Peninsula (3a). Lacking rivers and suffering a long season of drought Jaffna supports its prosperous and intensive agriculture – in some respects more properly termed horticulture – by great numbers of wells sunk in the Miocene limestone. Pumps and hand watering are used to irrigate the fields which man has made fertile by adding leaf mould and by penning livestock on the stubble and fallow weeds. The agricultural scene is an epitome of conditions in Tamilnadu: dry fields above the reach of water, carry millets or yams; low ground with grey soils is bunded to hold water for paddy cultivation during the rains and vegetable patches where water can be brought in the dry season, while red soils served by wells are used for multistoreyed garden crops – paddy, tobacco, yams, and chillies as ground crops, plantains, cassava as an upper storey, with betel vines, grown for their aromatic leaf, as climbers in shade structures.

The Jaffna Tamils are renowned for their diligence. The limitations of their region have encouraged them to migrate to the other parts of Ceylon, notably to Colombo and the east and west coast whence they remit their savings home to Jaffna. Their energy and business acumen are factors unlikely to make them very popular with the more easy-going Sinhalese. With a population of 94,248, the town of Jaffna is Ceylon's second largest after the Colombo conurbation.

The **West Coast** (3b) is the driest region of Ceylon. In contrast to the coast around Colombo, only 100 miles to the south, there is a very marked dry spell during the southwest monsoon, June–September (see data for Mannar, Fig. 2.2.7). It is this acute dry season and the lower rainfall total that distinguishes the climate of the west from that of the east coast. Much of the region has less than 50 inches of rainfall on average. The predominantly sandy soils in places overlying limestone, accentuate the tendency to climatic dryness. It is not surprising that many people here look seawards for a living. Fishing is important (there being a kind of seasonal transhumance practised between this coast and the east). Ceylon 'Moors' called 'seafarers' by the Sinhalese are present in some strength on both west and east coasts. This group, deriving originally from Arab traders, has a history probably longer than their Islamic faith itself, which followed in the wake of maritime settlers around the shores of the Indian Ocean, from East Africa and India to Malaya and Indonesia.

The whole coastal strip is scantily settled, there being only two areas of concentration of population. Around Puttalam Lagoon in the south, coconut groves provide almost the only alternative livelihood to fishing. Further north is Mannar, carrying the ferry service from Talaimannar to

Dhanushkodi on the Indian coast, at the other end of the Adams Bridge string of shoals. The island of Mannar is covered with coconuts, but on the adjacent mainland Giant's Tank (fed by the Aruvi Aru) waters the only extensive development of paddy-fields on the coast. Apart from these two nodes of settlement, the west coast is mostly scrub jungle with few villages served by poor roads.

The **East Coast** (3c) extending from the tenuous sandbars that make Jaffna a peninsula, south to Pottuvil, enjoys a heavier annual rainfall than the west coast and Jaffna, but with a similar regime. Trincomalee, with 6·5 inches has a simple northeast monsoon maximum in December, and a midsummer dry season when the coast lies to leeward of the southwest monsoon (Fig. 2.2.7 and Table 2.2.1). The only break in a rather monotonous coast of sandbar protected lagoons is at Trincomalee where quartzite ridges strike seaward and make possible the protected deep-water harbour, incomparable in Ceylon, but, alas, badly sited for modern economic use. Ceylon's European masters, Dutch and English, made good use of the harbour as a naval base, which came into its own in World War II as a bulwark against the Japanese naval threat to the Indian Ocean, but Trincomalee lacks an adequate hinterland. It is given artificial support by the routing of two-thirds of Ceylon's tea exports through the port.

The east coastlands south to Trincomalee show something of the same patchy development that characterises the west coast. Population is sparse and supported by sporadic areas of paddy and coconuts until Trincomalee (34,872) is reached, and the wider areas of paddy land along the rivers entering the bay. Tobacco is of some importance here. From about fifty miles south of Trincomalee, and thence continuously for some seventy-five miles, settlements with coconut groves line the sandbar coast, paralleled by their paddy lands lying generally on the inland side of the belt of lagoons. The greatest of postwar water-control projects in Ceylon, the Gal Oya scheme, guarantees irrigation to parts of this belt, which stands out as the most densely populated part of the dry zone (apart from Jaffna) with local densities of over 500 per square mile near the mouth of the Gal Oya estuary. Over wide areas however, the east coast has densities of under 25 per square mile, and in no district does the overall density exceed 200.

The **Southeast Coast** (3d): **Hambantota.** South of Pottuvil Bay, and west almost to Tangalla the coastlands, similar in physiography, again become sparsely settled. Rainfall is almost as low as on the west coast, Hambantota having a total of 43·2 inches and the whole district under 50 inches. However the rainfall is more evenly spread throughout the year, and is more reliable than in the west. Great numbers of abandoned tanks indicate closer settlement in former times – this was the core of the Ruhuna kingdom. It is undergoing a process of re-colonisation from the overcrowded wet zone to the west, in which direction it looks rather than towards the neighbouring dry belt regions. The Walawe Ganga (west of Hambantota) and the Kirindi Oya (fifteen miles east of the town) provide water for tanks that command perhaps two score thousand acres of paddy farms. Apart from these two blocks of development, the region is mainly jungle with very few small patches of coconut and tank-watered paddy.

Bintenne (3e) is the name given to the belt of low plateaus (25–40 miles wide, and rising to 3000–4000 ft. generally) that separates the southeast and Batticaloa coastlands from the hill country. It is a singularly empty region today, despite scattered evidence of former tank irrigation. From the level plateaus prominent rocky hills rise abruptly sometimes 1000 ft. The rivers crossing the region have small catchments within the wet zone, and what water can be brought under control can better be used further downstream in the coastal regions where alluvial soils are more extensive. The moderate rainfall – 50 inches in the south, 75 inches in the north – supports jungle in which the widely scattered population eke out a living by 'chena' cultivation, or on a few 'outliers' of the hill country plantations, here mostly rubber. Population densities are generally 25–50 per square mile, in parts lower; Moneragda Dt. has 60 per square mile overall.

North Centre (3f). The remainder of the dry belt, the north-central region, covers the interior of Ceylon north of the hill country and contains at its heart the ancient capitals of Anuradhapura (29,397) and Pollonaruwa. Eradication of malaria, the restoration of some of the old tanks, and a programme of resettlement have brought the region a new lease of life, but the capacity of the region to support a greater agricultural population is problematical.

48. Water buffalo teams *working a wet paddy field*, Anuradhapura. The ancient tank bund is in the background. White egrets are wading in the small fields between.

The small area illustrated in Fig. 5.2.5 is characteristic of much of the dry zone. With a rainfall reasonably reliable for only about four months of the year, rivers which dry up to an insignificant trickle and a shallow subsoil which may dry out down to bedrock, water is the principal but not the only problem. The upland soils are poor in nutrients and fragile in structure, requiring frequent fallowing (three to four years rest after three to four years cropping) to restore productivity, and minimal tillage to preserve the essential crumb structure. In the valley floors commanded by tank irrigation, high productivity is possible since the paddy derives nutrients and moisture from a much wider area than the field in which it grows. A third element in the agricultural landscape is the homestead garden, usually close to the tank bund, whose tree crops are able to reach the water-table (held artificially

high by the existence of the near-by tank) and whose shallow rooted vegetables and spices can be hand-watered from wells sunk to the water-table. (Fig. 5.2.5.)

Traditionally farmers have had access to all three types of land, obtaining their basic support from the irrigated paddy lands and homestead gardens, while supplementing their supplies by practicing rotational *chena* farming, using 'slash and burn' techniques, on the non-irrigated lands to grow millets and oil-seeds (gingelly). A satisfactory solution to the problem of economic permanent farming of the non-irrigated lands has yet to be found. The fragility, susceptibility to erosion by heavy rain or wind, and poverty of the soils makes it doubtful if a solution based on dry farming techniques using fertilisers and drought resistant crops would succeed. The most promising alternative suggested by

49. *Ploughing by a tractor* in Ceylon. In order to mechanise ploughing of wet paddy fields it is necessary to adapt machinery. As is seen here a tractor has to be equipped with extension wheels with steel paddles which will bite into the muddy soil. In place of a plough a form of harrow is used to work the soil deeply.

CEYLON
LAND USE : DRY ZONE

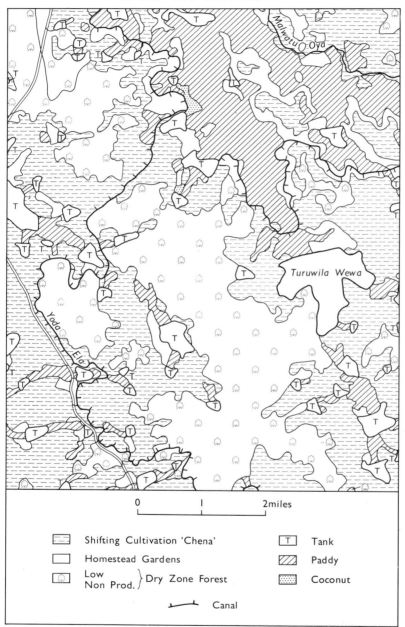

0   l   2miles

Shifting Cultivation 'Chena'   T   Tank

Homestead Gardens   Paddy

Low
Non Prod. } Dry Zone Forest   Coconut

Canal

Turuwila Wewa is a tank lying nine miles south of Anuradhapura in North Central Province. The area is a nearly level plateau averaging about 350 ft. above sea-level, from which occasional small rocky hills rise abruptly, e.g. to 570 ft. There are many tanks upon which the paddy lands depend for irrigation water. The Yoda Ela is an ancient canal, still in use, which derives water from the Kala Oya and leads it to Anuradhapura. The expanse of paddy lying immediately adjacent to the Malwata Oya is watered from Nachchaduwa Tank, one of Ceylon's largest, lying immediately to the east of the area shown on the map. The canal entering the area from the east is the high level channel from this tank and supplements irrigation supplies from Turuwila Tank.

Homestead gardens are almost invariably found adjacent to tanks or paddy. Away from the areas commanded by the tanks or canals much of the area of low interfluves is under dry monsoon forest, generally of very poor potential for timber. Shifting cultivation or *chena* is seen to occupy a considerable area, in most cases lying intermediate between the paddy-homestead garden belts and the forest. This may indicate that *chena* is invading the forest from settled bases where the possiblity for expansion of paddy farming is severely limited.

FIG. 5.2.5
Ceylon: dry zone land-use sample. Based upon a map of the Ceylon Survey Department with the sanction of the Surveyor General.

Dr. E. L. F. Abeyratne, who is responsible for much research into the problem, is the development of animal husbandry, in particular dairying. Grasses and leguminous fodder crops which protect the soil and are capable of increasing fertility could provide feed for cattle who would themselves add valuable manure to the soil. Integrated into the present village agricultural economy such a development could make the most of the upland areas, and at the same time (through the use of manures and composts) contribute to the improvement in output of the paddy lands and gardens. The large sum spent annually on imported milk products (Table 5.2.1 below) indicates a considerable potential market for dairy products.

The problems of low rainfall and its high unreliability increase northwards. The rivers become less capable of maintaining storage tanks and so agriculture becomes less secure. North of Vavuniya, much of the Wanni region is empty jungle with little prospect of more intensive settlement.

Economic Development

With the prospect of her population doubling to almost 20 million by the 1980s, Ceylon faces problems quite as difficult, although of less magnitude, as those facing India and Pakistan. In some respects the larger countries have certain advantages in that they possess resources which are in the process of being developed to provide industrial employment. Ceylon's resources for industry are poor by comparison. There is neither coal nor petroleum nor, so far, natural gas, and little potential for hydroelectric power development. The minerals she has – graphite, kaolin, ilmenite, monazite, glass sand – cannot be the basis of any substantial industry. The smallness of the home market compared with that in most industrialised countries is a further disadvantage, denying Ceylon the benefit of economies of scale such as can be looked forward to in India and Pakistan.

Ceylon's plans for the future are based on the need to export tree crops – tea, rubber, and coconuts – in increased quantities in order to earn foreign exchange with which to purchase whatever cannot be produced or made economically at home. In order to reduce the list of imports, the output of rice is being increased by improving yields per acre, with near self-sufficiency the first aim. The scope for raising yields is considerable: irrigation, flood control, artificial fertilisers, better seed, more intensive cultural methods. These are the familiar recipes elsewhere in South Asia. In the wet zone, agricultural improvement must rely mainly on intensification of production from the existing cultivated area, whether under rice or cash tree crops. The dry zone has perhaps one million irrigable acres which might

be developed at a cost, but here the great need is for the development of an agricultural technology which can make more effective use of the lands at present under chena cultivation.

When Ceylon published a ten-year plan in 1959 there was little large-scale industry in the country. A cement works on Jaffna Peninsula, a ceramics factory at Negombo, a small chemicals plant, a cotton textiles mill, a paper mill (using rice-straw and grass), and small undertakings in leather, plywood, and bicycles go a small way towards satisfying the local demand which must be the first basis of industrialisation in Ceylon. Tea factories, rubber mills, and vegetable oil mills (coconut and gingelly) process local produce for export. A wide range of small enterprises exists at or near the level of cottage industry making textiles, metal, and wooden goods, salt (by solar evaporation) soap, etc. Plans for development maintain a place for these small industries as a means to absorbing some of the seasonally surplus manpower of a predominantly agricultural country. An industrial estate has been developed at Colombo for a variety of modern light industries, and a steel re-rolling and wire drawing mill of 100,000 tons ultimate capacity came into production in 1967. Manufacture of motor tyres has begun.

The table below showing the main items of export and import trade (by value) in 1966 indicates clearly the country's heavy dependence on plantation products to earn exchange with which to buy not only manufactured goods, but a considerable amount of foodstuffs from abroad.

TABLE 5.2.1

Ceylon: External Trade 1967

(in million rupees and percentages of total)

Exports			Imports		
Tea	1061	62·8	Rice	211	12·0
Rubber	282	16·7	Wheat flour	229	13·2
Coconut products	167	9·8	Sugar	74	4·3
Cocoa	4	0·2	Milk products	66	3·8
Cinnamon	42	2·5	Grams and pulses	53	3·0
Plumbago	7	0·4	Fish products	53	3·0
Citronella	1		Chillies	29	1·6
			Fertilisers	80	4·6
			Petroleum products	112	6·4
			Textiles	73	4·2
			Machinery	175	10·1
			Transport equipment	89	5·1
Others	127	7·5	Others	494	28·4
TOTAL	1691	99·9	TOTAL	1738	99·9

(Source: Ceylon Customs Returns.)

APPENDIX

PLACE-NAMES IN INDIA

Since India achieved independence, many geographical names of places and features which during the period of British rule were transliterated in a fashion now considered over-anglicised or inaccurate, have been rendered in forms which more nearly represent the local pronunciation. Some of the main changes are listed below to help the reader locate places in atlases which give the old spelling.

New form	Old form
Ganga	Ganges (still used in Pakistan)
Jabalpur	Jubblepore
Kanpur	Cawnpore
Krishna	Kistna
Kozhikode	Calicut
Kutch	Cutch
Lakhnau	Lucknow
Madurai	Madura
Narmada	Narbada
Tamilnadu	Madras State
Tiruchirapalli, Tiruchchirappalli	Trichinopoly
Tirunelveli	Tinevelly
Varanasi or Banaras	Benares
Yamuna	Jumna

GENERAL INDEX

For place-names and regions see separate index.

Entries thus: 22 refer to text; *22* refer to Figures or Tables; 22n to footnotes; **22** refer to photographs. All are page numbers.

INDEX OF PLACE-NAMES AND REGIONS

Entries thus: 22 refer to text; *22* refer to Figures and Tables; **22** refer to Photographs. All are page numbers.